'Simply the most wide-rangii
of the impact of Pan on the We.   ...ugination yet written.'

RONALD HUTTON, author of *The Triumph of the Moon*

'We get the pleasure of seeing this goat-like god pop up everywhere from classic children's literature to romantic novels to early environmentalist tracts . . . The result is a tour de force.'

PERICLES LEWIS, author of
The Cambridge Introduction to Modernism

'The multiple identities and reincarnations of Pan are eloquently examined by Paul Robichaud in this fascinating book. Robichaud is not only an academic but a published poet and it shows in the elegance of his sentences – sensitive and careful attention is given to the shades of meaning attached to Pan . . . And it's not just the words but the images that captivate . . . If you are looking for a pleasurable source book on everything about Pan than Paul Robichaud's is it. An important and self-recommending study. I loved it.'

ALAN PRICE, *Magonia Review of Books*

'If you are interested in Pan in any way . . . then *Pan: The Great God's Modern Return* is simply a must-purchase. It is, without doubt, the most wide-ranging treatment of the goat-foot god I've ever read, combining thorough attention to detail and research, yet at the same time highly accessible to a general reader . . . This book is a tremendous achievement and deserves a treasured place on the bookshelf of anyone who hearkens to the call of Pan.'

Enfolding.org

'A fascinating account of a strange god with meme-like reach across the ages, and a study in the temporal shape-shifting of mythology itself.'

The Spectator

'Paul Robichaud's *Pan: The Great God's Modern Return* tracks the god from his origins as a guardian of Arcadian shepherds to his modern forms of trickster god primarily in the young adult genre of fiction. Along the way Robichaud examines the artwork, poetry, literature, and even music with Pan as the central figure. His prose paints a gorgeous picture of the misunderstood god and how changes in societal norms have erased or enhanced various aspects of the god over time.'

Folklore

PAN

The Great God's
Modern Return

Paul Robichaud

REAKTION BOOKS

For Natalie

Published by
REAKTION BOOKS LTD
Unit 32, Waterside
44–48 Wharf Road
London N1 7UX, UK
www.reaktionbooks.co.uk

First published 2021
First published in paperback 2023
Copyright © Paul Robichaud 2021

Printed and bound in Great Britain
by TJ Books Ltd, Padstow, Cornwall

A catalogue record for this book is available from the British Library

ISBN 978 1 78914 690 5

CONTENTS

PREFACE

It is late afternoon and the shadows falling on the pasture grow longer. You've herded the goats together and they're all accounted for – except little Simos. You hear a bleating from in the woods that stretch across the foot of the mountain, and make your way in, under the branches. He's in there somewhere. As the trees grow thicker around you, you realize how much darker it is here than in the open field. You think you might have seen the goat prancing ahead of you, going deeper and deeper into the forest, and follow reluctantly. Something, perhaps a small bird or animal, rustles the undergrowth nearby and you can feel the hairs on the back of your neck stand up. You again hear a bleating sound that echoes through the woods, but it is difficult to know from which direction. Looking around, you see nothing but trees and realize that you no longer know the way back to the pasture. The creeping darkness closes in around you, and you are seized by a sudden panic – then you hear Simos bleating close by. Stumbling through the brush, you enter a small clearing and there he is, chewing contentedly on some grass. The clearing is a little way up the mountain, and from here you can see the pasture below. You say a brief prayer of thanks to Pan for reuniting you with Simos as you pick up the kid and head back to your herd.

The Greek god Pan emerges into the knowable past as a guardian of flocks and inducer of panic terror, combining the physical features of goat and man. Yet from these remote origins he comes to have a rich variety of identities that shift and change through the centuries: cosmic god of All; symbol of bestial lust; demon; protector of forests; cipher for Stuart monarchs; symbol of the latent powers in nature; terrifying god of the abyss; source of occult knowledge; symbol of gay love; guardian of wild animals; Horned God of the witches; ruler of nature spirits; archetype of the unconscious; and many more. If these irreconcilable interpretations of the god have anything in common, it is that they register a powerful sense of otherness in the face of the radically different or unknown. Whether divine or demonic, animal or royal, this recognition of profound difference suddenly transfiguring the ordinary persists in representations of Pan into the twenty-first century.

This book explores the ways in which the Great God Pan has been imagined from antiquity to the present. Surveying Pan's role in mythology, art, literature, music, spirituality and popular culture, it shows how portrayals of the god reveal shifting anxiety about our own animality and our relationship to the natural world, whether this is understood as the wilderness beyond civilization or the cosmos as a whole. Pan is a god who transgresses the boundaries between human and animal, refusing to abandon the wilderness for civilization. After lurking in the shadows during the later Renaissance and eighteenth century, Pan returns in the Romantic era as a potent symbol of our instinctual life and the otherness of natural forces that live through us. At times he is a dangerous power threatening the order of modern civilization; at others, he is a power of fertility and renewal offering a new hope for our relationship with nature.

In surveying the god's changing identity in Western culture, I have chosen to focus on those works and individuals that re-imagine Pan in original ways, or are recognized as important in their own right. Others clearly articulate or explore aspects of the Pan tradition in ways that influence its later development. Occasionally I have included material simply because I thought it would interest any reader as fascinated by Pan as I am. In exploring Pan's role in occult and New Age spirituality, I have taken the accounts of believers seriously and do not attempt to explain them away. They strike me as valid examples of what the psychologist and philosopher William James called 'the varieties of religious experience'. How such experiences are understood, however, is shaped by a long tradition of cultural representation that culminates in the late nineteenth and early twentieth centuries. For Pagan readers who may believe in Pan (in one form or another), this book follows the historian Ronald Hutton's lead in leaving open the question of the existence of the gods. What are treated as changing representations of Pan in this book could, from a Pagan perspective, also be read as a gradual process of discovery – perhaps even of revelation.

In her magisterial study *Pan the Goat-God: His Myth in Modern Times* (1969), Patricia Merivale distinguished between 'benevolent' and 'sinister' traditions of representing the god. This is a valid contrast, particularly when considering the nineteenth- and twentieth-century literature that is her focus. Taking a somewhat more inclusive view, however, I have found the ancient distinction between Pan's pastoral and cosmic aspects more helpful, a distinction that I explore in the first chapter. As we'll see, both pastoral and cosmic aspects of Pan's character have been imagined in 'benevolent' and 'sinister' ways. A horror writer such as Arthur Machen depicts Pan as the terrifying power of the Abyss, while a visionary such as Robert Ogilvie Crombie sees a benign cosmic power nurturing life on Earth. How we experience Pan may depend much on our own assumptions and predispositions. A very few artists, D. H. Lawrence foremost among them, have attempted to convey Pan holistically, but even Lawrence rejected his more goatish associations. It is the tradition of depth psychology, and its focus on the unconscious, that has come closest to making sense of Pan in all his wild contradictions.

This book is written for readers interested in learning more about the goat-footed god and how he has been imagined through the centuries. While Merivale was writing for an audience of fellow scholars, I have not assumed that the reader has prior knowledge of the material explored here. My approach to individual texts, works of art and musical compositions is to introduce them and consider how they imagine Pan, relating them where possible to the larger tradition of which they form a part. Should the reader wish to follow up and read works in their entirety, I have referred where possible to readily accessible online editions. I am not a classicist, and in writing about the ancient world I have relied on the work of translators and scholars, especially Philippe Borgeaud, whose *The Cult of Pan in Ancient Greece* (1988) remains the major study of how Pan was conceived and worshipped in antiquity. In selecting visual works of art depicting Pan, I have been guided by John Boardman's *The Great God Pan: The Survival of an Image* (1998), a short but excellent survey.

1

MYTHIC PAN

Pan's written story begins with the ancient Greeks and the conflicting myths they told about the god's parentage. Before those myths were recorded, however, archaeological evidence in the form of bronze statues dedicated to Pan show that he was worshipped by shepherds in the region of Arcadia. His earliest representations in visual art depict him as an upright goat with human arms and torso, often with a prominent phallus. These start to appear in the fifth century BC as the cult of Pan begins to spread across Greece. At the same time, Pan makes his earliest literary appearance in the poetry of Pindar. A roughly contemporaneous hymn (mis-attributed to Homer by the Greeks) records the first known myth of Pan, an account of his birth, reception by the Olympians and pastoral character. That pastoral character is also reflected in the etymology of Pan's name, which clearly links him to pastures but was early on confused with the Greek word for 'all', a confusion with long-lived conse-quences for his later development. The god enters history in the work of the historian Herodotus, who records how Pan appeared to an Athenian runner, promising to help the Greeks in the Persian Wars – a promise that he fulfilled by instilling panic in the Persian army. The power to induce panic fear is among Pan's oldest attributes, persisting in his appearances through classical myth and literature, including pastoral poetry. His later mythology included the pursuit of several nymphs, but writers such as Longus and Apuleius portrayed him as a compassionate helper. In later antiquity, the misunderstanding of Pan's name as 'all' led to a variety of philosophical and mystical interpretations of the god that would echo down the centuries. In the reign of Tiberius, rumours of Pan's death began to circulate but, as this book will show, such rumours were greatly exaggerated.

ARCADIAN ORIGINS

With the horns and legs of a goat but the torso of a man, Pan is a god whose very form confounds the distinction between animal and divine. From his earliest appearances in the written record, Pan has been imagined in ways that are often irreconcilable. Even the stories of his birth and parentage vary wildly. According to the Homeric hymn 'To Pan', which may date from as early as the fifth century BC, when the newborn Pan's nurse first saw his goatish face, shaggy legs and cloven hooves she fled in terror, never to return. His father, Hermes, delighted by any sign of mischief, burst out laughing and picked up the strange child at once. He brought him straight to Mount Olympus, where the gods all shared in his mirth and welcomed Pan to their divine company, especially Dionysus. That is how he got his name, the hymn tells us, for the meaning of 'pan' is 'all'.[1]

Other ancient sources are not so sure. The Athenian playwright Aeschylus (525/524–456/455 BC) believed there were two Pans, one whose father was Cronos and one the son of Zeus. An Arcadian tradition identifies Pan's father as Aither, but pagan theologians knew this was just a local name for Cronos, the father of Zeus. It was because he was Zeus' half-brother that Pan was able to fight alongside him during the war with the Titans. As for Pan's mother, she may have been Amaltheia, Zeus' wet nurse, who was either a goat or a nymph who was changed into one.[2] It could also have been a nymph, such as Thymbris or Sose, or perhaps the famous Kallisto, who was transformed into a bear by Zeus and set among the stars.[3] Then there's Arcadian Penelope, also known as Dryope, daughter of Dryopos, himself either a mortal or a local oak-god from Mount Kyllene, sacred to Pan. This Penelope was the one whose beauty led Hermes to work as a labourer on her father's farm in order to win her hand. Some people confuse her with that other Penelope, wife of Odysseus, and tell a story about her that sounds more like a sailor's yarn than a proper myth. They say she wasn't the patient wife that the *Odyssey* would have us believe, but slept with all 108 suitors who courted her on Ithaca while Odysseus made his long way home from the Trojan War. It's no wonder Penelope's child looked more animal than human, given that she couldn't restrain her own bestial appetites – but surely that absurd tale is just an example of the same ancient misogyny that blamed the Trojan War on Helen? If Penelope, wife of Odysseus, was Pan's mother, it was more likely to have been because Hermes visited her in the form of a ram.[4]

There is no authorized version of the Greek myths, and most have several variants recorded across the ancient sources, but the multiplicity of accounts surrounding Pan's parentage is remarkable even by Greek standards. His outsider status may explain the conflicting attempts to bring him into the mythology of the dominant Greek pantheon, while the many accounts of his parentage might reflect intensely local cults of Pan in Arcadia itself. Never one of the Twelve Olympians – that quarrelsome family headed by Zeus – he was originally worshipped in Arcadia, although his cult would eventually spread throughout southern Greece. Arcadia is a forested and mountainous region in the centre of the southern Peloponnese, with pastures for grazing but little arable farmland. For most ancient Greeks, it was a wilderness whose rough inhabitants seemed to have survived from an earlier age. From this perspective, the Arcadians existed midway between a barbaric past and the full civic life typical of other Greek states. They spoke a dialect closer to Mycenaean than to classical Greek, and were believed to be the first Greeks in the Peloponnese. Regarded as 'older than the moon', Arcadians were hunters and eaters of acorns, suggesting to other Greeks that they were survivors from a time before farming was invented. In fact, the Arcadians did live in settlements surrounded by farms, as did other Greeks, but the difficult landscape meant they had to seek resources elsewhere. They had a reputation for being formidable warriors, and many sought their fortunes as mercenaries. Arcadians also – and perhaps most famously – herded goats and sheep, a major source of wealth.[5] For his earliest worshippers, Pan acted as sacred guardian of the flocks and presided over the hunt, the Arcadians' other major source of food. Mount Mainalos was especially sacred to Pan and there, according to the second-century AD geographer Pausanias, local people still heard him play on his pipes.[6]

The earliest archaeological evidence of the worship of Pan dates from the late sixth century. Discovered on Mount Lykaion in Arcadia, two bronze statuettes bear votive inscriptions to Pan, one of which identifies a ram and a jug as offerings.[7] These would have been costly to obtain, suggesting that at least some shepherds had considerable wealth. A fifth-century bronze sculpture from northern Arcadia depicts Pan with a goat head, shaggy mane and large testicles (goatish and suggesting fertility), although the lower parts of his legs are missing. The image conveys the inherently unsettling nature of the god, the way his divinity allows him to transgress the boundary between human and animal. He shields his eyes from the sun with one hand as though looking out over his flocks.[8] Although outside Arcadia Pan was generally worshipped in wild spaces such as grottoes and caves, there was an Arcadian temple dedicated to Pan and Apollo in the gorge where the River Neda runs down from Mount Lykaion.

Pan's name (in Greek, Πάν) provides some clues about his probable origins. As noted in the Homeric 'Hymn to Pan', the Greeks early on confused his name with their word for all, πᾶν, familiar to us as the prefix *pan-*, as in 'pandemic' and 'pan-European'. This confusion would eventually lead to elaborate speculation about Pan's true nature, as we'll see.

Bronze statuette from Arcadia, *c.* 525–500 BC, inscribed with a dedication to Pan from 'Aineas'. Statuettes such as this one are the earliest surviving evidence of Pan worship in Arcadia.

Today the derivation of Pan's name is generally acknowledged as πάειν (*paean*), a verb meaning 'to pasture'.[9] His name may also be cognate with ὀπάων (*opaōn*), 'companion'.[10] Considered together, these linguistic clues might suggest a deity who is first and foremost a companion to flocks and those who pasture them, which seems to fit well with the earliest archaeological and literary evidence. With some notable exceptions (such as Basque and Finnish), European and Indic languages all derive from a common ancestor, called by linguists 'Proto-Indo-European', that was probably spoken from about 4500 to 2500 BC on the Pontic-Caspian steppe north of the Black Sea. As its speakers became separated through migration, Proto-Indo-European gradually evolved into distinct languages. For example, the Irish *máthair*, Sanskrit *mātṛ* and English 'mother' all derive from a common Proto-Indo-European ancestor that accounts for their similarities. At one time scholars believed that Pan could be linked to the Indian Vedic god Pushan (Pūṣán) through a common reconstructed ancestor, but this has been rejected on linguistic grounds by scholars such as Willy Alfred Borgeaud.[11] Nonetheless, his son Philippe Borgeaud notes that the names of both Pan and Pushan 'refer to their pastoral function' and are 'approximate homonyms'.[12] According to the hymns in the *Rig Veda* (*c.* 1500–1200 BC), Pushan was a guardian of livestock, drove a solar chariot pulled by goats, and rewarded his worshippers with wealth and pasture land.[13] Pan and Pushan thus possess a few shared attributes – they both protect grazing animals and are associated with goats and pastures.

In addition to his name, Pan's epithets or cult titles provide clues about his early religious attributes. These include Agreus ('of the hunt' or 'hunter'); Agrotas ('giver of pasture'); Haliplanktos ('Sea-roaming'); Lytêrios ('releasing'); Nomios ('of the pasture'); Phorbas ('Terrifying One'); Sinoeis ('mischief' or 'bane'); and Skoleitas ('crooked').[14] While several of these are fairly straightforward, describing Pan's role as god of hunting and pastures and the source of panic terror, others are more mysterious. Why, for example, is he described as 'Sea-roaming'? Philippe Borgeaud points out that fishermen venerated 'Pan Aktios as god of riverbanks and ocean promontories where the goats come for fresh water and salt', so perhaps they imagined Pan roaming the seas just as shepherds envisioned him upon the mountains.[15] The epithet Lytêrios is explained by Pausanias as having the sense 'deliverer', and was a title given to Pan at his shrine in Troezen, where he had appeared in dreams to give people a remedy for the plague that was devastating their town.[16] Skoleitas may allude to Pan's goat horns or legs, or even his gait while walking. Like his purported father Hermes, Pan was fond of mischief, with an added twist of sudden fear, which would explain Sinoeis as a title.

GREECE AND BEYOND

Hermes' identity as Pan's father is described in what is probably the first literary or religious work specifically devoted to Pan, the Homeric 'Hymn to Pan' mentioned above. The first half of the hymn describes Pan in his natural habitat, while the second recounts the myth of his birth. Like many ancient Greek hymns, this one was mistakenly attributed to the poet Homer; its actual author is unknown. Its most recent translator, Peter McDonald, suggests that it may have been composed as the cult of Pan spread throughout Greece.[17] Addressing the Muse, the speaker asks to be told 'about Pan, the dear son of Hermes, with his goat's feet and two horns – a lover of merry noise'.[18] Here, Pan's characteristic physical features are noted, as is his preference for loud revelry – 'his taste for noisy parties' in McDonald's lively version.[19] Just as Pan's appearance crosses the line between human and animal, so his fondness for making noise resists the limits on behaviour imposed by civilized society. The hymn emphasizes the wild setting of Pan's rites: 'Through wooded glades he wanders with dancing nymphs who foot it on some sheer cliff's edge, calling upon Pan, the shepherd-god, long-haired, unkempt.' The cliffside setting adds an element of danger, while Pan's long, messy hair connects him with the wilderness, a domain including 'snowy crest and the mountain peaks and rocky crests' as well as 'close thickets'. These are all places uninhabitable by humans, but home to Pan.

The god has not forgotten us, however; at the end of his journey he 'climbs up to the highest peak that overlooks the flocks', presumably to strike the pose we see in the early Arcadian bronze, gazing out over the sheep and goats.[20] From his perch at the edge of the wilderness, he watches those animals that, as long ago as 8000 BC, were first brought from the wild into the human world through domestication. We may be surprised when the poet then describes Pan as killing wild animals, but this is consistent with his ancient title 'Agreus'. A statuette depicting Pan in a style common in the third century BC (with small horns and no hooves) portrays him brandishing a club and holding a dead hare. Arcadian hunters would ritually beat an image of Pan with squills (a Mediterranean relative of the lily) if they were unsuccessful in the hunt.[21] Given Pan's role as guardian of flocks, his killing of wild animals may also have been protective. Arcadia was known for its wolves; the name of Mount Lykaion, birthplace of Zeus and also sacred to Pan, means 'Wolf Mountain'. In the hymn's portrayal of his return from the hunt at evening, Pan plays on his pipes, surrounded by dancing and singing nymphs. The hymn punningly alludes to the nymph Echo, whom Pan pursues unsuccessfully in another myth. He wears a spotted lynx pelt, relaxing in a lush meadow that blooms with crocuses and hyacinths, delighting in the nymphs' song.

The second half of the hymn narrates the story of Pan's birth given at the start of this chapter. In the song sung by the nymphs, Hermes is described as 'swift messenger of the gods' who 'came to Arcadia, the land of many springs and mother of flocks, there where his sacred place is as god of Cyllene'.[22] In this telling, Hermes acquires his own pastoral role tending sheep for the mortal Dryops after falling in love with his daughter. The couple marries and, sure enough, Hermes' unnamed wife gives birth to a baby 'with goat's feet and two horns – a noisy, merry-laughing child'. This time, it is the nurse who flees on seeing 'his uncouth face and full beard'. The hymn includes the rather charming detail that Hermes wrapped his son 'in warm skins of mountain hares' before bringing him to Olympus. There, seated beside Zeus, the newborn delights all the gods, especially Dionysus, 'and they called the boy Pan because he delighted all their hearts.' The singling out of Dionysus is intriguing; the poet clearly recognized some affinity between the two gods, also suggested by Pan's wearing the pelt of a lynx, an animal traditionally sacred to Dionysus, who himself wore the pelt of a leopard. Pan and his nymphs offer a clear parallel to the wine god and his maenads, one of whom, Oenoe ('winy'), has the same name as one of Pan's possible mothers. Both gods are associated with irrational states of mind, Dionysus with drunkenness and Pan with sudden and overwhelming fear. They possess an 'otherness' distinct among the gods of ancient Greece.

Pan's cult had spread outwards from Arcadia by the early fifth century BC. In one of the earliest literary references to Pan, the poet Pindar (c. 518–438 BC) describes hearing girls singing in honour of Pan and 'the Mother' outside his home in Boeotia.[23] Pan's arrival in Athens as a venerated god is the subject of a remarkable story by Herodotus. Writing in around 440 BC, Herodotus claims that the cult of Pan came to Athens after the god helped the Athenians during the Persian War. While the Athenians considered how best to meet the Persian threat,

> the generals first sent to Sparta the herald Philippides, an Athenian and a long-distance runner who made that his calling. As Philippides himself said when he brought the message to the Athenians, when he was in the Parthenian mountain above Tegea he encountered Pan. Pan called out Philippides' name and bade him ask the Athenians why they paid him no attention, though he was of goodwill to the Athenians, had often been of service to them, and would be in the future. The Athenians believed that these things were true, and when they became prosperous they established a sacred precinct of Pan beneath the Acropolis. Ever since that message they propitiate him with annual sacrifices and a torch-race.[24]

The 'sacred precinct' was known as the Cave of Pan, while the site of Philippides' conversation with Pan also became a sanctuary to the god frequented by the thankful Athenians after their victory in the Battle of Marathon (490 BC). So established did the cult of Pan become in Athens that ninety years later Plato (428/427–348/347 BC) recorded a prayer to the god in his *Phaedrus*. In it, Socrates addresses the god directly: 'Dear Pan and all you gods of this place, grant me that I may become beautiful within; and that what is in my possession outside me may be in friendly accord with what is inside.'[25]

For Socrates, Pan is a 'dear' god with the power to reconcile our inner and outer worlds – a surprisingly philosophical development for a god associated with flocks and terror. Early artistic representations of Pan combine goat and human elements in a variety of ways, often suggesting characteristics described in the written sources. An Athenian black-figure vase fragment dated to circa 490 BC portrays Pan with a goat's head and legs but a human torso, playing a double-reeded pipe.[26] He closely resembles the bronze statuette from northern Arcadia. On a red-figure Attic vase from circa 470 BC, Pan has the head, tail and hooves of a goat, but a man's body and legs, with a prominent phallus. He extends his arms as he chases a local goatherd. Given the look of fear and surprise on the goatherd's face, the scene may well depict an experience of 'panic' – that sense of sudden terror that Pan's presence was believed to induce.[27] Pausanias reports that 'causeless terrors are said to come from the god Pan,' describing how the god had once brought panic to an invading army of Gauls, causing them to slay each other and flee.[28] Pan employed a similar tactic against the Persians when he brought victory to the Athenians at Marathon. Behind Pan on the Attic vase, the artist has depicted some rocks, atop which stands a Priapos, a further image of male sexual potency in a wild setting. Other early bronzes and pottery show Pan dancing, sometimes to the accompaniment of a satyr's piping.[29] He is also shown in duplicate, welcoming the goddess of spring.[30] By the end of the fifth century Pan was being depicted in ways that emphasize either his goatish or his human qualities, from a shaggy-looking Spartan marble of the god wrapped in a rustic blanket to a statue by Polyneices that portrays a male youth who looks fully human but for a pair of horns.

Representations of Pan early on established dramatic situations that artists would continue to portray throughout

Pan, Aphrodite and Eros (Greek, *c.* 100 BC Parian marble). Aphrodite, goddess of love, prepares to defend herself with a sandal against Pan's sexual advances, assisted by Eros, who grabs one of Pan's horns.

antiquity and rediscover in the Renaissance. By the fourth century BC Pan is depicted alongside Eros, the winged god of love. One bronze mirror back from this time depicts an armed Eros breaking up a fight between two Pans, but a contemporary Corinthian mirror cover shows Pan and Eros on more friendly terms, playing a game with Aphrodite.[31] The three figures are also portrayed in a Delian sculpture from about 100 BC, in which Aphrodite modestly covers her pudendum and holds up a sandal defensively while Pan grabs her arm. Eros tugs playfully at Pan's horn to help his mother fend off his advances.[32] That they are all smiling at each other suggests they are engaged in erotic play. A much later copy of a Hellenistic sculpture (second century AD) of Pan teaching the shepherd Daphnis to play the pipes portrays the god as sexually threatening.[33] A fascinating tradition of depicting female Pans begins as early as circa 400 BC, although it seems to have been confined to the visual arts.[34] According to the historian Robin Lane Fox, Roman women with several sexual partners were called 'Pan girls', so it is possible that these images reflect this popular tradition.[35] Roman depictions of Pan were more likely to foreground sexuality, as in the sculpture of Pan found at Herculaneum portraying the god copulating with a goat lying on her back.[36] The classicist Mary Beard has recently suggested that the image might be a clever pun on the name of Panyassis, a Greek poet whose bust was originally next to the Pan sculpture.[37] A Roman mural depicts Pan turning away in horror after discovering that what appears to be a woman is actually a hermaphrodite.[38]

The cult of Pan spread throughout the Roman Empire, far beyond Greece and Rome. Two sites sacred to Pan existed in the Middle East, one a temple at Apollonopolis Magna (present-day Edfu) in Egypt and the other a cave at Panion (now Banias in Israel), known as Caesarea Philippi in the Gospels. The cave at Panion contained a spring originally sacred to the Semitic god Ba'al, which may imply that the two gods were seen as equivalent by the Greeks and Romans who settled there.[39] In 2015 a large bronze mask believed to represent Pan was discovered near a Roman gate at Hippos-Sussita on the Sea of Galilee; subsequent digging has revealed a pagan sanctuary that archaeologists believe was dedicated to Pan or Dionysus, or possibly both.[40]

MYTHOLOGICAL NARRATIVES

Given Pan's half-goat appearance, it is intriguing that the foundational myths associated with Arcadia also blur the distinctions between human and animal. According to Pausanias, the first person in Arcadia was Pelasgos, who established the worship of Zeus on Mount Lykaion. Pelasgos was succeeded by his son Lycaon, who was turned into a wolf by Zeus when he sacrificed a human child.[41] (In the version recorded by Pseudo-Apollodorus, Zeus destroys Lycaon and his many sons with lightning, sparing only Nyktimos.[42]) Nyktimos succeeds his father as king at the time of the Great Deluge, which some traditions blame on Lycaon's crime.[43] The sister of Nyktimos was the nymph Kallisto, consecrated to Artemis, virgin goddess of the hunt. Kallisto is subsequently transformed into a bear, although there are different mythological explanations: some say Zeus transformed her in order to seduce her more easily, or to protect her from Hera, who was furious that he seduced her; others claim that Hera transformed Kallisto in punishment for having sex with Zeus; or that Artemis did, after discovering that Kallisto was pregnant. In any event, Kallisto's metamorphosis is intimately connected to her seduction by Zeus, after which she gives birth to a son,

Arcas, whose name means 'the Arcadian'. According to some accounts, Artemis hunts and kills Kallisto, possibly on behalf of Hera, while in others Arcas himself nearly slays his mother while hunting on Mount Lykaion. In the latter versions, Zeus intervenes at the last minute and sets Kallisto among the stars as the constellation we call the Great Bear.[44] Aeschylus thought Kallisto was the mother of Pan by Zeus, making him Arcas' twin; he also thought there was another Pan, a son of Cronos and so Zeus' brother.[45] Pan's birth and adventures are difficult to reconcile with Greek mythological time.

The surviving myths about Pan are relatively few and were recorded after his cult had spread beyond Arcadia. The illiterate Arcadian herders of goats and sheep left no written records, so there is no way of knowing if the myths recorded by Greek and Roman writers reflect their traditions accurately. Pan's dramatic role in classical mythology is primarily that of a seducer of nymphs. As we've seen, many of the earliest artistic representations depict him with large testicles and a prominent phallus, so his connection with sexuality is an early one. Goats were regarded throughout the ancient world as exceptionally libidinous animals, so it is unsurprising that a god with a body that is half-goat was also thought to be lustful. The best-known myth of Pan is relatively late, and tells of his attempt to seduce the nymph Syrinx. It was included by the Roman poet Ovid (43 BC–AD 17) in his *Metamorphoses*, a poetic retelling of classical mythology that has exerted enormous influence on Western culture. As Ovid tells it, Syrinx passed her days in Arcadia, where she followed the virgin goddess of the hunt, Diana (in Greek, Artemis), whom she resembled. Returning from Mount Lykaion, Pan saw her and was immediately smitten by her beauty. Although he begged her to yield to him, Syrinx refused, fleeing to the banks of the River Ladon with Pan in pursuit. Realizing that she would never escape a god, least of all one driven by sexual passion, she prayed to the nymphs of the river to be turned into a reed rather than submit to his desire. In the moment Pan grabbed hold of her, he found himself clutching a bunch of reeds. He sighed with grief and yearning, and the reeds made a haunting sound as his breath passed over them. Delighted with the notes, he bound the reeds with wax, promising Syrinx that they would always speak to each other in that way. And so Pan discovered the pipes that would forever accompany him, producing the strange and plaintive music for which he is known.[46] Ovid later tells how Pan entered into a musical contest with Apollo, who played so beautifully upon his lyre that the judge, Mount Tmolus, announced him victor, declaring that henceforth the pipes must bow to the lyre. All present agreed, except for Midas, who insisted that Pan's music was superior. In a fit of pique, Apollo transformed Midas' ears into those of an ass. The unfortunate king, who had already suffered having a golden touch, could only hide the consequences of his asinine judgement under a turban.[47]

Among the other nymphs pursued by Pan, two in particular caught the attention of ancient writers: Echo and Pitys. Echo was punished by Hera for helping to conceal Zeus' many love affairs; as punishment, instead of speaking, Echo could only repeat the last words said to her. When she fell in love with Narcissus, she was unable to tell him and so watched helplessly as he fell in love with his own reflection. Earlier, however, Echo had conceived a child by Pan, a nymph named Iynx, whom Hera would later transform into a bird (the Eurasian wryneck) as punishment for casting a love spell on Zeus.[48] As we have seen, Pan's relationship with Echo is alluded to in the 'Hymn to Pan', where she 'wails about the mountain-top' as he plays his pipes. A rival tradition has Echo torn apart by Pan's followers after she rejects his advances.[49] In the version told by Nonnos, an Alexandrian poet of the fifth century AD, Echo rejects Pan, who is tormented by his desire and apparently rapes her while she sleeps (or so the goddess Aura surmises), a detail not found elsewhere.[50] Nonnos was a Christian poet, whose epic *Dionysiaca* is regarded by classical scholars as dull and overwrought; it is impossible to know how much his faith led him to distort the mythical traditions available to him. He is one of only two written sources for the tale of the nymph Pitys (Pine), who planted herself in Gaia, the Earth, and turned into a pine tree in order to avoid Pan's sexual advances.[51] Further evidence of an ancient connection between Pan and Pitys is found in the Roman poet Sextus Propertius (55/43–after 16 BC), who mentions pine and beech as two trees sacred to Pan. In the version told in the tenth-century Byzantine compilation the *Geoponica*, Pitys is flung off a cliff by Boreas, god of the north wind, when she prefers the attentions of Pan.[52] Finally, Virgil (70–19 BC), following the Greek poet Nicander (second century BC), suggests that Pan successfully wooed the moon goddess Selene with a gift of wool.[53]

Pan occasionally plays a supporting role in myths devoted to other gods, appearing as a kind and helpful rustic. After her daughter Persephone was abducted by Hades, Demeter refused to bring fertility to the land, resulting in famine. The gods sought to plead with her, but Demeter could not be found. One day, as Pan hunted in the mountains of Arcadia, he chanced to see her hiding in a cavern on Mount Elaeus, dressed in mourning black. He went and told Zeus at once, and Zeus sent the Moirae (the three Fates) to persuade her to relent. Demeter's heart was moved by their pleas and, despite her grief over Persephone, she once again made the crops flourish.[54] Nonnos, in his *Dionysiaca*, places Pan in the army of Dionysus, where he acquits himself honourably during a war in India.

Pan's name and goatish appearance led him to be confused with another even murkier Greek god, Aegipan, who took the shape of a goat with a fish's tail when the gods were attacked by the titan Typhoeus. When Typhoeus removed Zeus' sinews during a particularly gruesome battle, Aegipan retrieved them. By way of reward, Zeus transformed him into the constellation we know as Capricorn.[55] Aeschylus attributed these deeds to Pan, and suggested that there were in fact two distinct Pans, as we have seen. Nonnos tells the same story with Pan loaning his pipes to Cadmus, who uses them to lure Typhoeus into a trap, while other sources identify Aegipan as one of the Panes.[56] Panes were multiplications of the god Pan himself, but were sometimes thought of as his children, or the children of Zeus or Hermes. They were imagined as rustic spirits of mischief and fertility, qualities that hardly distinguish them from the original Pan, although they were sometimes depicted differently, with just the horns and head of a goat and a fully human body. Distinct from satyrs (which have human heads and torsos, but small horns and the legs of a goat), the Panes could also be found in the retinue of Dionysus.[57] According to Flavius Philostratus (AD 170–c. 245) and Nonnos, the twelve sons of Pan were known as the Paneides and served Dionysus as warriors, journeying as far as India in his wars.[58] Of the remaining Panes, Agreus was probably a distinct god of hunting and prophecy; Nomios a Pan-like god of pastures; Pan Sybarios the unrelated offspring of an Italian shepherd and a goat; and Phaunos the Latin god Faunus, whom the Romans confusingly identified with Pan.[59]

PASTORAL PASTIMES

Pan is also a foundational presence, if not a central character, in the literary mode known as 'pastoral'. In its classical form, pastoral poetry envisions an idealized countryside populated by lovelorn swains and singing shepherds, far removed from the grinding poverty and hard lives faced by rural labourers in the ancient world. Despite its rural settings and rustic characters, pastoral literature is the creation of urban poets nostalgic for the perceived simplicity of country life. Its obvious artificiality can make ancient pastoral a difficult mode for modern readers to appreciate, but the examples of Theocritus and especially Virgil would inspire Western poets and artists from the Renaissance to the nineteenth century and beyond. In the collection of anonymous lyrics known as the *Greek Anthology* (third century BC to sixth century AD), Pan often appears as a literary version of his original Arcadian character, 'this yellow, bearded goat, a horned creature to the horned, a hairy one to the hairy-legged, a bounding one to the deft leaper, a denizen of the woods to the forest god'.[60] The Greek poet Theocritus (third century BC) alludes to Pan several times in his *Idylls*, which dramatize conversations and singing contests between rural characters.

In the first *Idyll*, the shepherd Thyrsis praises the piping of a goatherd as unrivalled except by Pan; nonetheless, the goatherd refuses to play: 'No, no man; there's no piping for me at high noon. I go in too great dread of Pan for that. I wot high noon's his time for taking rest after the swink o' the chase; and he's one o' the tetchy sort; his nostril's ever sour wrath's abiding-place.'[61] Theocritus here alludes to Pan's role as hunter, but also to the sensation of dread inspired by fear of his wrath should his sleep be disturbed. The goatherd persuades Thyrsis to sing a ballad called 'The Affliction of Daphnis', in which he addresses Pan directly, begging him to join their revels:

> And Pan, O Pan, whether at this hour by Lycee's
>   mountain-pile
> Or Maenal steep thy watch thou keep, come away to
>   the Sicil isle,
> Come away from the knoll of Helicè and the howe lift
>   high i' the lea,
> The howe of Lycáon's child, the howe that Gods in
>   heav's envye;
> *Country-song, leave country-song, ye Muses.*
> Come, Master, and take this pretty pipe, this pipe of
>   honey breath,
> Of wax well knit round lips to fit; for Love hales me to
>   my death.
> *Country-song, leave country-song, ye Muses.*[62]

Pan is urged to take up 'this pretty pipe' that the lovelorn Daphnis cannot bring himself to play. Daphnis and Pan also figure in two of Theocritus' inscriptions to pictures. The first portrays Daphnis honouring Pan with a gift of apples, while the second suggests a more disturbing encounter:

> You sleep there upon the leaf-strown earth, good Daphnis, and rest your weary frame, while your netting-stakes are left planted on the hillside. But Pan is after you, and Priapus also, with the yellow ivy about his jolly head; they are going side by side into your cave. Quick then, put off the lethargy that is shed of sleep, and up with you and away.[63]

The two gods are presented here as threatening figures in a scene strongly reminiscent of that depicted on the Athenian vase already mentioned, with a Priapos in the background and a sexually aroused Pan chasing a terrified rustic, perhaps suggesting an ancient myth that did not survive in narrative form.

Elsewhere in Theocritus, Pan is mentioned as the god to whom the shepherds swear oaths, honoured with milk and honeycombs. In the seventh *Idyll*, the narrator Simichidas offers a prayer to Pan to unite the lovers Philinis and Aratus:

> This do, sweet Pan, and never, when slices be too
> few,
> May the leeks o' the lads of Arcady beat thee back
> black and blue;
> But O if othergates thou go, may nettles make thy bed
> And set thee scratching tooth and nail, scratching
> from heel to head,
> And be thy winter-lodging nigh the Bear up Hebrus
> way
> I' the hills of Thrace; when summer's in, mid furthest
> Africa
> Mayst feed thy flock by the Blemyan rock beyond
> Nile's earliest spring.[64]

Theocritus is referring to the Arcadian ritual of beating an image of Pan after an unsuccessful hunt; note how Simichidas threatens Pan with a bed of itchy nettles and a very long journey with his flocks if he doesn't heed his prayer! Such a disrespectful attitude towards Pan seems to be part of the classical tradition.

In Virgil's *Eclogues*, modelled on Greek pastoral poetry, Pan is primarily invoked as a musician. In *Eclogue II*, Corydon attempts to persuade Alexis to live with him in the forest: 'With me in the woods you shall rival Pan in song. Pan it was who first taught man to make many reeds one with wax; Pan cares for the sheep and the shepherds of the sheep.'[65] Despite the brevity of this description, these few lines would shape literary perceptions of Pan for centuries to come. Virgil boasts in the fourth *Eclogue* that his skill as a poet is such that 'Even were Pan to compete with me and Arcady be judge, then even Pan, with Arcady for judge, would own himself defeated.'[66] In *Eclogue x*, Virgil's Arcadian speaker describes seeing Pan 'crimsoned with vermilion and blood-red elderberries' – a vision that is at once frightening and rather messy.[67] The god also makes a brief appearance in the third of Virgil's *Georgics*, the main source of the myth of Pan's seduction of the moon goddess Selene. After praising the virtues of white-woolled sheep and rams, Virgil comments, ''Twas with gift of such snowy wool, if we may trust the tale, that Pan, Arcadia's god, charmed and beguiled you, O Moon, calling you to the depths of the woods; nor did you scorn his call.'[68] That conditional 'if we may trust the tale' perhaps suggests some scepticism on Virgil's part, and it is possible that the original seducer of the Moon was Endymion rather than Pan.

ANCIENT COMEDY AND FICTION

Although classical dramatists such as Aeschylus and Euripides make passing references to Pan, the god doesn't really find a home in the high seriousness of the tragic mode. Comedy is a more promising venue for a god who thrives on incongruity. He appears as a central figure in just one surviving ancient play, the *Dyskolos* (Grouch) by the comic playwright Menander (*c.* 342–*c.* 292 BC). Despite being present on stage just once, to introduce the play, Pan is very clearly working behind the scenes to orchestrate the action throughout. His prologue has little to say about the god, but establishes the setting in Phyle, a wild region of Attica where farmers live a hard life on rocky soil. There, a grouchy old man named Knemon has a farm beside a shrine dedicated to the nymphs and Pan. The main plot is straightforward: a rich young man named Sostratos has fallen in love with Knemon's daughter Myrrhine, and in order to win her father's approval agrees to work as a labourer. This dramatic scenario parallels that of Hermes in the Homeric 'Hymn to Pan', where a disguised Hermes labours for Dryopos in order to marry his daughter. Meanwhile, Sostratos' mother has preparations made to sacrifice to Pan after dreaming of him. (Philippe Borgeaud suggests that the ritual worship of Pan provides the

Votive relief from the Cave of the Nymphs, Mount Penteli, Attica, *c.* 330 BC, marble. From left to right: three nymphs; Hermes with his cadaceus; Pan; a servant pouring wine; and Agathemeros, the dedicator of the relief. In Menander's *Dyskolos*, *c.* 317–316 BC, Pan also shares a cave with the nymphs, where his worshippers gather to honour him.

underlying dramatic structure of the play as a whole.[69]) In the first act, Myrrhine expresses her piety towards the nymphs: 'dearest Nymphs, I must borrow water from you. / [hesitates] I'd be ashamed, though, to disturb the prayers / of anyone inside the shrine.'[70] This gives Sostratos the opportunity to offer to carry the water for her, making a good first impression. The act concludes with his friend Daos expressing concern over 'a group of somewhat drunken / worshippers of Pan carousing toward us'.[71] Drunkenness was considered a fitting part of the worship of Pan, one more connection he has with Dionysus.

In Act Two, Sostratos approaches Knemon's stepson Gorgias, pledging his good intentions by invoking Pan: 'If I came here intent on evil, or to do you some secret / harm, my friend, may Pan here and his Nymphs / avenge the deed by striking me right down / beside this house.'[72] His survival is a clear indication that his motives are pure. The mysterious procession of Pan worshippers is revealed to be preparing a sacrifice on behalf of Sostratos' mother. Her slave Geta reveals that she had a mysterious dream in which she saw Pan shackle Sostratos 'and then equip him with a farmer's / cloak and mattock, and order him to work / the neighbour's land.'[73] Fearful for Sostratos, his mother clearly wishes to propitiate the god with sacrifice, but we in the audience understand that the dream has a positive meaning: Pan is actively helping Sostratos win Myrrhine by bringing him to labour on Knemon's farm.

Unsurprisingly, the cranky Knemon is upset by all the noise being made by the cook and slaves who are preparing the sacrificial feast. Just as Sostratos and Myrrhine signalled their devotion to Pan and the Nymphs earlier in the play, in Act Three, Knemon disparages them: 'God damn you all! You're making me fall idle! / I can't be off and leave the house with them / around. These Nymphs are nuisances as neigh-bours.'[74] His impious comments and his refusal to lend a pot for Pan's feast do not bode well for him. In the fourth act, Knemon has fallen down a well – a misfortune we can con-nect to his disdain for Pan and the Nymphs. Lucky for him, Gorgias and Sostratos are there to rescue him. After this mis-adventure, Knemon decides to move in with his estranged wife, allowing Gorgias to decide whom Myrrhine should marry (in patriarchal Greek society, a right traditionally belonging to the father).[75] The fifth and final act takes place just as the sacrifice and feast in honour of Pan are about to begin, with the women planning to keep vigil all night while the men drink in the god's honour. Sostratos' father jokes that it will probably be the other way around. He gives his blessing to Sostratos' marriage plans, and encourages Gorgias to marry his daughter.[76] So often unsuccessful in his own amorous pursuits, Pan succeeds as matchmaker for the main characters of Menander's play.

Stepping out from behind the scenes, Pan makes two appearances as a character in novels from the second century AD. In the tale of Cupid and Psyche, as told in *The Golden Ass* by Lucius Apuleius (*c.* AD 124 – after 170), Pan assists Psyche when she attempts to end her life after Cupid abandons her for disobeying his command never to look upon him. Overcome by grief, Psyche throws herself into a river, which lifts her back on to its banks, refusing to let her drown. Pan, described in William Adlington's translation from 1566 as 'that rustical god', is 'sitting on the river-side, embracing and teaching the mountain goddess Echo to tune her songs and pipes'. Seeing the distraught Psyche, Pan uses his powers of divination to discern the cause of her unhappiness. He coun-sels her to 'go not about to slay yourself, nor weep at all, but rather adore and worship the great god Cupid, and win him to you by your gentle promise of service.' Psyche does not answer, 'but made reverence to him as to a god, and so departed'. She follows Pan's directions and has a joyful reunion with Cupid. At the celebratory feast, the gods all have a part, with Pan and the satyrs providing music on their pipes.[77]

Pan also appears as a protector in *Daphnis and Chloe*, the only surviving work by the Greek novelist Longus (second century AD). Longus portrays Pan as kindly disposed towards the two lovers, a protective god who instils panic in their enemies. The novel is among the most influential ancient portrayals of Pan, and inspired later writers and artists. The one-act ballet *Daphnis et Chloé* (1912) by Maurice Ravel adapted Longus' story, and the painter Marc Chagall completed 42 colour lithographs illustrating the novel between 1956 and 1961.[78] Longus tells the story of two young people who were each separated from their parents at birth and raised by shepherds. When they meet as adolescents, they fall in love. Guided by Philetas, a wise old man from the countryside, they come to understand their condition and, after many adventures, are finally united in wedlock. Longus dedicates his book 'as an offering to Love, the Nymphs, and Pan'.[79]

When Chloe is kidnapped by a party of raiders from Methymna, Daphnis seeks out the nymphs for help. They appear to him in a dream and assure Daphnis that they have already appealed to Pan, 'whose statue is under yonder pine, to whom you have never offered so much as a chaplet of flowers in token of respect, to go to the assistance of Chloe'. With a nod to Pan's power to cause panic among soldiers, the nymphs note that he 'is more used to the ways of camps' than they are. Daphnis wakes and, worshipping at the statues of Pan and the nymphs, promises them the sacrifice of a goat if Chloe is rescued. Meanwhile, Chloe's kidnappers have anchored their ships and been given permission by their captain to make merry. After a round of heavy drinking, they decide to go to sleep, but Pan soon reveals his power:

> when night began to fall and put an end to their enjoyment, suddenly the whole earth appeared in flames: the splash of oars was heard upon the waters, as if a numerous fleet were approaching. They called upon the general to arm himself: they shouted to each other: some thought they were already wounded, others lay as if they were dead. One would have thought that they were engaged in a battle by night, although there was no enemy.

What Longus describes is a classic example of the kind of military panic attributed to Pan. When panic broke out at night or in adverse weather conditions, soldiers might accidentally attack one another. Such had been the fate of Gauls and Persians when they attempted, at different times, to invade Greece. Their self-slaughter was attributed to Pan's intervention.

The next day Pan reveals his divine power at work through a series of strange occurrences that employ his traditional symbolic associations. The pirates are terrified as they witness the evidence of his direct intervention:

> They saw Daphnis's goats with ivy-branches, loaded with berries, on their horns: while Chloe's rams and ewes were heard howling like wolves: Chloe herself appeared, crowned with a garland of pine. Many marvellous things also happened on the sea. When they attempted to raise the anchors, they remained fast to the bottom: when the oars were dipped into the water

to row, they snapped. Dolphins, leaping from the waves, lashed the ships with their tails, and loosened the fastenings. From the top of the steep rock over-hanging the promontory was heard the sound of a pipe: but the sound did not soothe the hearers, but terrified them, like the blast of a trumpet.

This episode suggests a similar myth about Dionysus, in which the god, disguised as a boy, is kidnapped by sailors, who are then terrified by a series of supernatural events aboard ship. Note, however, the number of elements in this supernatural visitation that are traditionally connected with Pan: the goats, rams and ewes; the wolves, associated in particular with Mount Lykaion; the pine, symbol of the nymph Pitys; and the pipe, Pan's musical instrument. This pipe is not the usual relaxing accompaniment to rural pursuits, but a source of sudden terror; it literally induces a state of panic in its hearers, when 'smitten with affright they ran to arms, and called upon their invisible enemies to appear'. Those with insight realize that these bizarre disturbances 'were the work of God Pan'.

Having revealed himself symbolically, Pan now com-municates directly with the pirates to let them know that Chloe is under his protection. At noon the following day the exhausted men fall asleep, and an angry Pan appears in a dream to their leader, Bryaxis. Having realized the source of Pan's anger, Bryaxis wastes no time in returning Chloe home, personally rowing her to shore in his own small boat. The pipes of Pan are again heard, playing a pastoral air this time, and the Methymnian ships mysteriously lift anchor and follow a dolphin to shore, where the sheep and goats disem-bark. A joyful reunion ensues, and Daphnis duly sacrifices to Pan and the nymphs. In the celebration that follows,

Daphnis and Chloe take the parts of Pan and Syrinx in a dance that retells their myth to the accompaniment of Philetas' piping. Longus' Pan shows the god in his most appealing aspect, kind-hearted and protective, and the terror he inspires in the pirates has the quality of a practical joke; they lie 'as if dead', rather than actually being killed. This pastoral version of the god, friend to shepherds and devoted lovers, was, however, just one aspect of Pan as he was conceived in the ancient world. He was also given more profound qualities by a variety of religious and philosophical traditions.

PAGAN RELIGION AND PHILOSOPHY

Cultures in the ancient world did not hesitate to identify gods from one place with those of another. The Greeks themselves identified Pan with the Egyptian god Min, a horned god of fertility and the desert (the Egyptian wilderness), depicted with a prominent phallus. Ipu or Khent-Min, a site of his worship, was later known as Panopolis.[80] Herodotus identified Pan with the Egyptian city and god the Greeks called Mendes (Banebdjedet).[81] He claims that

> the Mendesians reckon Pan among the eight gods who, they say, were before the twelve gods. Now in their painting and sculpture, the image of Pan is made with the head and the legs of a goat, as among the Greeks; not that he is thought to be in fact such, or unlike other gods; but why they represent him so, I have no wish to say.[82]

Even in describing an Egyptian god, Herodotus reveals his embarrassment over Pan's scandalous form. In his account, goats are especially sacred to the Mendesians, who never sacrifice them. With his usual gift for combining sober information with sensational anecdote, he tells us: 'In the Egyptian language Mendes is the name both for the he-goat and for Pan. In my lifetime a strange thing occurred in this district: a he-goat had intercourse openly with a woman. This came to be publicly known.'[83] It is impossible to know if Herodotus is describing a ritual in honour of the god or merely reporting a local story.

In the second and third centuries BC the Roman upper classes began to adopt Greek culture, identifying the traditional Latin gods with those of Greece – Jupiter with Zeus, Juno with Hera, Mars with Ares and so on. Pan was identified with two semi-distinct Roman gods: Faunus, the horned god of forests, pastures and flocks, and Inuus, the god of sexual intercourse. Faunus and Inuus were sometimes understood as different aspects of the same god, called Inuus when overseeing the fertility of flocks. The Roman historian Livy (59 BC–AD 17) identifies Faunus with Lupercus, whose name means 'one who wards off wolves', celebrated at the annual Lupercalia on 15 February. Livy also claims that the festival was introduced by an Arcadian named Evander, who 'derived from Arcadia, that youths should run naked about in playful sport, doing honour to Lycaean Pan, whom the Romans afterwards called Inuus'.[84] The priests of Lupercus wore goatskins and wielded goatskin whips against passers-by at the festival. Unlike Pan, Faunus has no distinct myths, but was believed to have been an early king of the Latins. He was celebrated by name at two Roman festivals called the Faunalia, held on 13 February and 5 December.[85]

In addition to the kind of public worship associated with festivals and temples, religion in the ancient world offered devout pagans the opportunity to be initiated into various mystery cults. Apuleius, for example, was an initiate of the mysteries of Isis; the main narrative of *The Golden Ass* culminates in a redemptive vision of the goddess. The best known of the ancient mysteries were those practised at Eleusis, devoted to Demeter and Persephone. By living a moral life and practising certain rites, initiates of the various ancient mysteries could aspire to immortality in the Elysian Fields, instead of just twittering forever in the darkness of Hades or enduring a series of endless incarnations.[86]

Pan was one of many gods worshipped by adherents of Orphism, named after the legendary Thracian poet Orpheus. In Greek legend, Orpheus was a poet who could enchant people and animals with the power of his lyre. After his wife, Eurydice, died, he journeyed to the underworld to retrieve her. He nearly succeeded but at the last minute looked behind him to see if she was there, breaking a condition imposed by Hades and so losing her forever. Overwhelmed with grief, Orpheus refused to remarry and was torn to pieces by furious maenads.[87] Orphics believed that humans possessed a divine soul that could be liberated from the cycle of rebirth through ascetic practices. They rejected the most typical practice of ancient Greek religion, the sacrifice of an animal and ritual meal. Orphic mythology adapted existing myths in a cosmic or philosophical way. For example, Dionysus, their central god, was believed to be the source of the human soul. He was torn to pieces and devoured by the Titans during their wars with the gods, and subsequently reborn. In Orphic cosmology, the Titans are the source of our physical bodies, which imprison the Dionysian soul. Initiates learn the rites and practices necessary to liberate the Dionysus within.[88] While details of Orphic ritual remain unknown, some 87 Orphic hymns survive, including one dedicated to Pan. The scholars Apostolos N. Athanassakis and Benjamin M. Wolkow date the hymns to the mid-third century AD, identifying Eastern Anatolia as their probable place of origin, based on the inclusion of regional gods who were known only locally.[89]

Like its companions, the Orphic hymn to Pan is an invocation, or summoning, of the god. This could be a dangerous activity; the ancient writer Porphyry records that nine of Pan's worshippers died of fright when the god suddenly appeared to them.[90] The hymn opens with what appears to be an allusion to a ritual context: 'The Fumigation from Various Odours'. Athanassakis and Wolkow suggest that the hymns may have been recited over the course of an entire night as a kind of liturgy, accompanied by a variety of incense appropriate to each god.[91] Ritual invocation of the pagan gods was known as 'theurgy', and was common throughout the ancient world, where it often blurred into magic. The hymn itself is remarkable for its development of the idea that Pan's name signifies 'all', imagining him as a foundational god comprising all things. In its eighteenth-century translation by Thomas Taylor, the Orphic hymn to Pan would exert enormous influence on English Romanticism:

> I call strong Pan, the substance of the whole,
> Etherial [sic], marine, earthly, general soul,
> Immortal fire; for all the world is thine,
> And all are parts of thee, O pow'r divine.[92]

Somewhat obscured in Taylor's translation, Pan is here envisioned as the basis of the ancient elements of air, water, earth and fire, which make up the physical universe, described as 'parts' of the god himself. Later in the hymn Pan is credited with securing the elemental forms of the world through his power over all:

By thee the earth wide-bosom'd deep and long,
Stands on a basis permanent and strong.
Th' unwearied waters of the rolling sea,
Profoundly spreading, yield to thy decree.
Old Ocean too reveres thy high command,
Whose liquid arms begirt the solid land,
The spacious air, whose nutrimental fire,
And vivid blasts, the heat of life inspire;
The lighter frame of fire, whose sparkling eye
Shines on the summit of the azure sky,
Submit alike to thee, whole general sway
All parts of matter, various form'd obey.[93]

Even the sun (that 'sparkling eye') submits to the will of cosmic Pan. While the hymn also describes Pan in more familiar mythological terms as the 'goat footed, horned' god of shepherds, lover of 'rural haunts', the nymph Echo and the hunt, as ruler of the material universe he transcends these more homely associations. The poet even identifies Pan with Zeus himself. Nonetheless, the speaker of the hymn concludes by asking Pan to 'Drive panic Fury too, wherever found, / From human kind, to earth's remotest bound.'[94] Even amid the subtleties of Orphism, Pan retains his original connection to the sensation of panic and is asked to spare us from it. Throughout the other hymns, allusions to Pan connect him with Dionysus and other gods who induce madness or ecstasy.

Through the influence of Stoic philosophy, Pan would also find his way from the wilderness to the groves of academe. Stoics believed that virtue was the only way to happiness, and that the universe itself was a living substance endowed with reason. Their philosophical interpretation of Pan closely parallels the version we encounter in the Orphic hymn, hinging as it does on the identity of Pan with 'all' – the universe in its totality. This Pan first appears in the work of Lucius Annaeus Cornutus (*fl.* AD 54–69), a Stoic teacher and writer during the reign of Emperor Nero. He interprets Pan's appearance as an allegory of the universe: 'The lower part of this god is hairy, and recalls a goat, to designate the roughness of the earth. The upper part, however, is like a man, for heaven holds sway over the entire world, because in heaven itself reason is placed.'[95] Classical philosophers, medieval theologians and Renaissance humanists would all echo and expand on this basic allegory. Writing in AD 636, Isidore of Seville describes a more detailed allegory originally composed by the grammarian Servius, who wrote in about AD 400:

Pan [is] the god of the rustics, whom they have formed in the shape of Nature; wherefore he is called Pan, that is, All. For they form him out of every kind of element. For he has horns in the shape of the rays of the sun and the moon. He has skin marked with spots, because of the stars of the sky. His face is red, in the likeness of the upper air. He carries a pipe with seven reeds, because of the harmony of heaven in which there are seven notes and seven distinctions of tones He is hairy, since the earth is clothed and is stirred by the winds. His lower part is filthy, because of trees and wild beasts and herds. He has goat hoofs, to show forth the solidity of the earth, he whom they desire as the god of things and of all nature: whence they call him Pan, as if to say Everything.[96]

While the cosmic parallels are inventive, the passage is perhaps most interesting as an inventory of Pan's various physical characteristics as understood in late antiquity. Most are consistent over a thousand years, but Servius and Isidore include a few that are less common, such as 'skin marked with spots', presumably a reference to the lynx skin that Pan is reported to wear. The red face is a detail also reported by Virgil, who, as we have seen, attributes it to 'vermilion and blood-red elderberries'.[97] Given that Servius wrote commentaries on Virgil's poetry, it seems likely that he is the source of this colourful detail. In terms of the cosmic parallel, the connection between Pan and the 'solidity of the earth' is also suggested by the Orphic hymn, which makes Pan responsible for keeping the Earth 'on a basis permanent and strong'.

DEATH OF A GOD

Of all the events in Pan's varied career in ancient religion, myth, history and philosophy, none is more incredible than the last: his death. There were gods, such as Dionysus, who died and were reborn. Persephone spent the winter months in Hades and returned every spring to bring fertility to our world. In the Gospels, Jesus was crucified, died and was buried before returning from the dead three days later. Of all the gods worshipped in the ancient world, however, only Pan was reported simply to have died. The event is recorded by Plutarch in his treatise *On the Failure of the Oracles* (c. AD 100). He cites as his source a man named Epitherses, father of a prominent orator named Aemilianus. Here is the story in full:

> He said that once upon a time in making a voyage to Italy he embarked on a ship carrying freight and many passengers. It was already evening when, near the Echinades Islands, the wind dropped, and the ship drifted near Paxi. Almost everybody was awake, and a good many had not finished their after-dinner wine.

Suddenly from the island of Paxi was heard the voice of someone loudly calling Thamus, so that all were amazed. Thamus was an Egyptian pilot, not known by name even to many on board. Twice he was called and made no reply, but the third time he answered; and the caller, raising his voice, said, 'When you come opposite to Palodes, announce that Great Pan is dead.' On hearing this, all, said Epitherses, were astounded and reasoned among themselves whether it were better to carry out the order or to refuse to meddle and let the matter go. Under the circumstances Thamus made up his mind that if there should be a breeze, he would sail past and keep quiet, but with no wind and a smooth sea about the place he would announce what he had heard. So, when he came opposite Palodes, and there was neither wind nor wave, Thamus from the stern, looking toward the land, said the words as he had heard them: 'Great Pan is dead.' Even before he had finished there was a great cry of lamentation, not of one person, but of many, mingled with exclamations of amazement. As many persons were on the vessel, the story was soon spread abroad in Rome, and Thamus was sent for by Tiberius Caesar. Tiberius became so convinced of the truth of the story that he caused an inquiry and investigation to be made about Pan; and the scholars, who were numerous at his court, conjectured that he was the son born of Hermes and Penelopê.[98]

Plutarch's retelling reads like straight reportage, which is apparently how the Emperor Tiberius understood the story when told by Thamus. If Pan was really dead, however, why were his worshippers carrying on as usual when Pausanias toured Greece during the next century? Robert Graves, following earlier scholars, suggests that Thamus 'apparently misheard the ceremonial lament *Thamus Pan-megas Tethnēche* ("the all-great Tammuz is dead!") for the message: "Thamus, Great Pan is dead!"'[99] Tammuz (Dumuzid) was a Mesopotamian god of shepherds and the divine consort of Ishtar (Inanna). In Sumerian mythology he dies but, like the Greek Persephone, is able to return from the underworld for half of the year.[100]

While the reported death of Pan appeared not to trouble his worshippers, for the followers of a newer faith it appeared as vindication. Eusebius (d. AD 340), an early historian of the Christian Church, argued that Pan's death occurred even as Jesus was exorcising demons through his ministry. Christians typically viewed the pagan gods as demons in disguise, so this historical coincidence seemed to provide clear evidence of the efficacy of Christ's power.[101] While some later writers would wholeheartedly endorse the Eusebian view of Pan's death, for many others Plutarch's account would be understood symbolically or vehemently rejected.

Eusebius also reports the story told by the pagan philosopher Porphyry, who 'affirms that Pan is a servant of Dionysos, and that he being one of the good daemons appeared once upon a time to those who were working in the fields'.[102] If this seems an unlikely anecdote for a Christian apologist to relate, the tables are quickly turned: 'Did then any good result to the beholders of this good daemon, or have they found him an evil daemon, and learned this by practical experience? This admirable witness says indeed that those to whom this blessed sight was vouchsafed all died at once.'[103] As mentioned earlier, Porphyry reports that nine people were discovered dead, and when the locals consulted the oracle of Apollo of Branchidae, they received the following verses:

Lo! where the golden-horned Pan
In sturdy Dionysos' train
Leaps o'er the mountains' wooded slopes!
His right hand holds a shepherd's staff,
His left a smooth shrill-breathing pipe,
That charms the gentle wood-nymph's soul.
But at the sound of that strange song
Each startled woodsman dropp'd his axe,
And all in frozen terror gaz'd
Upon the Daemon's frantic course.
Death's icy hand had seiz'd them all,
Had not the huntress Artemis
In anger stay'd his furious might.
To her address thy prayer for aid.[104]

This oracle presents a characteristic image of Pan, but specifies that while his pipes have the power to charm nymphs they are a source of danger to men, who, on hearing them, are frozen in place, apparently unable to look away, and so perish. Death was the fate conventionally meted out to mortals who beheld the true form of a god or goddess. The last four lines of the oracle imply that at least some of those who beheld Pan were spared death through the intervention of Artemis. Eusebius glosses over this detail, however, casting aspersions on all the pagan gods and their supposed blessings.

A sudden, sharp note pierces the warm summer evening, making the hairs on the back of your neck stand on end. You've travelled the length and breadth of Greece, gathering accounts of the gods and debating their origins with other learned men, not to mention several women well versed in the traditions of their districts. One, however, remains elusive: the goat-footed god of the Arcadians with that mysterious name meaning 'all'. No one agrees about him. Those surly Arcadians, so boastful about their wealth in goats and their prowess in battle, become curiously reticent when asked about their god. As the twilight deepens, another note and then another floats through the air. The melody is indescribably beautiful and – perhaps it was that exceptionally strong wine – you find your eyes filling with tears. Then, among the trees, you see lithe figures dancing, and in a moment of panic you press up against an enormous pine, lest you be seen. You peer cautiously around the tree and witness bright female forms dancing in circles to the music. The background fades and those circles become the seven spheres of the cosmos, one for each note that sounds on the invisible pipes. In your reverie, you see the stars emerge against a sky black as an animal's pelt, and, further up, the curved shape of a horn appears in brilliant silhouette.

When you wake it is the crescent of the moon that greets your eye, and you could swear you hear a distant music fade into the wind. You sigh as you recall your failed search for the god's true origins, and then it all comes back: the music, the nymphs, the circling planets. Now you know those rumours from Rome are false: the Great God Pan lives on!

2

MEDIEVAL AND EARLY MODERN PAN

Classical visions of Pan came to an end along with the pagan religion that had sustained and inspired them. In AD 323 the emperor Constantine proclaimed Christianity the official religion of the Roman Empire, and for the next two centuries paganism lived a kind of half-life, until the emperor Justinian finally closed the Academy of Athens in AD 529. Pan disappeared from public view along with the other pagan gods. He is depicted in a few manuscript images, but when later medieval poets such as Chaucer bring in pagan deities, Pan is not among them. With the rediscovery of pagan antiquity in the Renaissance, Pan takes his place among the other gods, interpreted in a variety of allegorical senses that echo Orphic and Stoic tradition. The sixteenth-century revival of pastoral poetry in England features occasional appearances of Pan in his Virgilian character, but also in an allegorical role symbolizing Christ. This Christian appropriation of Pan opened the way for identifying the god with the Stuart monarchy, an identification that lasted throughout the Jacobite rebellions. At the dawn of the Scientific Revolution, Francis Bacon argued that pagan mythology encoded scientific knowledge, and that Pan offered insight into the composition of the material universe. Painters of the seventeenth century were drawn to Pan as the embodiment of sexual desire, whether in allegories of the struggle between love and lust or in depictions of his pursuit of Syrinx. Contemporary poets tended to shy away from him, but Milton and Marvell in particular found remarkably inventive ways to bring him into their verse. The decorous neoclassicism of the eighteenth century proved unwelcoming for the god of the wild, but it provides us with our first glimpse of Pan as protector of the forests.

MEDIEVAL IMAGES AND RENAISSANCE REDISCOVERIES

The horns and hooves that Pan shares with conventional modern images of the Devil might lead us to conclude that medieval Christians followed Eusebius in imagining Pan as a kind of demon. Medieval devils, although usually horned, are typically scaly rather than shaggy, and often have bat-like wings. While Pan's appearance would eventually become synonymous with the Devil's, the few images of Pan surviving from the Middle Ages hold some surprises. In the ninth-century Stuttgart Psalter, one of the treasures of Carolingian religious art, an unexpected scene unfolds below Psalm 77. On the left are the twelve Tribes of Israel, roaming in the wilderness, looking at a monkey in the upper right-hand corner of the illumination. Below that monkey, with a mischievous gleam in his eye, is an image of Pan, just as we've come to know him, complete with horns and hooves. He plays on his pipes, a faint smile lighting up his face. Around his torso is wrapped some kind of skin, perhaps intended to be that of a lynx. He is cheerful rather than diabolical, at home in the wilderness that is such an ordeal to the wandering Tribes. If he offers any temptation, it would seem to be nothing other than the wilderness itself, or perhaps he hints at the pleasures of the flesh. An orthodox Christian interpretation might see in the image of Pan a reference to the sin of lasciviousness, which was also symbolized by the monkey. A less interesting manuscript image from the eleventh century portrays Pan with enormous goat hooves, playing his pipes while he stands beside Venus and Cupid, symbolizing love and desire.[1]

The rediscovery of classical antiquity in the Renaissance led to fresh contact with the pagan gods and goddesses. Christian Europeans would create mystical interpretations of pagan mythology, avoiding the question of literal belief in the pagan gods. By interpreting myths allegorically, they could find spiritual meaning in them without directly challenging the authority of the Church or their own faith. The Renaissance philosopher Giovanni Pico della Mirandola (1463–1494), for example, imagined Pan as symbolizing the 'One' and the shape-shifting Proteus as 'the Many', leading him to remark that 'He who cannot attract Pan approaches Proteus in vain.'[2]

Depicting these allegories in painting rather than words was another way to avoid religious controversy. Sandro Botticelli's *Birth of Venus* (*c.* 1485) and *Primavera* (*c.* 1480) are perhaps the best-known examples of Renaissance paintings that can be viewed as illustrations of classical myth or as allusions to deeper philosophical truths.[3] In *The School (or Court) of Pan*, a painting unfortunately destroyed in the Second World War, Luca Signorelli (*c.* 1450–1523) depicts Pan in a way that is recognizable as the cosmic or Orphic Pan. He sits enthroned at the centre of the painting, with the reflective and fully human face of a Renaissance prince. Out of his abundant hair protrude two stylized horns that resemble lunar crescents. In place of an animal skin, he wears a fine cloak ornamented with stars. In one hand he holds a shepherd's crook, in the other his pipes. From the waist down,

Luca Signorelli, *The School (or Court) of Pan*,
Florence, *c*. 1490, tempera on canvas. This painting, destroyed
in the Second World War, depicts the cosmic or Orphic Pan
dispensing wisdom to his followers.

Pan is shaggy and cloven-hoofed. His very appearance
encompasses Heaven and Earth, god and beast – truly the
Pan of 'all'. As though seeking his wisdom, young and old
men gather around him, and Pan appears engaged in earnest
conversation with one of them. In the foreground, a naked
female figure holds a long reed; she may represent Syrinx or
Echo. A reclining young man gazes up at her yearningly with
a reed protruding from his mouth. The art historian Michael
Levey describes these various figures as 'banished creatures
of mythology, who had always existed and who have now
crept back into the welcoming Renaissance air'.[4]

That welcoming air also fostered a new way of reading
Plutarch's account of the death of Pan, one that challenged
the Christian absolutism of Eusebius. A few decades before

Signorelli painted his *School of Pan*, the poet and humanist Paulus Marsus wrote a commentary on Ovid's extended poem *Fasti*. Citing the authority of 'holiest men', Marsus claims that Plutarch's story did indeed take place at the exact moment of Christ's death, because the death of Pan is really the death of Christ. Marsus claims that if Pan means 'all', then 'the lord of all and of universal nature had died,' so Pan and Christ are in a sense identical.[5] This somewhat awkward attempt to reconcile Christian and pagan belief is typical of Renaissance humanism. Marsus' interpretation offered yet another way to bring Pan back into Western culture, and would prove influential for later writers, among them François Rabelais (*c.* 1494–1553). Rabelais is most famous for his uproarious, hard-to-classify tale *Gargantua and Pantagruel*, which ostensibly tells the story of two giants, father and son, while satirizing the received pieties of his time. Our adjective 'Rabelaisian', meaning something earthy, gross or even obscene, succinctly captures the pungency of his creation. While Pan the shaggy, goat-footed, nymph-chasing god would seem to fit well in Rabelais' imaginative world, he appears in a more reflective context that develops the ideas of Marsus, which he probably encountered through his mentor Cardinal Jean du Bellay.

In Book IV, Chapter 28, the giant Pantagruel retells Plutarch's story of the death of Pan and provides his own explanation. In his view, the story refers to

> that great Saviour of the faithful who was shamefully put to death at Jerusalem by the envy and wickedness of the doctors, priests and monks of the Mosaic law. And methinks my interpretation is not improper; for he may lawfully be said in the Greek tongue to be Pan, since he is our all. For all that we are, all that we live,

all that we have, all that we hope, is him, by him, from him and in him. He is the good Pan, the great shepherd, who, as the loving shepherd Corydon affirms, hath not only a tender love and affection for his sheep, but also for their shepherds. At his death, complaints, sighs, fears and lamentations were spread through the whole fabric of the universe, whether heavens, land, sea or hell.[6]

Rabelais here plays not only on the idea of Pan and Christ as gods of all, but on their role as divine shepherds. That these reflections are put into the mouth of the giant Pantagruel may, however, give us pause. Is Rabelais hiding his own heterodox belief behind a fictional character? Or is he satirizing the excesses of Renaissance humanism by attributing that belief to Pantagruel? Whatever he was doing, Rabelais has been read as everything from a strident atheist to a pious Catholic, so we should perhaps keep an open mind.

Renaissance literature also revitalized the pastoral side of Pan's character. The sixteenth-century Renaissance in England brought a new interest in pastoral and mythological poetry, with Virgil and Ovid offering new models and sources of inspiration. The *Countess of Pembroke's Arcadia*, a pastoral romance by Philip Sidney (1554–1586), includes several conventional invocations of Pan ('Thy pipe, ô Pan, shall helpe, though I sing sorilie'), hailing him as 'ever carefull of the chiefe blessings of Arcadia'.[7] Act IV of John Lyly's play *Midas* draws on Ovid to dramatize the musical contest between Apollo and Pan. While Apollo, like a Renaissance gentleman, sings the praises of Daphne to the accompaniment of the lute instead of his traditional lyre, Pan must lay down his pipes to sing a rustic ballad, which begins, unpromisingly, 'Pan's Syrinx was a girl indeed, / Though now she's turned into a reed.'[8] To get the satirical tone, we might imagine these lines sung by Baldrick from *Blackadder*. Pan here is a figure of fun – a simple country bumpkin. Despite a new interest in the pastoral mode, however, few English poets before Edmund Spenser (1552/3–1599) allude to the Great God Pan beyond the usual Virgilian oaths and prayers.

Spenser's innovation in portraying Pan is to employ pastoral literary conventions to suggest that the god is in reality Christ himself. His allusions to Pan in *The Shepheardes Calender* were inspired by Rabelais as well as by the French poet Clément Marot (?1496–1544), who wrote a lengthy poem linking Pan to François I, King of France, and another praising God as Pan.[9] In the eclogue for 'July', Spenser alludes to Christ as Pan, playing on Christ's traditional role as the good shepherd:

MORRELL
And wonned [lived] not the great God Pan
Upon Mount Olivet;
Feeding the blessed Flock of Dan,
Which did himself beget?

THOMALIN
O blessed Sheep! O Shepherd great!
That bought his Flock so dear:
And them did save with bloody Sweat,
From Wolves that would them tear.[10]

The goatherd Morrell imagines Pan's herds as the Israelites ('Flock of Dan') who begot Christ; Thomalin's response retains the pastoral conceit while alluding to Christ's suffering on the Cross ('bloody Sweat'). The examples from Rabelais and Spenser expose the limits to imagining Pan as Christ; no reference at all is made to Pan's goatish appearance or nature, irreconcilable as it is with Christ's promise that when the Son of Man returns, 'before him shall be gathered all nations: and he shall separate them one from another, as a shepherd divideth his sheep from the goats.'[11] One imagines the goat-footed god shrugging sadly and taking up his pipes as he leads his unwanted goats away.

Something truer to the classical image of Pan is found in *The Book of Emblems* by Andrea Alciato (1492–1550), a collection of symbolic images accompanied by poems that explain their meaning. The emblem 'Nature' is represented by an image of Pan in all his glory, with horns, beard and goatish legs, holding his pipes as he sits on a flat rock far from the two cities that appear in the background. He is clearly a god of the wilderness. Unlike some of his sixteenth-century contemporaries, Alciato acknowledges Pan's animal sexuality:

> The people reverence Pan (that is to say, the nature of things), a man who is half-goat, a god who is half-man. He is a man down to his loins because the virtue implanted in us, rising from the heart, is seated in the high citadel of the head. Below, he is a goat, because nature continues us through time by means of copulation, like birds, fish, brute animals and wild beasts. Because this is common to other living creatures, the goat is the sign of lechery and bears the open marks of Venus. Some give wisdom to the heart, others to the brain. No moderation or reason rules the baser things.[12]

Despite its relative brevity, Alciato's emblem reconciles the Orphic Pan who is 'the nature of things' with the Pan whose body combines the distinctly human with the bestial. This generous symbolic interpretation of Pan neither excludes nor dismisses the god's wilder aspects: his hairy sexuality expresses the way 'nature continues us through time by means of copulation.' The lecherous goat on its own may lack 'moderation or reason', but, as with us, Pan's sexual nature is balanced by the virtues associated with heart and head. Alciato's holistic vision of the Great God has an authenticity and completeness rare among the work of writers and artists of the Renaissance. Not until D. H. Lawrence would another writer embrace Pan's nature and spirit so fully.

ALLEGORIES IN THE LATE RENAISSANCE AND RESTORATION

Pan is a sporadic presence in Western culture from the seventeenth to the nineteenth century. Francis Beaumont and John Fletcher's pastoral comedy *The Faithful Shepherdess* (c. 1608) includes a couple of conventional hymns to Pan, in the first of which the swains hail him as 'Father of our Sheep' and, more surprisingly, praise him for keeping them 'chaste and free'. This Pan is guardian of both Christian virtue and English liberty. In the second hymn, Pan 'defends our flocks from blame', his traditional role as guardian of sheep and goats.[13] On 19 June 1620 the dramatist Ben Jonson celebrated the birthday of King James I with an elaborate masque entitled *Pan's Anniversary; or, The Shepherd's Holiday*, designed by the architect Inigo Jones. It imagines James himself as a presiding Pan, amused and praised by nymphs, a shepherd, a fencer, various Arcadians and Echo. The masque opens with three nymphs strewing flowers, encouraged by an elderly shepherd: 'Thus, thus begin the yearly rites / Are due to Pan on these bright nights.'[14] After a brief comical anti-masque, the shepherd alludes to James as a bringer of civilization and peace:

> And come, you prime Arcadians forth, that taught
>   By Pan the rites of true society,
> From his loud music all your manners wrought,
>   And made your commonwealth a harmony.[15]

Jonson echoes the classical view that the wild Arcadians were civilized by the power of rustic music. One can imagine the royal pleasure as the Arcadians hail Pan as 'best of singers', 'best of leaders', 'best of hunters' and 'best of shepherds'.[16] This sycophancy, as it must seem to us, is dwarfed by that of the Arcadians' second hymn:

> Pan is our All, by him we breathe, we live,
>   We move, we are; 'tis he our lambs doth rear,
> Our flocks doth bless, and from the store doth give,
>   The warm and finer fleeces that we wear.[17]

The first two lines play on the ancient pun identifying Pan with 'all', appealing to James the classical scholar; this is the Orphic or cosmic Pan who is the substance of the material universe, on whom all living things depend. Pan is then imagined as the 'Good Shepherd', both guardian and provider, alluding to James's pastoral role as head of the Church of England. The remainder of the hymn celebrates Pan's power over the fertility of flocks, a traditional role for the god, although perhaps a surprising one for the Stuart monarch. The connection between royalty and fertility is, however, a very ancient one; in the Arthurian legend, to cite one example, the Fisher King's lands perish because of the wound he has received in his thigh, and can be renewed only by the Grail. After the main dance, which dramatizes royal and cosmic order, the arrival of Echo initiates the 'revels'. The masque concludes with a fourth hymn to 'Great Pan, the father of our peace and pleasure', praying once again for protection and fecundity.[18] The reference to peace would have been especially flattering to James, who prided himself on being a peaceful monarch.

Outside imaginative literature, prose writers continued to develop philosophical interpretations of Pan. The naturalistic vision of Pan explored by Francis Bacon (1561–1626) reflects his own sensibility as a pioneer of the scientific method. In *The Wisdom of the Ancients* (1609), Bacon attempts to make sense of classical mythology as a kind of poetic explanation of nature and the cosmos. Because they lacked scientific language and concepts, Bacon argues, the ancients expressed their knowledge in the language of myth, a development of the earlier Renaissance notion that the ancients possessed a secret or hidden wisdom. In Chapter Six, 'Pan; or, Nature Explained of Natural Philosophy', Bacon begins by offering a brief survey of Pan's origins and appearance, and the myths associated with him. His account of the mythic lore associated with Pan is brief but inclusive; he also includes an allegorical myth in which Pan 'challenged Cupid at wrestling, and was worsted', representing the triumph of love over lust, also depicted by the sixteenth-century artist Agostino Carracci (see p. 64).[19]

Bacon's approach can perhaps best be illustrated by his convoluted interpretation of three myths of Pan's parentage, Mercury (Hermes) and Penelope, Penelope and her suitors, and Jupiter and Hybris:

> these three several accounts of Pan's birth may seem true, if duly distinguished in respect of things and times. For this Pan, or the universal nature of things, which we view and contemplate, had its origin from the divine Word and confused matter, first created by

God himself, with the subsequent introduction of sin, and consequently corruption.

He understands Pan's half-human, half-goat appearance as reflecting the 'superior and inferior parts' of nature, 'as the former, for their beauty, regularity of motion, and influence over the earth, may be properly represented by the human figure, and the latter, because of their disorder, irregularity, and subjection to the celestial bodies, are by the brutal'. Each of Pan's physical attributes is explained in terms of some aspect of the physical universe, as it was understood in Bacon's time. For example, 'the beard of Pan is exceeding long, because the rays of the celestial bodies penetrate, and act to a prodigious distance, and have descended into the interior of the earth so far as to change its surface.' Pan inspires terror, 'for nature has implanted fear in all living creatures'. If Bacon's quasi-scientific explanations remove all the wonder and mystery from our experience of Pan, that is really the point; for Bacon, what seem like mysteries are really just coded observations of the natural world. The action of myths describes natural processes or imparts moralistic lessons, as when the musical contest between Apollo and Pan is read as teaching us 'to humble the human reason and judgment, which is too apt to boast and glory in itself'. This rationalizing approach to myth would become more common in the eighteenth century and be echoed in the Romantic poetry of William Wordsworth.

For other writers in literary and popular culture, Pan was simply one more otherworldly being. For the French poet Pierre de Ronsard (1524–1585), in his *Hymne des Daimons*, 'Pan' is but one of many demons, a category that includes fairies, satyrs, nymphs and fauns. In English popular culture, the image of Pan (or a faun) appears in the guise of Robin

Robin Good-fellow, His Mad Prankes and Merry Jests, 1639, woodcut.
The mischievous spirit from English folklore is given the form of Pan or
a faun in this anonymous woodcut. In the twentieth century Margaret A.
Murray would argue that such similarities were evidence of the persistence
of the worship of a Horned God since Palaeolithic times.

Goodfellow. *Robin Good-fellow, His Mad Prankes and Merry Jests* was printed in London by Thomas Cotes. The title page depicts a bearded male with the horns, ears and legs of a goat – as well as two large testicles and a curiously tapered phallus. In one hand he holds a lit candle, while the other clasps a broom that he has positioned behind his head. Some sort of necklace hangs around his neck, and across his chest is a hunting horn – the one accessory that at least suggests the classical Pan. He is surrounded by a circle of dancing elves, fitting company for the mischievous hobgoblin. The image shows how the half-goat form of Pan could be repurposed to accommodate other supernatural beings. It is also worth noting that Robin Goodfellow is a mischievous but helpful spirit, by no means an evil one, evidence against the assumption that Pan's form was identified with the Devil.

Pan appears in Baroque art in a less flattering allegorical light than Bacon provides. Annibale Carracci (1560–1609) includes an image of Pan and Diana among his ceiling frescoes in the Galleria of the Palazzo Farnese, Rome. Standing with a goat at his side, Pan offers up some bright wool to the goddess Diana (the Roman Selene), who appears delighted with the offering. In the allegorical scheme of the frescoes, Pan is generally interpreted as representing bestial love, also symbolized by the goat.[20] He had appeared in a similar role in an engraving by Annibale's brother Agostino Carracci (1557–1602), *Omnia Vincit Amor* (Love Conquers All), where Cupid restrains him from approaching two naked female figures. John Boardman notes that the title of the work includes a pun: if love conquers all, and 'all' is Pan, then the meaning of the title is that love conquers Pan – that is, that love overcomes mere bestial lust.[21]

Peter Paul Rubens (1577–1640) produced the rather sinister drawing 'Pan Reclining' (1610), portraying the god stretched out with his head upon a goat and his legs sprawled over a tree. Working with Jan Brueghel the Elder (1568–1625), Rubens also depicted a Pan human in form except for his grotesque face and horns, in *Pan and Syrinx* (c. 1617). The painting depicts the moment Pan surprises a naked Syrinx, who modestly covers her privates as she smiles upon the god.[22] A leering, ruddy-faced statue of Pan appears at the

Agostino Carracci, *Omnia Vincit Amor* (Love Conquers All), 1599, engraving.
Pan's defeat by Cupid was read as an allegory of the triumph of love
over lust, while the Latin title puns on the traditional understanding
of Pan's name as 'All'.

centre of the orgiastic revels depicted in Nicolas Poussin's
The Triumph of Pan (1636), a painting that Pablo Picasso would
revise in his work *La Bacchanal* (1944).[23] Luca Giordano presents an intriguing allegory in his painting simply titled
Allegory (c. 1675). In it, Venus points to a mirror held up by
Cupid, into which Pan gazes through the eyes of a mask. The
mask is that of a handsome youth, whose appearance contrasts with that of the goatish, pointy-eared god. Does love
transform the way we see ourselves, or how we perceive the
more brutish aspects of our nature? Boardman draws our
attention to a Hellenistic epigram by Zeuxis, in which Pan
asks, 'Am I a goat deformed not only in leg but in heart too?'[24]
Perhaps the mask paradoxically reveals an inner beauty.

Although Pan remained a subject of direct interest to
seventeenth-century European painters, he retreated from
contemporary English poetry as the fashion for pastoral verse

gave way to the more complex lyrics of the Metaphysicals. For the Puritan poet John Milton (1608–1674), Pan could offer metaphorical possibility even while belonging to the world of pagan error. In Milton's masque honouring chastity, *Comus* (or, *A Masque Presented at Ludlow Castle*; 1634), the evil Comus enters accompanied by 'a rout of Monsters headed like sundry sorts of wilde Beasts, but otherwise like Men and Women'.[25] They are monstrous because they combine the human with the animal, in the manner of the goat-footed god. After the monsters engage in a 'wild, rude, & wanton' dance, the chaste Lady enters, having mistaken their revels for those of Pan's devotees:

> This way the noise was, if mine ear be true,
> My best guide now, me thought it was the sound
> Of Riot, and ill-manag'd Merriment,
> Such as the jocund Flute, or gamesom Pipe
> Stirs up among the loose unleter'd Hinds [farm
>   labourers],
> When for their teeming Flocks, and granges full
> In wanton dance they praise the bounteous Pan,
> And thank the gods amiss.

'Riot, and ill-manag'd Merriment' can only betoken trouble in a ceremonious courtly masque. Although she describes Pan as 'bounteous', the Lady makes it clear that the shepherds are 'amiss' in thanking him and the other pagan gods. For Puritans such as Milton, all blessings come from the one true God, and attributing them to Pan is (at best) a serious mistake; the 'unleter'd Hinds' cannot, of course, read the Bible. In Book IV of *Paradise Lost* (1667), Milton draws metaphorically on the Orphic Pan to describe the unchanging perfection of the Garden of Eden: 'Universal *Pan* / Knit with the *Graces* and the *Hours* in dance / Led on th'Eternal Spring.'[26] This stately procession of Graces and Hours is remote indeed from Pan's revels in the woods and mountains of Arcadia.

Milton's most surprising use of Pan, however, is in 'On the Morning of Christ's Nativity' (1629). For the most part, this poem argues that Christ's birth banishes the pagan gods altogether: 'The Oracles are dumm, / No voice or hideous humm / Runs through the arched roof in words deceiving.'[27] *On the Failure of the Oracles* (*De defectu oraculorum*) is the title of Plutarch's work in which he describes the death of Pan. Yet Milton himself follows the tradition of Marsus, Rabelais and Spenser, seeing the pagan Pan as a metaphor for Christ:

> The Shepherds on the Lawn,
> Or ere the point of dawn,
> Sate simply chatting in a rustick row;
> Full little thought they than,
> That the mighty *Pan*
> Was kindly com to live with them below;
> Perhaps their loves, or els their sheep,
> Was all that did their silly thoughts so busie keep.[28]

These chatty shepherds are portrayed as innocent worshippers of Pan, who little imagine that the God they have been (mistakenly) honouring as Pan has in fact been born on Earth. Like Pan's followers described in *Comus*, these are 'unletr'd Hinds'. Milton imagines them as conventionally pastoral swains, preoccupied with 'their loves, or els their sheep'. Christ's birth in a sense redeems their misplaced religious faith and the 'silly thoughts' that distract them.

Whereas Milton's poetry offers a Christian interpretation of pastoral conventions, the poetry of Andrew Marvell (1621–1678) reverses pastoral tradition by portraying Pan as a strictly anti-sensual god. In 'Clorinda and Damon' (1650–52), Clorinda attempts to entice Damon to join her in a cave that she designates as 'Love's shrine', but he sternly rejects the site as 'virtue's grave'.[29] The reason he gives for this 'late change' in attitude is a surprising one: 'The other day / Pan met me.' Contrary to the classical vision of Pan, Damon's encounter with the god has led him to reject the pleasures of 'pastures, caves, and springs', as well as sex. What is going on here?

Marvell's poetry doesn't always reject sensual pleasure (see, for example, 'To His Coy Mistress'), but the poem's concluding stanzas suggest that he has in mind the cosmic Pan, rather than the shaggy god concerned with fertility. Both Spenser and Milton identified Pan with Christ, and it may be that Marvell is implying a similar identification without saying it. When Clorinda asks Damon what Pan told him, he can only reply, 'Words that transcend poor shepherds' skill, / But he e'er since my songs does fill: / And his name swells my slender oat.' A Chorus chants the end of the poem, which explicitly identifies Pan with 'all':

> Of Pan the flowery pastures sing,
> Caves echo, and the fountains ring.
> Sing then while he doth us inspire;
> For all the world is our Pan's choir.

Marvell imagines pastures, caves and fountains singing of Pan, whose choir is 'all the world'. Pan's physical appearance is never mentioned in the poem, but note how Marvell slyly alludes to the myth of Pan and Echo in the second line in much the same way as the author of the Homeric hymn.

Damon's rejection of (heterosexual) sex undergoes a strange twist in 'The Garden' (first published in 1681), a poem that exhibits a strong sexual attraction to trees and other plants. The fourth stanza re-imagines the metamorphoses of Daphne and Syrinx as though their transformation was the real purpose of their pursuit by Apollo and Pan:

> The gods, that mortal beauty chase,
> Still in a tree did end their race:
> Apollo hunted Daphne so,
> Only that she might laurel grow;
> And Pan did after Syrinx speed,
> Not as a nymph, but for a reed.[30]

Far from being a consolation for failing to obtain the love of Syrinx, the reed is here portrayed as the real object of Pan's desire all along. Marvell's erotically charged celebration of solitude in nature makes this poem a curiously fitting tribute to the goat-footed god. Unlike Pan, however, the poem's speaker seems content without any companionship at all: 'Such was the happy garden-state / While man there walked without a mate!'[31] The poet also makes one oblique allusion to the death of Pan. In 'The First Anniversary of the Government under O.C.' (1655), Marvell imagines all of nature mourning the fall of Cromwell: 'all about was heard a panic groan, / As if that Nature's self were overthrown.'[32] That 'panic groan' of Nature links Cromwell to Christ as well as to Pan.

The revival of interest in Pan and the other pagan gods that began in the Renaissance was complicated by Christianity, leading Pan to be interpreted allegorically as nature or as Christ himself. While the identification of Pan with Christ did not outlast the seventeenth century, the vision of Pan as a symbol of nature would undergo yet another rebirth in the Romantic era. In between, the eighteenth century was less hospitable to the goat-foot god, and his appearances tend to be idiosyncratic or politically charged.

THE LONG EIGHTEENTH CENTURY

With its fetishizing of the ancient world, we might expect the neoclassical eighteenth century to have brought a rebirth of Pan in all his pagan glory; however, the Augustan Age, as it is sometimes called, looked back to the orderly Rome of Caesar Augustus, not the wilds of ancient Arcadia. Eighteenth-century Arcadias, like those of the French painter Poussin in the previous century, are the idealized landscapes of pastoral verse. For the expanding British Empire, any perceived threat to established order – whether from Jacobites in Scotland or Acadians in Nova Scotia – was likely to face the sharp end of a bayonet. The eighteenth century was also the Age of Enlightenment, which upheld Reason as the source of all virtue. A god whose very form irrationally combines goat and man, a visible reminder of our own animality, was unlikely to endear himself to neoclassical writers, artists or their patrons. Nonetheless, Pan endures as a conventional presence in the pastoral verse and classical translations of the eighteenth century, and is sometimes made to serve more political purposes.

For John Dryden (1631–1700), Pan covertly symbolizes the exiled James II, banished by Parliament in the 'Glorious Revolution' of 1688, which gave the throne to William of Orange. Supporters of the Stuart dynasty were known as 'Jacobites', from the Latin for James, 'Jacobus'. It was politically dangerous to be suspected of loyalty to the Stuarts, so Jacobites relied on symbols and allegories to signal their allegiances to one another. As we saw earlier in this chapter, Ben Jonson had represented James I as Pan in his masque of 1620. In Dryden's 'The Lady's Song', the abandoned kingdom is symbolized by 'Phillis', who refuses a gift of flowers, saying 'I'll not wear a garland while *Pan* is away.'[33] The fact that the speaker is female is yet one more way that Dryden distances himself from the poem's political implications. Pan is away because James II fled to France after being finally defeated by William's forces at the Battle of the Boyne in 1690. In the second stanza, Phillis presents a vision of a land that languishes in Pan's absence:

> While *Pan* and fair *Syrinx*, are fled from our shore,
> The Graces are banish'd, and Love is no more:
> The soft God of Pleasure that warm'd our Desires
> Has broken his Bow, and extinguish'd his Fires,
> And vows that himself, and his Mother will mourn,
> Till *Pan* and fair *Syrinx* in Triumph return.

Dryden's song links the Stuarts' exile to the disappearance of civility and fertility from the land; Jonson similarly connected James I with Pan and a fertile Britain, although not in such erotic terms. The 'God of Pleasure' is Cupid, whose broken bow and extinguished fires suggest a lack not just of fertility, but of sexual desire itself. He and his mother, Venus or Aphrodite, mourn the loss. A shared interest in sex occasionally brought these figures together in classical art, although usually in a more playful way. Mythologically, Syrinx (representing Mary of Modena, second wife of James II) seems to be imagined as a nymph rather than a musical instrument, Pan's willing partner instead of terrified victim. As with Jonson's masque, out of respect for the Stuart monarch, Dryden's song makes no reference to Pan's goatish appearance.

Pan as a disguised James II also appears in a poem by Alexander Robertson of Struan (*c.* 1669–1749), thirteenth chief of Clan Donnachaidh, who led his clansmen in both the 1689 and 1715 Jacobite uprisings in Scotland. In 'The Consolation: An Eclogue' (first published in 1749), Struan dramatizes a conversation between two shepherds, Damon and his friend, Strephon, who is overcome with grief at the departure of Pan. Struan draws on the imagery used by Dryden in 'The Lady's Song' to imagine Pan and Syrinx as parents fleeing from political turmoil:

> When honest PAN withdrew from factious State
> (Curs'd was the Hour, and fatal was the Date)
> When virtuous SYRINX, vilest Rage to Shun,
> Fled to preserve herself and infant Son,
> Then our unguarded Flocks became the Prey
> Of rav'nous Wolves, and Men more Wolves
>   than they.[34]

Struan's political purpose renders the myth of Pan and Syrinx virtually unrecognizable. His Syrinx (Mary of Modena) flees not libidinous Pan, but the 'vilest Rage' of Britain's 'factious State'. She has also gained an 'infant Son' (James, the future 'Old Pretender') in the course of her allegorical transformation. As with Dryden, the Stuart exile leaves Britain a wasteland. Without Pan's protection, the unguarded flocks are vulnerable not only to actual wolves (suggesting a land suffering from famine), but to men whose lupine behaviour makes them even more dangerous. Damon counsels Strephon, 'Tune up thy manly Pipe as heretofore,' as he muses on his beloved Fidelia (faithfulness to the Stuart cause).[35] Given that Struan wrote many bawdy poems, 'manly Pipe' may well be the double entendre it appears.

As well as enlisting Pan in the Jacobite rebellions, the eighteenth century also brought the first appearance of the god as outraged defender of the environment against human despoilment, a role he would assume again in the late twentieth century. 'Pan and Fortune' (1732) is a verse fable by John Gay (1685–1732), the poet and dramatist best known for *The Beggar's Opera* (1728). The fable is addressed 'To a Young Heir', urging him to avoid gambling so that he does not have to plunder his estates or end up in debtor's prison. It begins with a forest being made into a 'wasteful ruin' as its trees are felled at the squire's command: 'Through the long wood loud axes sound, / And eccho groans with ev'ry wound.' The presence of 'eccho' is a strong hint that Pan is near. The god dutifully appears, and he is not happy:

> To see the desolation spread,
> *Pan* drops a tear and hangs his head:
> His bosom now with fury burns,
> Beneath his hoof the dice he spurns;
> Cards too, in peevish passion torn.
> The sport of whirling winds are born.[36]

Pan's sorrow over the ruined forest quickly changes to anger, which he directs at the dice and cards that have driven the squire to this grim act of spoilage. This is a robustly physical Pan, weeping with emotion that surges through his body, a body that terminates in the familiar hooves. As we saw in Chapter One, his potential for anger was noted as early as Theocritus. In Gay's fable Pan expresses his hatred for snails, caterpillars and locusts, all of whom destroy his beloved woods, but saves his greatest scorn for Fortune, whom he blames for the scourge of gambling that has his 'kingdom's pride defac'd, / And all its antient glories waste.'[37] The goddess utterly rejects Pan's accusations, insisting that such destruction is the fault of those who gamble with 'knaves', not Fortune herself. She concludes the fable by addressing Pan directly: "'Tis Folly, *Pan*, that is thy foe. / By me his late estate he won, / But he by Folly was undone.'[38] Human greed and foolishness, not bad luck, have laid waste to Pan's beloved woods. This is an ecological lesson that can apply to our own age as well.

You have watched the choruses of shepherds sing and the shepherdesses respond coyly. The painted scenery, with its mountains and ruined temples, suggests a vanished Arcadia, provoking dreams of summer on this chilly winter night. Among the figures depicted is the god Pan, held down by a triumphant Cupid and surrounded by laughing nymphs. High above the stage, a trapdoor swings open and creaking pulleys lower an elaborately designed throne, its legs terminating in realistically carved goat hooves. The audience around you gasp as they recognize the figure of the king himself, wrapped in an animal pelt with spots indistinguishable from stars. In his hand he clasps not a sceptre but musical pipes made of reeds. You join the applause enthusiastically as the king's eyes meet your own – they are deeper and darker than any you have seen before. In them you perceive the elemental fire of the cosmos burning steadily. You realize that the king's face is but a festive mask, and a gloved hand lifts it away to reveal a face that is at once man and goat, complete with horns curling back through a head of thick hair. His eyes twinkle and his smile gives way to a goatish laugh at your obvious terror. Why has no one else noticed? The choruses of shepherds and shepherdesses criss-cross in front of the throne, and when they depart, you behold the king as you have always known him, smiling with royal pleasure. You shift awkwardly as his eyes meet yours again, and he gives you a knowing wink.

3

PAN'S ROMANTIC REBIRTH

The later eighteenth century brought a reaction against Enlightenment rationalism that would create an artistic and literary climate much more amenable to Pan. Unlike the neoclassicism of the Augustan Age, Romanticism valued wild nature, passion and imagination – all of which were conducive to a rebirth of enthusiasm for the god, as was a revival of interest in all things Greek, including the irrational mysteries of Greek religion. The 'Hymn to Pan' attributed to Orpheus provided Romantic poets with an image of the god as a cosmic power animating the natural world. All the major Romantic poets from Blake to Byron wrote about Pan, as did many of their lesser-read contemporaries. The Romantic Pan is typically an invisible power whose presence is intuited in nature, although some, such as Thomas Love Peacock, would employ Pan satirically. For their Victorian heirs, Pan could be a troubling figure, but a return to the classical sources also provided material for fresh imagining of ancient stories. Pan crosses the Atlantic at this time, making his first appearance in the belated Romanticism of Emerson and Hawthorne. In both England and America, Pan could provide an encoded way to explore sexuality without directly confronting Victorian morality, a tendency carried further by writers associated with the *fin de siècle*, for whom Pan could symbolize forbidden desire and the instinctive life. In visual art, Pan makes appearances in the work of Edward Burne-Jones and Aubrey Beardsley, as well as in numerous paintings by Arnold Böcklin. Pan also begins his modern musical career in operetta and orchestral music. At the turn of the century, the first major modern study of Pan, *Ephialtes* by Wilhelm Heinrich Roscher, argues that the god embodies the experience of nightmare. These nineteenth-century developments provide the foundations for Pan's resurgence in the early twentieth century and his surprising role in the occult revival, which we will explore in the next two chapters.

Romantic re-imaginings

The most important eighteenth-century poem about Pan, and one that would shape perceptions of the god for the Romantic poets and their heirs, was Thomas Taylor's translation in 1787 of the ancient Orphic 'Hymn to Pan' in *The Mystical Initiations or Hymns of Orpheus*. As we saw in Chapter One, this hymn presents Pan as the cosmic embodiment of 'all'. Taylor's work was read by most of the major Romantic poets, and offered a vision of the god that rhymed with their own philosophical ideas about the nurturing power of the imagination and nature. Taylor's claim, in his introduction to the *Hymns*, that 'in the universe, there is one harmony though composed from contraries' resonated with the poet and artist William Blake (1757–1827), whose *Marriage of Heaven and Hell* (*c.* 1790) explores the dual nature of reality.[1]

Pan himself is mentioned only once in Blake's poetry, in his 'Imitation of Edmund Spenser' (1793), where the god appears in his rustic-comical role as Apollo's rival in song. Blake's poem addresses the god Apollo, and invokes Pan in the second stanza, only to dismiss him as patron of 'tinkling rhimes' and poor critical judgement:

> For brutish Pan in vain might thee assay
> With tinkling sounds to dash thy nervous verse,
> Sound without sense; yet in his rude affray,
> (For ignorance is Folly's leesing nurse,
> And love of Folly needs none other curse;)
> Midas the praise hath gain'd of lengthen'd eares,
> For which himself might deem him ne'er the worse
> To sit in council with his modern peers,
> And judge of tinkling rhimes, and elegances terse.[2]

This 'imitation' is clearly apprentice work, with the musical contest between Apollo and Pan symbolizing a conflict between good and bad poetry, as well as the critical power to distinguish between them. In Blake's view, ass-eared Midas has many 'modern peers' similarly lacking judgement.

Although unsympathetic to Pan in this early poem, in the same year Blake engraved a delightful illustration for John Gay's 'Pan and Fortune', one of a series he did for Gay's *Fables*.[3] The engraving depicts Pan in the act of tearing up a deck of cards, looking over his shoulder at the smiling goddess Fortune, who gazes kindly at him from atop her wheel. She points to a symbol of Folly in the lower half of the engraving, a puppet with a jester's head and cap. Pan smiles back at her, perhaps convinced that Fortune is not responsible after all for the grim-faced man chopping a tree in the background. The god does not directly appear again in Blake's work, but it is hard to imagine a more Pan-inspired sentiment than that of his 'proverb of Hell' from *The Marriage of Heaven and Hell*: 'The lust of the goat is the bounty of God.'[4]

In contrast with Blake's early representations of the god, the Pan of Wordsworth and Coleridge is an intuited presence or cosmic power in nature, witnessed or experienced only indirectly. For William Wordsworth (1770–1850), 'universal Pan' is invisible but retains his associations with wild nature, music and the protection of flocks. In Book VIII of his long autobiographical poem *The Prelude*, Wordsworth imagines that 'Smooth life had flock and shepherd in old time,' perhaps taking too literally the idealized world of pastoral verse.[5] In this nostalgic vision,

> the goat-herd lived
> As calmly, underneath the pleasant brows
> Of cool Lucretilis, where the pipe was heard
> Of Pan, Invisible God, thrilling the rocks
> With tutelary music, from all harm
> The fold protecting.

This goatherd lives in Italy, rather than Arcadia, beneath the mountain referred to by Horace as 'Lucretili Mons', probably Monte Zappi in Lazio. As in many classical narratives, including that of Daphnis and Chloe, the pipes of Pan are heard while the god himself remains unseen. Uniquely, Wordsworth's Pan is identified as 'Invisible God', as though invisibility were his defining feature. He nonetheless remains one of nature's powers, with his music 'thrilling the rocks' as he protects the fold of goats.

Pan appears in his familiar role as the source of panic when Wordsworth envisions the ancient pastoral world in Book IV of *The Excursion*. In this part of the poem, he imagines how the 'unenlightened Swains' of pagan Greece came to transform natural forces into pagan gods through the power of imagination.[6] For example, a lonely hunter calls upon the moon above

> to share his joyous sport:
> And hence, a beaming Goddess with her Nymphs,
> Across the lawn and through the darksome grove,
> (Not unaccompanied with tuneful notes
> By echo multiplied from rock or cave)
> Swept in the storm of chase.

'Echo' is herself one of the nymphs, tangled up with Pan in Greek mythology. Approaching nature with an active imagination peoples the world with divinities. Pan appears at the end of this passage on the origins of the gods, appropriately embodying a somewhat frightening experience:

> Withered Boughs grotesque,
> Stripped of their leaves and twigs by hoary age,
> From depth of shaggy covert peeping forth
> In the low vale, or on steep mountain side;
> And, sometimes, intermixed with stirring horns
> Of the live Deer, or Goat's depending beard;
> These were the lurking Satyrs, a wild brood
> Of gamesome Deities! or Pan himself,
> The simple Shepherd's awe-inspiring God.

Despite the imaginative power of this poetry, Wordsworth is in effect offering a completely naturalistic, even banal, explanation: ancient shepherds saw deer or goats among the twisted boughs of dead trees and imagined they were 'lurking Satyrs', 'or Pan himself'. This uncanny experience inspires feelings of 'awe' attributed to the god's presence, although this is not quite the right word to capture the sensation of sudden dread the ancient sources all attribute to Pan.

Where Francis Bacon saw in the myth of Pan an encoded expression of ancient wisdom, Wordsworth sees evidence of an original, poetic form of consciousness transforming its perception of natural phenomenon. His naturalism attempts to expound Pan and the other gods, but does not quite explain them away. Wordsworth's 'unenlightened Swains' have a richer, more authentic experience of the world than us, perceiving nature in its many aspects and responding with feeling and imagination. They have an almost mystical relationship with the natural world around them. For Wordsworth, our loss of such a relationship is a form of spiritual poverty that contact with nature might renew. He would agree with Blake that 'All deities reside in the human breast,' but that does not diminish their imaginative reality.[7] More puzzling is Wordsworth's brief allusion in Book VII to the presence of 'Pan or Apollo' in mortal guise, revealed through 'a Scholar's genius' or the 'spirit of a Hero' – neither of which fits well with traditional ideas of Pan.[8]

Despite his early creative collaborations with Wordsworth, Samuel Taylor Coleridge (1772–1834) imagines Pan in a more allegorical mode, blending symbolism and psychology in ways that register the god's associations with lust and darkness. In 1805 he made a brief entry in his notebook, perhaps an idea for a poem that he never developed. In it, he envisions Pan and Syrinx as symbolizing 'Disappointment turning sensual into purer pleasures – disapp: Lust by regret, refining into Love & ending in Harmony'.[9] His reading of the myth of Pan and Syrinx describes an almost Freudian process of sublimation, where sexual desire is frustrated and finds symbolic release in music. This combination of symbolism and psychology would also inform Coleridge's comments on Pan in his *Biographia Literaria* (1817), which are brief but prophetic of later portrayals of the Great God. In Chapter XXI he recalls visiting the tomb of Pope Julius II with a Prussian artist, where they spent time looking at Michelangelo's statue of Moses, whom he depicts with horns. The two observers call to mind 'the horns of the rising sun', and Coleridge cites a passage from a book by Thomas Taylor (translator of the Orphic hymns) called *Holy Dying*, which claimed

> That horns were the emblem of power and sovereignty among the Eastern nations, and are still retained as such in Abyssinia; the Achelous of the ancient Greeks [god of rivers and fresh water, often depicted with bull's horns]; and the probable ideas and feelings, that originally suggested the mixture of the human and the brute form in the figure, by which they realized the idea of their mysterious Pan, as representing intelligence blended with a darker power, deeper, mightier, and more universal than the conscious intellect of man; than intelligence; – all these thoughts and recollections passed in procession before our minds.[10]

Note how Coleridge initially interprets Moses' horns naturalistically ('the horns of the rising sun'), as does Francis Bacon, before considering them symbolically ('the emblem of power and sovereignty'). Coleridge then explores what Pan's blending of man and beast might symbolize. The horned and hairy aspect of the god's form represents 'a darker power, deeper, and more universal than the conscious intellect of man,' language evoking the instinctual life that we share with animals. Coleridge here anticipates Pan's portrayal by both Arthur Machen and D. H. Lawrence. While Machen finds the 'darker power' a source of genuine terror, for Lawrence such power is both alienating to us as individuals and necessary for the continued existence of life itself. It is testimony to Coleridge's strange genius that this brief anecdote simultaneously reaches back to Renaissance and classical allegories of Pan and looks forward to modern psychological interpretations.

The next generation of Romantic poets builds on the Wordsworthian sense of Pan as an invisible natural power, but makes him a more central figure. The Pan portrayed by John Keats (1795–1821) combines elements of the philosophical and mythic-pastoral traditions – an imaginative synthesis that is Keats's original contribution to Romantic portrayals of the Great God. Despite Keats's greater attention to Pan's character, however, his portrayal remains strangely disembodied, with no horns, hooves or hair in sight. This feels disappointing in a poet known for the sensuousness of his language. As an incorporeal presence, Keats's Pan is consistent with Wordsworth's 'Invisible God' in *The Prelude*, but he is also more dynamic as an active guardian of flocks and leader of the dancing satyrs. Keats was probably inspired by Taylor's translation of the Orphic hymn, which similarly combines a cosmological vision of Pan with elements from traditional mythology. Keats's major exploration of Pan's nature is undertaken in his poem *Endymion* of 1818.

Pan appears in *Endymion* as a hidden power in nature who has temporarily been forgotten by his worshippers. Book I opens in Latmos, a beautiful and rugged country whose inhabitants are thriving under the bountiful rule of Endymion, their handsome but melancholy 'chieftain-king'. A 'venerable priest' warns his people that their 'vows are wanting to our great god Pan', offering up a sacred fire, libations of wine and incense.[11] Responding to his summons, a chorus gathers to sing their hymn to the Great God, each stanza of which focuses on a different aspect of Pan's character. The first stanza sets the scene by describing the wild home of Pan, 'whose mighty palace roof doth hang / From jagged trunks'. Keats presents us with three different sites, all of them uncultivated and uninhabitable. The roof of Pan's rugged palace 'overshadoweth / Eternal whispers, glooms, the birth, life, death / Of unseen flowers in heavy peacefulness'. His realm is one where we might hear 'whispers' of the immortal, while that word 'glooms' suggests a sombre, melancholy mood. The cycle of floral life here takes place unseen and drowsily. Pan's domain is a world of nature beyond direct human knowledge. He watches 'the hamadryads dress / Their ruffled locks where meeting hazels darken', or else spends hours listening to 'The dreary melody of bedded reeds – / In desolate places, where dank moisture breeds / The pipy hemlock to strange overgrowth'. Keats's rather voyeuristic Pan is in keeping with the many ancient images of the god as observer or bystander. The 'dreary melody' heard by Pan and the 'desolate' location echo the 'glooms' of his palace, while the references to music and reeds (and the language of 'pipy hemlock') bring us closer to the source of the god's melancholia. The final lines of the first stanza allude to Pan's failed pursuit of the nymph Syrinx, acknowledging 'how melancholy loth / Thou wast to lose fair Syrinx.' This acknowledgement is a prelude to the chorus asking for Pan to hear them 'By thy love's milky brow! / By all the trembling mazes that she ran.' Keats's use of 'trembling' describes the reeds that Syrinx runs through, while also suggesting her fear at Pan's approach.

The second stanza of the hymn situates Pan in the natural world, while the third focuses on the 'fawns and satyrs' who do his bidding. As Pan listens to the mournful song of turtle doves, he feels the seasons changing even amid the bounty of summer. The chorus addresses him at the end of the second stanza in language that subtly alludes to another of Pan's loves: 'be quickly near, / By every wind that nods the mountain pine, / O forester divine!' Keats's reference to the wind-blown pine suggests the nymph Pitys, and perhaps also Pan's contest with Boreas for her affection. 'Forester' here would seem to be meant in the archaic sense of one who dwells in a forest, although it is possible that Keats had the more modern sense of one who looks after the trees in mind as well. The fauns and satyrs who clamour to serve Pan in the third stanza include among their duties surprising hares while they sleep, rescuing lambs from eagles and gathering shells to toss into Naiads' caves. This light-hearted picture of Pan's followers concludes with them 'leaping' for his entertainment, as 'they pelt each other on the crown / With silvery oak apples, and fir cones brown.' The chorus swears 'By all the echoes that about thee ring', allowing Keats another subtle allusion to one of Pan's loves, addressing the god as 'satyr king'. While Pan is sometimes depicted on Greek pottery in the company of satyrs, Keats's portrayal overlooks his more usual followers, the nymphs.

Keats then acknowledges Pan as the god who presides over pastoral activity and (unexpectedly) farming, before daringly presenting him as the guardian of forbidden knowledge. The chorus primarily recognizes him as a pastoral god, 'Hearkener to the loud clapping shears, / While ever and anon to his shorn peers / A ram goes bleating.' True to Pan's mythological character as god of the hunt, the chorus addresses him as 'Winder of the horn, / When snouted wild-boars routing tender corn / Anger our huntsman'. While he is not traditionally associated with farming, the next two lines envision Pan breathing on the people's farms 'To keep off mildews, and all weather harms', a new power seemingly invented by Keats. The chorus then turns to the darker, more uncanny aspects of Pan's character that were evoked in the opening lines of the hymn, addressing him as

> Strange ministrant of undescribed sounds,
> That come a swooning over hollow grounds,
> And wither drearily on barren moors:
> Dread opener of the mysterious doors
> Leading to universal knowledge.

The sounds to which Pan ministers are 'undescribed', and so necessarily mysterious, but the strange landscapes they inhabit ('hollow grounds', 'barren moors') are appropriately desolate haunts for him to tend. In the lines that follow, Keats anticipates the feeling of horror that Machen associates with Pan, while gesturing towards Pan's ancient connection with 'all'. The god is portrayed as the guardian of 'universal knowledge', but one who should be feared. Is such knowledge meant for us to have? Or is the 'Dread opener' of its 'mysterious doors' there to keep us away? What happens when those doors are opened? Keats does not tell us, but Machen's *The Great God Pan* will imagine a terrifying answer. In the concluding lines of the stanza, Keats identifies Pan's mother as Dryope – just one of many possible candidates, as we saw in Chapter One.

The final stanza is an invocation of the cosmic Pan of the Orphic hymn. Keats conveys a sense of Pan's unfathomable depths first by invoking him as

> the unimaginable lodge
> For solitary thinkings; such as dodge
> Conception to the very bourne of heaven,
> Then leave the naked brain.

These 'solitary thinkings' elude conception altogether; they are intuitions or insights too profound to be captured in words. As such, they are unmediated perceptions of a reality beyond language – the domain of cosmic Pan. Keats portrays Pan as a spiritual 'leaven' that provides 'a touch ethereal' to the mud and muck of our physical world. He may have in mind ether as the traditional 'fifth element' that binds the others together, just as Pan binds the universe together in the Orphic hymn. The chorus prays for Pan to 'Be a symbol of immensity; / A firmament reflected in a sea; / An element filling the space between.' Pan is here conceived of as a liminal power, neither sky nor sea but an element between them. In twenty-first-century terms, we might think of this Pan as a kind of dark matter, impossible to perceive or describe, but necessary for keeping the forces of our visible universe behaving as they should.

Although Percy Bysshe Shelley (1792–1822) was usually a more philosophically complex poet than Keats, his 'Hymn of Pan' is a much simpler, more straightforward presentation of the god in his traditional mythological role. What distinguishes Shelley's poem is that it is spoken by Pan himself, who addresses his words to Apollo. Shelley composed hymns for both gods for the play *Midas* (1820) by his wife, Mary Wollstonecraft Shelley (1797–1851). The first act of the play depicts the musical contest between Pan and Apollo, with Midas describing Pan as 'my guardian God, old-horned Pan'.[12] Even before the contest begins, Midas has decided to award him the prize. Pan introduces himself as a leader of a band of supernatural revellers who follow where his pipes lead:

> From the forests and highlands
> > We come, we come;
> From the river-girt islands,
> > Where loud waves are dumb
> > Listening to my sweet pipings.[13]

All of nature, from 'The wind in the reeds' to insects and animals, is 'silent as old Tmolus was' during his competition with Apollo as Pan plays. In the second stanza, Pan reminds Apollo of his ancient presence in the earlier ages of the world, before boasting of the hypnotic effect of his music, which draws followers who listen in silent awe:

> The Sileni, and Sylvans, and Fauns,
>> And the Nymphs of the woods and the waves,
> To the edge of the moist river-lawns,
>> And the brink of the dewy caves,
> And all that did then attend and follow,
> Were silent with love, as you now, Apollo,
>> With envy of my sweet pipings.

Pan's retinue more closely resembles that of Dionysus, but Shelley (unlike Keats) remembers to include the nymphs. Apollo's envy of Pan's music is an invention of Shelley's, unless we imagine that Pan is blinded by his own sense of its worth.

The third and final stanza of the poem explores the dual nature of Pan's cosmic and mythological identities. The first several lines suggest the 'universal knowledge' that Keats associated with Pan, as the god sings of cosmic history and the mysteries of life itself:

> I sang of the dancing stars,
>> I sang of the daedal Earth,
> And of Heaven, and the giant wars,
>> And Love, and Death, and Birth.

(The unusual adjective 'daedal' has the sense of 'ingenious', and is derived from the mythological figure Daedalus, the legendary inventor whose son Icarus flew too close to the sun wearing his father's waxen wings.) These few lines span a cosmos that includes the stars, Earth and heaven, looking back in time to 'the giant wars', when Pan helped Zeus in his struggle against Typhoeus. Pan also sings of the primal mysteries of human life, 'Love, and Death, and Birth', all reflections of the dark power of sexual desire. The mention of these mysteries leads Pan to change his song to one more sorrowful, 'Singing how down the vale of Maenalus / I pursu'd a maiden and clasp'd a reed. / Gods and men, we are all deluded thus!' Sexual desire, frustration and music are intertwined in this allusion to Pan's pursuit of Syrinx. Such desire 'breaks in our bosom and then we bleed', a line that echoes a more famous sentiment from Shelley's 'Ode to the West Wind', 'I fall upon the thorns of life, I bleed.'[14] The poem concludes with Pan telling Apollo that he too would weep 'If envy or age had not frozen your blood, / At the sorrow of my sweet pipings.' In Mary Shelley's play, Tmolus judges that 'wisdom, beauty, & the power divine / Of highest poesy' reside in Apollo's hymn, even if 'Fauns may dance / To the blithe tune of ever merry Pan.' After hearing this judgement, Pan appeals to the judgement of Midas, who praises Pan's 'sprightly song' as superior to Apollo's 'drowsy tune', which sends him to sleep.[15] As in Ovid's story, Apollo punishes Midas by giving him the ears of an ass.

Pan makes a brief appearance in Shelley's poem 'The Witch of Atlas' (1820) as a disembodied but responsive power, when the mysterious witch summons with her 'low voice' a variety of animals and supernatural beings, including Pan in his cosmic aspect:

> And universal Pan, 'tis said, was there,
> And though none saw him, – through the adamant

Of the deep mountains, through the trackless air,
And through those living spirits, like a want,
He passed out of his everlasting lair
Where the quick heart of the great world doth pant,
And felt that wondrous lady all alone, –
And she felt him, upon her emerald throne.[16]

This Pan is a typically incorporeal Romantic vision of the god, who cannot be seen or pictured, but whose presence can nonetheless be sensed. He travels through landscapes and atmospheres that are characteristically wild or remote: 'deep mountains' and 'trackless air'. There is a strange mutuality between the witch and 'universal Pan', as they 'feel' each other without physical contact.

Shelley's posthumously published translation of the Greek poet Moschus, 'Pan, Echo, and the Satyr', presents a dramatic situation in which each of the three figures is in love with one who is in love with someone else. Pan is not so much a character in this poem as an archetype of the failed lover: 'As Pan loved Echo, Echo loved the Satyr, / The Satyr, Lyda; and so love consumed them.'[17] Because of their unrequited passion, each hates his or her rival, leading to this conclusion: 'Ye that love not / Be warned – in thought turn this example over, / That when ye love, the like return ye prove not.' The network of sexual desire mapped out in the poem must have resonated with Shelley's own complex erotic life.

Although his engagement with Pan is minimal compared with that of Keats and Shelley, Lord Byron (1788–1824) is the sole Romantic poet to write directly on the death of Pan, if only in a fragment written while on Cephalonia in 1823. It is a single verse, part of the first canto of a projected poem entitled 'Aristomenes' after a seventh-century Messenian king who resisted the Spartans. Byron doesn't mention Aristomenes in the verse, which reflects on the death of Pan to create a melancholy nostalgia for a lost pagan world:

> The Gods of old are silent on the shore.
> Since the great Pan expired, and through the roar
> Of the Ionian waters broke a dread
> Voice which proclaimed 'the Mighty Pan is dead.'[18]

The silence of the gods is a direct reference to the subject of Plutarch's book *On the Failure of the Oracles*, which Byron sees as coinciding with the death of Pan. He laments the passing of the ancient pagan world, where imagination transformed the landscape into the home of gods and nymphs:

> How much died with him! false or true – the dream
> Was beautiful which peopled every stream
> With more than finny tenants, and adorned
> The woods and waters with coy nymphs that scorned
> Pursuing Deities, or in the embrace
> Of gods brought forth the high heroic race
> Whose names are on the hills and o'er the seas.

Byron doesn't care whether 'the dream' was 'false or true' – what matters is that it was 'beautiful'. The pagans dreamed a world where gods pursued nymphs and sired the eponymous heroes of the Greek landscape. For Byron, Greek mythology shows us what Wordsworth called 'The face which rural Solitude might wear / To the unenlightened Swains of pagan Greece', but Byron emphasizes the beauty of that face rather than the 'unenlightened' state of those who envisioned it.[19] Pan himself may be somewhat incidental to Byron's conception of the pagan imagination, but his death symbolizes the end of a whole mode of consciousness that perceived meaning and beauty in the natural world we inhabit.

Byron's nostalgia for a world where Pan had his place among other pagan glories is matched in the work of Leigh Hunt (1784–1859) by an earnest desire for his return. In a letter to his friend Thomas Jefferson Hogg, dated 22 January 1818, Hunt expresses his wish that the cult of Pan would be revived again in England:

> I hope you paid your devotions as usual to the Religio Loci, and hung up an evergreen. If you all go on so, there will be a hope some day . . . a voice will be heard along the water saying 'The Great God Pan is alive again,' – upon which the villagers will leave off starving, and singing profane hymns, and fall to dancing again.[20]

However humorous his intention, Hunt imagines a dancing English peasantry revitalized by a voice countering that which was heard in the age of Tiberius, proclaiming that Pan lives.

Hunt is the most likely author of an anonymous poem (signed 'L.') from 1820 called 'The Universal Pan', a charming but not entirely successful attempt to fuse the god's pastoral and Orphic characters. As in Shelley's hymn, here Pan himself is the speaker, sounding like a rather genial English country-man. The poem also alludes, often indirectly, to several of the myths involving Pan that are by now familiar to us. The god opens the poem by distancing himself from urban life: 'Not in the Town – not in the busy Town / Am I, but come upon the woodlands / And thou shalt find me.'[21] He might also be found 'upon the hills / Topped with the clustering pines' (suggesting the nymph Pitys), or by rivers or fountains too cold for Apollo. Hunt domesticates Pan by imagining him loitering 'by the hedgerow-side' at noon and evening. At this point, however, the English countryman reveals himself as 'the universal Pan', an incorporeal power. After an indirect allusion to the myth of Selene, where the moon comes to Pan 'like a maid / A vestal maid', he shows himself to be the god of poetic inspiration and the force behind all natural phenomenon:

> For I, although a humbler Deity
> Usurp the honours that belong to me,
> Am the pervading and surrounding power
> Of the great earth – the universal Pan.[22]

Like the Pan portrayed by Wordsworth, Keats, Shelley and Byron, Hunt's Pan lacks horns, hair and hooves; he is a god of nature, but lacking form. Were the Romantics embarrassed by Pan's outrageous physical appearance, or were they simply more drawn to the philosophical idea of Pan as a natural or cosmological power? It is striking that while the Orphic hymn itself accommodates Pan's traditional appearance ('Goat-footed, horned'), most of the Romantic poets writing in the wake of Taylor's translation suppress these attributes altogether. Only Coleridge, in *Biographia Literaria*, reflects on the significance of Pan's form. The rest of Hunt's poem is pleasant enough, with Pan inviting us (particularly if we 'are tired of life, / Noise, and the trouble of cities') to join him and receive his joyful blessings, but the disembodied Romantic god lacks the physicality and uncanniness of his authentically pagan self.[23]

Although, like Hunt, a less central figure in English Romanticism than Wordsworth, Keats and Shelley, Thomas Love Peacock (1785–1866) has the distinction of being the Romantic writer who alludes to Pan most frequently. He writes about the god in four different works, encompassing an astonishing tonal range from outright satire to nostalgic melancholy. Pan makes a brief appearance in Peacock's fragment of Arthurian romance, *Calidore* (*c.* 1816), set on an island where the defeated knights of the Round Table consort with unworshipped gods. As the members of Arthur's court arrive at the island, they see Pan and Bacchus walking together on a beach. Peacock, unlike the other Romantics, describes Pan's appearance admiringly as 'a wild singular figure in a fine state of picturesque roughness with goat's horns and feet and a laughing face'.[24] Merlin introduces Arthur, Guinevere and their company to the gods, who welcome them with a sad story. Bacchus tells them how mankind abandoned the ancient gods, despite their affection for human beings. The ancient temples were destroyed and the gods labelled with 'frightful and cacophonous names – Beelzebub and Amaimon and Astaroth'. After an emergency meeting on Olympus, the gods decided to retreat to the island to be left in peace. Bacchus explains,

> That mountain on which the white clouds are resting is now Mount Olympus, and there dwell Jupiter and the Olympian deities. In these forests and valleys reside Pan and Silenus, the Fauns and the Satyrs, and the small nymphs and genii. I divide my time between the two, for though my home is Olympus, I have a most special friendship for Pan.

Peacock here recalls the tradition reflected in the Homeric 'Hymn to Pan', where Dionysus (Bacchus) is delighted with the infant Pan when Hermes brings him up to Olympus. After the gods warn Arthur's court not to pull any long faces, Merlin asks Bacchus and Pan to take them under their protection, ending this episode of the fragment. Despite the brevity of his appearance, the Pan of *Calidore* is important to our story, since he 'may well be the first (non-dramatic) fictional Pan character in English', according to Patricia Merivale.[25]

Peacock's allusions to Pan in the satirical novel *Melincourt* (1817) are brief, but address questions that are central to Pan's identity as a figure whose appearance bridges the divine, human and animal. The relevant part of the satire focuses on an orangutan named Sir Oran Haut-Ton, who becomes a candidate for parliamentary election by mimicking human behaviour. Peacock's satire thus raises questions about what exactly distinguishes humans from animals, as well as about how we form judgements of others. As Sir Telegraph makes his way to Melincourt Castle to visit his recently widowed cousin, he encounters his old friend Mr Forester, who has brought an orangutan back from Angola and bought him the title of baronet. Forester categorically rejects the idea that such creatures are monkeys, when their characteristics and behaviour so strongly suggest that they are human beings: 'It is still more curious to think that modern travellers should have made beasts, under the names of Pongos, Mandrills, and Oran Outangs, of the very same beings whom the ancients worshipped as divinities under the names of Fauns and Satyrs, Silenus and Pan.'[26] Such 'beings' are deserving of far more respect. It is worth pointing out that although Peacock is writing satire, Forester is himself among the least satirized characters in the novel. The attempt to advance the career of an orangutan is clearly absurd, but Forester also demonstrates an understanding of animals as sentient beings worthy of respect. Peacock's own views are hard to pin down, because his satires are typically written as conversations between characters representing different philosophical viewpoints, but we might well wonder if Forester (however absurdly) makes an early case for animal rights.

When Forester introduces 'Sir Oran' to a mythologist friend, 'he immediately conceived a high veneration, and would never call him by any name but Pan.' The mythologist greets him by quoting the Orphic hymn to Pan, a passage translated by Peacock as

> King of the world! enthusiast free,
> Who dwell'st in caves of liberty!
> And on thy wild notes of glee
> Respondest Nature's harmony!
> Leading beneath the spreading tree
> The Bacchanalian revelry![27]

These lines are carefully chosen, the mythologist tells Forester, for the passage

> alludes to the existence of the dancing Pans, Fauns, Orans, *et id genus omne* [and everything of that kind], whose dwellings are the caves of rocks and the hollows of trees, such as undoubtedly was, or would have been, the natural mode of life of our friend Pan among the woods of Angola.[28]

Having identified the higher primates with 'Fauns and Satyrs, Silenus and Pan', Peacock's mythologist infers that the orangutan's dwelling places were similar to theirs. This naturalistic approach to the beings of Greek mythology resembles Wordsworth's, but in reverse, inferring things about nature from 'information' in the Orphic hymn. The mythologist also sees in the hymn an allusion 'to their musical powers, which in our friend Pan it gives me indescribable pleasure to find so happily exemplified'.

Peacock opens Book III of his long poem *Rhododaphne* (1818) with a sustained reflection on how the death of Pan has left a landscape that, while beautiful, has lost its spiritual power. In common with other Romantic poets, Peacock laments the loss of imaginative perception that breathed life into nature, a process he believed was furthered in his own time by the rise of science, which threatened to make poetry itself obsolete. The passage opens with a lament that the nature gods and spirits of ancient Greece are no longer called upon:

> By living streams, in sylvan shades,
> Where winds and waves symphonious make
> Sweet melody, the youths and maids
> No more with choral music wake
> Lone Echo from her tangled brake,
> On Pan, or Sylvan Genius, calling,
> Naiad or Nymph, in suppliant song.[29]

Nature itself continues to make 'Sweet melody', but 'the youths and maids' no longer respond in kind by singing to Pan and the nymphs. As in *Melincourt*, the gods have been forgotten. No 'pious hands' carve a basin or build a 'grassy altar' for the 'traveller' to refresh himself or honour the 'Sister Nymphs'. Instead, the world has been evacuated by any trace of divine presence:

> In ocean's caves no Nereid dwells:
> No Oread walks the mountain dells:
> The streams no sedge-crowned Genii roll
> From bounteous urn: great Pan is dead:

The life, the intellectual soul
Of vale, and grove, and stream, has fled
For ever with the creed sublime
That nursed the Muse of earlier time.[30]

Pagan spirits and gods have disappeared along with the faith that sustained them. What is original about Peacock's interpretation of the death of Pan is that he identifies it as the ultimate source of that very modern experience, disenchantment. With Pan dead, the landscape has lost its very 'life' and 'intellectual soul'. Nature is hollowed out of all meaning with the demise of paganism, symbolized by Pan's death.

In 'Pan in Town', from his collection *Paper Money Lyrics* (1825), Peacock restores Pan to his primordial role as cause of 'Panic Terrors', although the panics here are financial ones.[31] Peacock satirizes financial panic by imagining it as the arrival of Pan in the city: 'The country banks are breaking / The London banks are shaking.'[32] Although the opening passage is spoken by 'Pan and Chorus of Citizens', the dramatic poem makes no reference to Pan's character or mythology, reducing him simply to a source of financial panic. Peacock's footnote to the poem, however, offers a gently satirical rebuke to Hunt's 'The Universal Pan'. Referring to its author as 'the Cockney poet', Peacock describes the poem as 'a most original demonstration of his universality'. Reflecting on Pan's claim that he is 'not in the busy town', Peacock suggests that 'the Cockney poet' has had 'a good opportunity, since he wrote that poem, of seeing that Pan can be in town sometimes. Perhaps, according to his mythology, the Pan in town was the Sylvan Pan; a fashionable arrival for the season.'[33] In London Hunt's countryman becomes, according to Peacock's reimagining, a stylish man about town, bringing financial ruin in his wake.

Like Peacock, Felicia Dorothea Hemans (1793–1835) lamented the passing of the ancient pagan world, contrasting past and present in her long poem *Modern Greece* of 1817. Pan has a cameo in the stanza on Arcadia, in which Hemans emphasizes his lingering power to evoke terror: 'Yet brooding fear and dark suspicion dwell / 'Midst Pan's deserted haunts, by fountain, cave, and dell.'[34] Pan may be gone, but the 'fear and dark suspicion' his presence invokes remain. Hemans's allusion to Pan is admittedly slight, but her sense of the god as primarily connected to the darker side of pagan feeling is notably different from that of most of her male Romantic contemporaries.

The final word on Pan and Romanticism must go to the essayist William Hazlitt (1778–1830), for whom the goat-footed god symbolizes the 'unequal and irregular' qualities he sees as characteristic of English poetry itself: 'Perhaps the genius of our poetry has more of Pan than of Apollo; "but Pan is a God, Apollo is no more!"'[35] The quotation is from John Lyly's sixteenth-century play *Midas*. As we've seen, the myth of Pan and Apollo's musical contest is one in which sophisticated art triumphs over rustic tradition, but Hazlitt reverses these values to celebrate the way English poetry diverges from classical order and regularity. Pan thus stands as the embodiment of alternative Romantic values of nature and organic form.

Most of the Romantics viewed Pan as an invisible power within nature, or nature transformed by the imagination, variously a source of inspiration and wonder. Since 'natural' was the most positive Romantic value, implying an authenticity that fostered both individuality and imagination, sustained by powerful feelings, Pan was generally regarded as a force for good. The Romantic view of Pan is, however, a partial one, mostly ignoring his traditional physical appearance and its goatish associations. Although Wordsworth provides a naturalistic explanation for Pan's association with the emotion of fear, the Romantic poets are mostly uninterested in the experience of panic that is inseparable from Pan's origins. Such feelings are found in Romantic poetry – Wordsworth's sudden dread while paddling a stolen boat in Book I of *The Prelude* is the most famous example – but they are typically unrelated to Pan. The exception of Hemans, who evokes 'brooding fear and dark suspicion' as lingering traces of Pan's uncanny presence, may raise the question of gendered responses to the god. Those mythological aspects of Pan suppressed by male poets were perhaps less easily ignored by women. Pan as half-bestial pursuer of nymphs, lurking in dark and wild places and emerging suddenly to satisfy his lusts, violently if need be, is a much less benign figure than the nurturing power imagined by most male Romantics. Hemans's brief allusion is a partial corrective to their view, but it also diminishes Pan to a pair of negative emotions. Her scepticism of Pan would, however, be echoed in Victorian poetry, nowhere more strongly than in the work of Elizabeth Barrett Browning (1806–1861).

Victorian versions

Pan is at once everywhere and nowhere in Elizabeth Barrett Browning's poem 'The Dead Pan' (1844), which views the death of Pan and the other pagan gods as a cause of joy. He is everywhere because each of its 39 stanzas ends with a line terminating in the phrase 'Pan is dead'; and nowhere because Pan himself is completely absent. He doesn't even figure in the catalogue of dead gods that comprises most of the poem. This absence is in many ways the point, for 'The Dead Pan' is a gleeful example of Christian triumphalism, celebrating the demise of the pagan gods in the wake of Christ's resurrection. Browning's point is that they should stay dead, and that modern Christian poets shouldn't be seduced by calls for a revival of antiquity by poets such as Friedrich Schiller ('Let no Schiller from the portals / Of that Hades call you back').[36] Browning devotes three stanzas of the poem to retelling Plutarch's account of the death of Pan. Her language casts the event in implicitly Christian terms:

> Calm, of old, the bark went onward,
> When a cry more loud than wind,
> Rose up, deepen'd, and swept sunward,
> From the piléd Dark behind;
> And the sun shrank and grew pale,
> Breath'd against by the great wail –
>   'Pan, Pan is dead.'

Out of this darkness comes the voice announcing Pan's demise, and in the following stanza the sailors fall from their benches in shock. Browning follows the ancient Christian tradition that the death of Pan coincided with the death of Christ, occurring at 'the hour of one in Sion / Hung for love's sake on a cross'. In a Miltonic touch, she envisages the Olympians as 'false gods' who in that moment 'fell down moaning / Each from off his golden seat'. In death, Christ triumphs over paganism.

A mellower attitude to Pan emerges in Browning's late poem 'A Musical Instrument', published in 1860, which nonetheless portrays Pan as a destructive force towards nature until his music acts as a healing balm. 'A Musical Instrument' also offers an original version of the myth of Pan and Syrinx, from which the nymph herself is absent. Browning presents us with a Pan who is very much a corporeal presence, complete with hooves, fooling about by the riverside:

Engraved by the Dalziel Brothers after a drawing by Lord Leighton
(1830–1896), *The Great God Pan*, 1860. This illustration appeared in
Cornhill Magazine, II (July–December 1860) to accompany Elizabeth Barrett
Browning's poem 'A Musical Instrument'. The image depicts the moment
Pan first plays upon the transformed Syrinx.

What was he doing, the great god Pan,
    Down in the reeds by the river?
Spreading ruin and scattering ban,
Splashing and paddling with hoofs of a goat,
And breaking the golden lilies afloat
    With the dragon-fly on the river.[37]

The incongruity between the epithet 'great god' and Pan's 'Splashing and paddling' lends an ironic tone to Browning's portrayal. Yet such incongruity has been integral to Pan's character since at least the time when Attic painters first depicted him as part-human, part-goat. The later Orphic and philosophical versions of Pan, so distant from his pastoral origins, add yet another layer of inconsistency, one that is resolvable only through strained allegorical interpretation. Browning's phrase 'great god' is used either wryly or scoffingly, depending on how we understand her tone, but it is impossible to reconcile with Pan's clumsy play.

In place of the myth of Pan's pursuit of Syrinx, Browning's poem claims that Pan simply 'tore out a reed', bringing it to the side of the river where he 'hacked and hewed as a great god can' until it was completely leafless. The violence of Browning's verbs is matched by the 'hard bleak steel' that Pan uses to shape the reed. We get a detailed account of how to turn a reed into a flute as Pan removes the pith and notches holes (he seems to be making a flute rather than his traditional pipes). His transformation of raw nature into a musical instrument is necessary for the creation of music itself. Browning's poem suggests that such transformations of nature into art happen in a kind of solitary, violent frenzy; there is a sublimated, masturbatory eroticism in Pan's lonely splashing and his shaping of the reed. When he plays on his flute, the result is both beautiful and restorative:

> Sweet, sweet, sweet, O Pan!
>   Piercing sweet by the river!
> Blinding sweet, O great god Pan!
> The sun on the hill forgot to die,
> And the lilies revived, and the dragon-fly
>   Came back to dream on the river.

Pan's music prolongs the day, brings the lilies back to life and summons the dragonfly, undoing the wanton destruction earlier in the poem. The Pan of this stanza resembles Kenneth Grahame's Piper at the Gates of Dawn in *The Wind in the Willows*, also a joyful preserver of the life of the river (see Chapter Four).

Despite the ecstatic joy of Pan's music, Browning concludes her poem on a melancholy note. The final stanza also raises a number of troubling questions. It begins by reminding us of Pan's half-bestial nature, linking it to his laughter:

> Yet half a beast is the great god Pan,
>   To laugh as he sits by the river,
> Making a poet out of a man:
> The true gods sigh for the cost and pain, –
> For the reed which grows nevermore again
>   As a reed with the reeds in the river.

Where previously Pan was carving a flute from a reed, now he is turning a man into a poet, seemingly through the power of his laughter. Her reference to the figure of the male poet is enigmatic – as a woman, is Elizabeth Barrett Browning somewhat immune to Pan's charms? It is worth noting that she returns quickly to her senses after being briefly overcome by the 'sweet' music he plays. The last three lines of the poem contrast Pan's laughter with the sighing of the 'true gods', who (unlike Pan) understand 'the cost and pain' that come with making art. Despite her evident delight in Pan's music, Browning is clearly on the side of the 'true gods', a group that does not include Pan, implying that there is something suspect about his divinity. The gods are sighing for the reed that will never again grow alongside others – but why lament a single reed at all, especially one that now provides music? Perhaps the conclusion of the poem is haunted by the suppressed myth of Syrinx, a feminine absence that is a counterpoint to the male poet created by Pan's laughter.

Victorian poetry is not all earnestness and regret over life's fleeting pleasures (although much of it is). For devotees of Pan, there are surprises, particularly in the rich variety of myths explored by Victorian poets, not always approvingly. Robert Browning (1812–1889), for example, has a poem on the myth of Pan's seduction of the moon goddess Luna, and includes the story of Pheidippides' encounter with Pan in a lengthy narrative poem about the Battle of Marathon. 'Pan and Luna' (1880) is Browning's attempt to flesh out the story briefly alluded to by Virgil. He follows his Romantic predecessors in naturalizing the myth, before suddenly introducing a corporeal Pan that incarnates the myth in a dramatically shocking way. He opens by responding to Virgil's conditional clause, in *Georgics*, book III, line 390, 'if it is worthy to believe' (*si credere dignum*), referring to the myth itself: 'O worthy of belief I hold it was, / Virgil, your legend in those strange three lines!'[38] Imagining a particularly dark night, Browning introduces the 'Maid-Moon, with limbs all bare', banishing the darkness before her until she is distracted by what appears to be a white cloud 'tethered' to a pine. (The pine, you'll recall, is the tree sacred to Pan.) She finds herself trapped, drawn deeper into the cloud by the 'downy swathes' twisting about her. Like a pearl collected by divers, 'So lay this Maid-Moon clasped around and caught / By rough red Pan, the god of all that tract.' The colour red alludes to another poem by Virgil, *Eclogues* x, in which Pan is described as 'crimsoned with vermilion and blood-red elderberries.'[39] Although Virgil's language in *Georgics* III suggests that Luna acquiesces willingly to Pan's charms, Browning's poem turns the encounter into a rape, in which the 'Girl-moon' is 'Bruised to the breast of Pan, half-god half-brute, / Raked by his bristly boarsward while he lapped / – Never say, kissed her! that were to pollute / Love's language.'[40] Limited by Victorian ideas of womanhood, Browning cannot conceive of the goddess desiring a sexual encounter – least of all with 'half brute' Pan.

The poem returns from the mythic to the natural, speculating that perhaps the myth is really about the origins of the lunar eclipse. Browning's attempt to make sense of the story ends in rueful frustration mixed with pleasure at the poem it has given him:

> Ha, Virgil? Tell the rest, you! 'To the deep
> Of his domain, the wildwood, Pan forthwith
> Called her, and so she followed' – in her sleep,
> Surely? – 'by no means spurning him.' The myth
> Explain who may!

Browning can only imagine Luna following Pan's summons in her sleep, not of her own volition. The obvious implication of Virgil's lines – that the moon goddess lay with Pan to satisfy her own sexual desire – is so beyond Victorian propriety that Browning cries out for another explanation rather than acknowledge it. Not only does he rewrite Virgil's myth, turning one of Pan's few successful seductions into a rape narrative, but also the poem completely disempowers Luna, turning a goddess into a passive victim. Browning's puzzlement concludes the poem, which ends with him keeping just 'one verse of five words, each a boon, / Arcadia, night, a cloud, Pan, and the moon'. Retrospectively, one might interpret the poem as Browning's attempt to arrange these terms into a coherent narrative, ultimately acknowledging his failure to make sense of Virgil's story.

'Pheidippides' (1879) is a dramatic monologue spoken by the Athenian runner (also known as Philippides), telling the story of his encounter with Pan and the victory at the Battle of Marathon. Browning's poem also has the distinction of inspiring the founders of the modern Olympic Games to invent the 42.2-kilometre (just over 26 mi.) race they called a 'marathon'.[41] Pheidippides opens the poem by invoking the gods who protect Athens, including Pan: 'Present to help, potent to save, Pan – patron I call!'[42] He encounters Pan on his way back to Athens from his mission to recruit the Spartans' help against the Persians. Browning describes the god in delightful detail:

> There, in the cool of a cleft, sat he – majestical Pan!
> Ivy drooped wanton, kissed his head, moss cushioned
>   his hoof;
> All the great God was good in the eyes grave-kindly
>   – the curl
> Carved on the bearded cheek, amused at a mortal's
>   awe
> As, under the human trunk, the goat-thighs grand
>   I saw.

Unlike the variously demonic or frenzied Pan portrayed by his wife, Elizabeth, or the bestial figure who appears in his own 'Pan and Luna', here Robert Browning's Pan is described as unqualifiedly 'good'. As in the version of the story given by Herodotus, Pan wants to know why Athens doesn't worship him or build temples, although he remains 'forever her friend'. Pan charges Pheidippides with a message for the Athenians:

> Go, say to Athens, 'The Goat-God saith:
> When Persia – so much as strews not the soil – is cast
> in the sea,
> Then praise Pan who fought in the ranks with your
> most and least,
> Goat-thigh to greaved thigh, made one cause with
> the free and the bold!'

As a token of his promised help, Pan gives Pheidippides some fennel, then disappears. The runner addresses the assembly of Athenian generals, presenting them with the token. Browning does not include the Battle of Marathon itself in his narrative, but fast-forwards to the aftermath of the Athenian victory. Pheidippides is commanded to run back to Athens, where his heart bursts with joy, and he dies. These last details are given not by Herodotus, but by Plutarch, and Browning's poem combines the traditions reported by the two ancient authors. The distance between Marathon and Athens would subsequently provide the template for the modern marathon run.[43]

Just as Browning elaborated on the myth of Pan and Selene from the barest hints provided by Virgil, the poet Walter Savage Landor (1775–1864) retells two of the less frequently related myths of Pan in 'Pan and Pitys' and 'Cupid and Pan', from his collection *Hellenics* (1859). Landor's classicism distinguishes his work from that of most other nineteenth-century poets, and his interest in lesser-known myths reflects the depth of his knowledge of classical sources.

'Pan and Pitys' begins with a rather playful lovers' quarrel as Pitys looks at Pan 'With a sly fondness' while upbraiding him for his 'fickle mind'.[44] She then describes Pan's deception of the moon goddess (here named Cynthia). In this retelling, Pan conceals his best sheep deep in a cave, covered with dust, while offering Cynthia his worst animals, washed and arranged on the riverbank. Landor adds the amusing detail that Pan scraped his knee while moving his flock and had to conceal the injury with a bit of ivy.[45] Pan responds ('blushing thro' both ears as never before') that the wind god Boreas, his rival for Pitys' love, frightened his goats, causing him to fall. He denies attempting to woo Cynthia – rather, he insists that the moon goddess pursued him. When Pitys challenges him over the quality of his gift, Pan again explains that it was all a misunderstanding: Cynthia had only asked for half the flock, and chose the sheep with 'weightier fleece', though these were louder and smellier.[46]

Unusually for a Victorian poet, Landor includes a moment of apparent sexual candour as Pan recalls more pleasant times he has enjoyed with the nymph:

> Pitys! a time there was when I was heard
> With one long smile, and when the softest hand
> Stroked down unconsciously the lynx-skin gift
> Of Bacchus on my lap, and blushes rose
> If somewhat, by some chance, it was removed.[47]

Landor is no more explicit, but his lines suggest that the removal of the lynx skin from Pan's lap revealed something that made Pitys blush. In his own lifetime, Landor was accused of writing indecent verse in Latin, and he particularly admired the erotic poetry of Catullus. The sexually charged quality of Pan's mythology was generally ignored or heavily

sublimated in nineteenth-century verse, so Landor's suggestive lines are a breath of classical fresh air, even if not sexually
explicit in themselves.

After sharing these playful recollections, Pan begins to
stroke Pitys' hair, and she asks him to play something for her
on his pipes. It is clear that he has won her over, for Pitys
states, 'I will sing of Boreas, whom I hate,' before listing all
his misdeeds.[48] Her singing precipitates the tragedy with
which the poem closes, as an enraged Boreas hurls a rock at
Pitys: 'It smote the Dryad, sprinkling with her blood / The
tree they sat beneath.'[49] Pan is grief-stricken. Landor writes
that 'faithful Pan', redeemed from the earlier charge of fickle-
ness, 'often called aloud the name / Of Pitys, and wiped off
tear after tear / From his hoarse pipe, then threw it wildly
by.' No poet before Landor writes of Pan with such sympathy
for his loss. He concludes by noting that Pan 'never from that
day wore other wreath / Than off the pine-tree darken'd with
her gore.' The pine becomes a permanent symbol of Pan's
grief. In a short lyric simply called 'Pan', Landor imagines
the god responding appreciatively to his retelling of the myth.
Pan leads the poet to the woods and, 'bending both hoofs
under him', invites Landor to sit beside him, telling him, 'I
heard thee tell my loss / Of Pitys,' relating how a mutual
friend in Sicily claimed that only Landor could 'contend' with
him in song.[50] Pan joins the friend's praise of Landor as a
poet, assuring him that he holds few 'higher since thou hast
breath'd / Thy gentle breath o'er Pitys and her Pan'.

Although he depicts Pan with great sympathy in 'Pan and
Pitys', Landor can also portray the god as a figure of ridicule.
In 'Cupid and Pan', Cupid initiates the conflict with a sleep-
ing Pan when he 'snatcht the goatskin hung about his loins
/ And now and then pluckt at a cross-grain'd hair / Bent
inward.'[51] Pan nonetheless sleeps on, failing to wake even

when Cupid steals his favourite pipes from underneath his head. When he finally rouses Pan by playing the pipes, the goat god is angry, grabbing Cupid and warning him to respect his elders. Cupid responds by attempting to shoot an arrow at Pan, and a comical wrestling match ensues: 'Cupid, now faint and desperate, seiz'd one horn; / Pan swung him aloft.'[52] The image of Pan flinging Cupid up into the air with his horn is comical, but it is Cupid who has the last laugh as he plucks a feather from his wing and jabs Pan in both eyes. Nature echoes with the sound of Pan's cry, and the god despairs of ever seeing again. A repentant Cupid offers to heal Pan with a wreath of flowers, on condition that he keep them over his eyes until he is given permission to remove them. As Pan rests, however, he begins to fantasize about the Hamadryads and decides to tidy himself up so that he can go and see them. After exchanging his goatskin for a faunskin, Pan removes the garland from his eyes, discovering too late that the remedy has not yet worked. He visits the temple of Venus, who tells him that he shall have to begin the remedy again, leaving him with a scolding: 'Goat-foot! He who scorns / Our gifts, scorns never with impunity: / Round that horn'd brow, to ake again ere long, / A wreath less soft and fragrant thou shalt wear.'[53] Although this poem is placed after 'Pan and Pitys' in *Hellenics*, Venus appears to prophesy the wreath of pine that Pan will wear after the death of his beloved nymph.

AMERICAN VISIONS

Across the Atlantic, Pan arrived in America through the writings of Ralph Waldo Emerson (1803–1882). Emerson argued for a radically Romantic relationship with the natural world, most famously in *Nature* (1836), in which he claimed, 'I become a transparent eyeball; I am nothing; I see all;

the currents of the Universal Being circulate through me; I am part or parcel of God.'[54] Given his fascination with nature and his desire to experience 'all', it makes sense that Emerson was drawn to Pan, the god who in his various guises haunts the local wilderness and embodies the cosmos. It was, however, the latter form of Pan that most engaged Emerson's imagination. In his poem 'Woodnotes II' (1841) he imagines his speaker being addressed by a pine tree, which presents a vision of cosmic order. The pine's association with Pan through the god's love of the nymph Pitys makes the tree an appropriate one for reflections that culminate in a vision of the god. The pine presents a creation myth in which the voice of God commands, 'Throb!', changing inert mass into an ocean.[55] It is at this point that Pan makes his appearance:

> Onward and on, the eternal Pan,
> Who layeth the world's incessant plan,
> Halteth never in one shape,
> But forever doth escape,
> Like wave or flame, into new forms
> Of gem, and air, of plants, and worms.

This 'eternal Pan' is not bound by his conventional form with horns and hooves; as Patricia Merivale notes, he is more like the shape-shifting god Proteus.[56] Where the Orphic hymn to Pan imagined the cosmic Pan as holding the elements of the universe together, Emerson sees him as enacting 'the world's incessant plan', a role that seems more dynamic. His shape-shifting drives the dynamic processes of geological and biological evolution on Earth.

A stranger version of Pan appears in an undated fragmentary poem by Emerson that imagines the god as suppressor of the primal fires of the Earth. It begins with a conventional enough portrayal of Pan lying drunk and asleep:

> The patient Pan,
> Drunken with nectar,
> Sleeps or feigns slumber,
> Drowsily humming
> Music to the march of time.[57]

The 'nectar' could be ambrosia, the traditional drink of the gods, or it might simply be the more ordinary kind secreted by flowers. That Pan is 'humming' perhaps suggests that he is merely pretending to sleep. Emerson then compares Pan (surprisingly) to a 'tooting, creaking cricket' that never really sleeps, but only 'feigns' doing so: ''Tis his own manner, / Well he knows his own affair.' What this 'affair' turns out to be is the mysterious process of 'Piling mountain chains of phlegm / On the nervous brain of man.' Whatever is Emerson describing, and why is Pan doing it? The image is certainly bizarre, particularly for modern readers, for whom 'phlegm' is normally the sputum we cough up when ill. Emerson's phlegm, however, is one of the four traditional bodily humours of ancient medicine (the others being blood, black bile and yellow bile). Phlegm was believed to cause apathy, and was associated with old age, winter and the element of water. The image of 'mountain chains of phlegm' therefore indicates something like 'vast amounts of apathy'. Pan is engaged in oppressing our minds with the heaviness of apathy or indifference – an activity that no one but Emerson has ever attributed to the god. While he does so, Pan also 'holds down central fires / Under Alps and Andes cold'. This last image suggests the cosmic god who controls the elements, and that 'cold' links him once again with the humour of phlegm.

A Pan who both induces apathy and suppresses fire beneath mountains is idiosyncratic, to say the least; taken together, these ideas imply a god who suppresses potentially eruptive forces in us and in nature, 'Haply, lest we could not live, / Life would be too wild an ode.' Maybe so, but the god who inspires sudden terror is a poor fit with the phlegmatic trait of apathy – and 'too wild an ode' sounds more like Pan's music than a form of life that he would help us to avoid. The fragment as a whole fails to present a cohesive vision of Pan, distorting too many irreconcilable ways of imagining him while adding just a dash too much Emersonian originality to be convincing.

In Emerson's late essay 'Natural History of Intellect', Pan symbolizes 'the unscrutable force we call Instinct,' a force that embodies a divine potential not yet fully realized.[58] Emerson follows Wordsworth in regarding Greek myths as expressing feelings and intuition inspired by imaginative perception of the natural world. The passage attempts to account for both the mythic and Orphic traditions concerning Pan:

> The mythology cleaves close to Nature; and what else was it they represented in Pan, god of shepherds, who was not yet completely finished in godlike form, blocked rather, and wanting the extremities; had emblematic horns and feet? Pan, that is, All. His habit was to dwell in mountains, lying on the ground, tooting like a cricket in the sun, refusing to speak, clinging to his behemoth ways. He could intoxicate by the strain of his shepherd's pipe, – silent yet to most, for his pipes make the music of the spheres, which, because it sounds eternally, is not heard at all by the dull, but only by the mind. He wears a coat of leopard spots or stars. He could terrify by earth-born fears

called panics. Yet was he in the secret of Nature and could look both before and after. He was only seen under disguises, and was not represented by any outward image; a terror sometimes, at others a placid omnipotence.[59]

Emerson draws on allegorical readings of Pan (such as that of Francis Bacon, whom he quotes at the beginning of the essay), but makes subtle modifications. Pan's horns and hooves symbolize his closeness to nature as well as the incompleteness of his 'godlike form'. Acknowledging Pan as 'All', Emerson then describes him in much the same situation as portrayed in his poetic fragment, 'lying on the ground, tooting like a cricket in the sun'. His description of Pan 'refusing to speak' seems to be his own invention, since Pan was among those gods who spoke to mortals, most famously to Philippides. In describing Pan as 'clinging to his behemoth ways', Emerson must be using 'behemoth' as a synonym for 'monstrous'. Despite his silent, monstrous character, he has the power to 'intoxicate' by playing his pipes, which produce no rustic music but rather 'the harmony of the spheres', which Emerson's awkward syntax implies can be heard only by those with sharp mental perception. Although Bacon and other allegorists had interpreted the spots on Pan's cloak as symbols of the stars, rather than as a leopard skin, Emerson gives the god a choice between the two. Unlike the fragmentary poem, where Pan brings only apathy, this passage recognizes Pan's power to inspire fear. Emerson also alludes to the gift of prophecy that Pan taught to Apollo by noting that the god could see 'both before and after'. Ignoring more than two millennia of visual representations, Emerson concludes this passage by claiming that Pan was 'not represented by any outward image', appearing only in disguise. Is he suggesting that the familiar representation with goat horns, shaggy legs and hooves is merely a disguise for a god beyond appearances? Oscillating between 'terror' and 'a placid omnipotence' (qualities of his mythic versus his Orphic identities), for Emerson Pan eludes definitive form. The familiar image we have of Pan is a symbolic one: 'Such homage did the Greek – delighting in accurate form, not fond of the extravagant and unbounded – pay to the unscrutable force we call Instinct, or Nature when it first becomes intelligent.'[60] Emerson's linking of Pan with our instinctual life would be echoed by D. H. Lawrence, as well as the modern tradition of depth psychology.

Pan is a disturbing presence, allusively and thematically, in the final 'romance' by Emerson's sometime neighbour in Concord, Nathaniel Hawthorne (1804–1864). *The Marble Faun* (1860) concerns three American artists in Italy – Miriam, Hilda and Kenyon – and their friend the Count di Monte Beni, whom they call Donatello. The romance opens with the three Americans being struck by the uncanny resemblance between the sculpted Faun of Praxiteles and Donatello himself, who keeps his ears hidden discreetly under curls. We later learn that the count's family is an ancient one said to be descended from the union of a woman and a faun, but whether Donatello has inherited the physical traits of his purported forebear remains a mystery. Like much of Hawthorne's fiction, *The Marble Faun* explores the consequences of repressing instinct in favour of what society considers to be virtue. In Chapter ix Pan symbolically arrives in the form of music overheard while Miriam and Donatello play in the park, racing and weaving each other garlands of flowers. Their play evokes not the innocence of Eden but the 'eternal mirthfulness' of Arcadia:

It was a glimpse far backward into Arcadian life, or, further still, into the Golden Age, before mankind was burdened with sin and sorrow, and before pleasure had been darkened with those shadows that bring it into high relief, and make it happiness.

'Hark!' cried Donatello, stopping short, as he was about to bind Miriam's fair hands with flowers, and lead her along in triumph, 'there is music somewhere in the grove!'

'It is your kinsman, Pan, most likely,' said Miriam, 'playing on his pipe. Let us go seek him, and make him puff out his rough cheeks and pipe his merriest air! Come; the strain of music will guide us onward like a gayly colored thread of silk.'

'Or like a chain of flowers,' responded Donatello, drawing her along by that which he had twined. 'This way! – Come!'[61]

For Miriam, the 'glimpse' of Arcadia afforded by their play imaginatively transforms Donatello into a 'kinsman' of Pan, who seems to be summoning them to further revels with his music. The scene continues into the following chapter, 'The Sylvan Dance', in which the pair join in with musical revelry.

Whereas Miriam's movements contain 'an artful beauty', in Donatello's, as in Pan himself, 'there was a charm of indescribable grotesqueness hand in hand with grace.' Hawthorne's narrator concludes that 'Miriam resembled a Nymph, as much as Donatello did a Faun.' At the level of language, as well as narrative incident, Hawthorne blurs distinctions between the mundane and the supernatural. The festivities are thus joined by 'a shaggy man in goat-skin breeches, who looked like rustic Pan in person, and footed it as merrily as he.'[62] This Arcadian interlude ends as unexpectedly as it began, however, when the string of a harp suddenly breaks. In Miriam's memory, the episode is immediately transformed into a strange 'fantasy':

> It was as if a company of satyrs, fauns, and nymphs, with Pan in the midst of them, had been disporting themselves in these venerable woods only a moment ago; and now in another moment, because some profane eye had looked at them too closely, or some intruder had cast a shadow on their mirth, the sylvan pageant had utterly disappeared. If a few of the merrymakers lingered among the trees, they had hidden their racy peculiarities under the garb and aspect of ordinary people, and sheltered themselves in the weary commonplace of daily life. Just an instant before it was Arcadia and the Golden Age.

Hawthorne's Pan is seen with the eye of imagination, a transformation of the ordinary into the fantastic. He is experienced in an erotically charged moment of heightened emotion, music and revelry – and vanishes along with the feeling. The tenuous reality of Pan in the novel is treated with greater scepticism in Chapter xii; when Hilda speculates excitedly that Donatello might really be a faun after all, Kenyon replies sarcastically, 'A Faun! a Faun! Great Pan is not dead, then, after all!' The romance as a whole suggests that 'Great Pan is not dead' and may erupt at any moment from beneath the surface of ordinary life.

LATE VICTORIAN AND DECADENT DEPICTIONS

As the nineteenth century progressed, the thought of Pan's presence in the everyday world, or of his imminent return, began to appeal to a greater variety of writers. In 'Pan's Pipes' (1881), Robert Louis Stevenson (1850–1894) offers a sustained prose reflection on Pan that seeks to embrace the god in all his contrariness. Stevenson argues that the incongruity of our experience of life is what makes Pan such a compelling embodiment of its powers:

> The Greeks figured Pan, the god of Nature, now terribly stamping his foot, so that armies were dispersed; now by the woodside on a summer noon trolling on his pipe until he charmed the hearts of upland ploughmen. And the Greeks, in so figuring, uttered the last word of human experience. To certain smoke-dried spirits matter and motion and elastic aethers, and the hypothesis of this or that other spectacled professor, tell a speaking story; but for youth and all ductile and congenial minds, Pan is not dead, but of all the classic hierarchy alone survives in triumph; goat-footed, with a gleeful and an angry look, the type of the shaggy world: and in every wood, if you go with a spirit properly prepared, you shall hear the note of his pipe.[63]

Unlike so many other nineteenth-century writers, Stevenson attempts to understand Pan holistically, as 'the type of the shaggy world' in all its contradictions. The god who disperses armies and the god who pipes cheerfully in the afternoon are one and the same, and he can look both 'gleeful' and 'angry'. The future author of *The Strange Case of Dr Jekyll and Mr Hyde* is clearly fascinated by the duality embodied by Pan, who brings together those human and bestial qualities that are expressed separately by the divided personality of his famous protagonist. Without integration, the human tends to become insipid, while our animal nature manifests as the merely brutal.

Stevenson goes on to contrast the sweet and sour aspects of Pan. He cautions those who would resist the lure of Pan's call, for 'here is not a man but has his pulses shaken when Pan trolls out a stave of ecstasy and sets the world a-singing.' It is better, therefore, to participate willingly and passionately. And yet there is also a dark side to Pan, which we experience when nature threatens us or seems to betray its promise of happiness with disease and sudden death: 'It is no wonder, with so traitorous a scheme of things, if the wise people who created for us the idea of Pan thought that of all fears the fear of him was the most terrible, since it embraces all. And still we preserve the phrase: a panic terror.' Despite this, Stevenson suggests that rejecting Pan is a grave error, and he associates such rejection with Victorian bourgeois respectability. Those 'who flee life's pleasures and responsibilities and keep, with upright hat, upon the midway of custom, avoiding the right hand and the left, the ecstasies and the agonies', are really fleeing from Pan in abject terror. Hearing the pipes of Pan, the banker conceals himself 'in the bank parlour'. Stevenson warns us that 'to distrust one's impulses is to be recreant to Pan,' a claim also made, in different language, by D. H. Lawrence some forty years later.

Stevenson's rejection of Victorian bourgeois respectability is shared by those writers of the 1880s and 1890s known as the Decadents. Decadence was a *fin-de-siècle* literary and artistic movement that combined formal artifice with excess of various kinds (often emotional or sexual), arguing for the primacy of creative or artistic truth over the merely scientific or natural. The movement began in France, with the poetry of Théophile Gautier (1811–1872) (whose poem 'Bûchers et Tombeaux' mentions the death of Pan) and Charles Baudelaire (1821–1867). Among its defining works is Joris-Karl Huysmans's novel *À Rebours* (*Against Nature*; 1884), whose protagonist rejects the natural in favour of a private world shaped by his own aesthetic tastes.

Oscar Wilde (1854–1900) is the major English-language Decadent, and, as did his French contemporaries, sought to distance artistic creation from ordinary life. Wilde claimed that 'Art never expresses anything but itself.'[64] Although he includes brief allusions to Pan in several poems, in 'Pan', written in 1881 – the same year as Stevenson's essay – Wilde offers a kind of prayer to the ancient god to come and renew the dreary present of modern England. Reflecting the Decadent emphasis on the artificiality of art, Wilde's poem takes the elaborate form of a double villanelle. The villanelle is a fixed form of French origin consisting of nineteen lines divided into five tercets (a stanza of three lines) and a quatrain (a stanza of four lines). The rhyming first and third line of the opening tercet alternate as the closing line of each of the following tercets, and repeat as the final two lines of the last quatrain. To complicate matters further, the second line of the first tercet provides the rhyme for the second line of each stanza that follows. Wilde's astonishing double villanelle keeps the first rhyme going across *two* villanelles, varying only the second rhyme. The complexity of the form announces its distance from the world of nature, and from any romantic notion of 'spontaneity' as the source of art.

Wilde's 'Pan' opens with a direct address to the god:

> O goat-foot God of Arcady!
> This modern world is grey and old,
> And what remains to us of thee?

No more the shepherd lads in glee
Throw apples at thy wattled fold,
O goat-foot God of Arcady![65]

As the second line suggests, the poem is really a comment on modernity itself, characterized as 'grey and old'. The rhetorical question of the third line asks what remains of Pan in such a world as late Victorian England. Its geriatric qualities contrast with those of Arcadian antiquity, when 'shepherd lads' mischievously tossed apples at the 'wattled fold', where, presumably, Pan kept his goats. It is worth noting in the context of Wilde's life and work that 'lad' could have homoerotic connotations in the late nineteenth century, designating a youthful object of gay male desire. As we saw in Chapter One, Pan himself directed his sexual desire towards young men in some of his earliest artistic representations. When we consider the traditional Christian symbolism connecting the apple with temptation, the second stanza reads as a lightly coded celebration of uninhibited homoerotic play. In this reading, the sexual possibilities available in antiquity stand in stark opposition to the conjugal propriety of nineteenth-century England. Pan cannot be found anywhere in modern England, not even a glimpse of his 'soft brown limbs' or 'beard of gold'. The climate itself rules out the god's life-affirming presence: 'dull and dead our Thames would be, / For here the winds are chill and cold.' And so the speaker tells Pan to keep 'the tomb of Helice' (a willow nymph who nursed Zeus on Crete), as well as his 'olive woods' and 'vine clad wold'. The final quatrain concludes with a recognition that 'many an unsung elegy / Sleeps in the reeds our rivers hold,' suggesting a dormancy that would require the musician Pan to release them through his playing. The first villanelle ends on a note of despair with the repeated line, 'Ah, what remains to us of thee?'

As if in answer to this sad rhetorical question, the second villanelle begins with a prayer for Pan's return: 'Ah, leave the hills of Arcady, / Thy satyrs and their wanton play, / This modern world hath need of thee.' Wilde characteristically imagines Pan dancing not with the female nymphs, but among his playful male satyrs. The god's revitalizing power is needed because, in England, 'Faun and nymph are old and grey.' The next two stanzas appeal to England's literary past, where liberty and chivalry inspired a poetic tradition represented by John Milton and Philip Sidney:

> This is the land where liberty
> Lit grave-browed Milton on his way,
> This modern world hath need of thee!
>
> A land of ancient chivalry
> Where gentle Sidney saw the day,
> Ah, leave the hills of Arcady!

The oppressive dreariness of modern England contrasts with the older land of liberty and chivalry that nurtured English poetic genius. Wilde's prayer implies that Pan's return would revitalize English culture and restore the greatness of its poetic tradition. Although Wilde characterizes England as 'fierce sea-lion of the sea', it yet 'lacks some stronger lay'. Its strength as a naval power has perhaps come at the cost of its poetic prowess. Wilde implores Pan to lay aside his traditional rural instrument in favour of something more martial:

> Then blow some trumpet loud and free,
> And give thine oaten pipe away,
> Ah, leave the hills of Arcady!
> This modern world hath need of thee!

Wilde's trumpet-blowing Pan distantly echoes the god's ancient identity as one who instils sudden terror in battle or military camp; his role as potential restorer of English poetry is Wilde's own happy invention.

The return of Pan, or at least of Pan-worship, took a more literal form in 1885, a year that brought one of the strangest incidents of the whole Pan revival. According to Ronald Hutton, who cites an article from *Country Life*, when a vicar named W. H. Seddon took over the parish of Painswick in Gloucestershire, he learned of a village procession in honour of Pan that had last been held in 1830. The procession had been created in the eighteenth century by Benjamin Hyett, a classical enthusiast, and villagers had tramped through the woods to his country estate, chanting 'Highgates! Highgates!' – most likely a corruption of Hyett's name. Seddon, however, thought it was an ancient chant derived from the Greek *aig aitis*, 'goat-lover', in honour of Pan himself. In his enthusiasm for all things pagan, the vicar not only revived the ceremony in what he believed was its original form, but had a statue of Pan erected by the church tower, where it stood until 1950, when a less tolerant successor had it removed.[66]

As this incident suggests, Pan fever was spreading, and the god assumed an even more central role in the poetry of the *fin de siècle*. The poet Algernon Charles Swinburne (1837–1909) wrote three poems about Pan, 'Pan and Thalassius', 'A Nympholept' and 'The Palace of Pan'. His major innovation in portraying Pan is, Patricia Merivale suggests, to unite the experience of terror associated with Pan and the Orphic understanding of Pan as a cosmic god of all, particularly in 'A Nympholept'.[67] Nonetheless, Swinburne is fascinated by Pan's terror-inducing power in all three poems. 'Pan and Thalassius' dramatizes a dialogue between the god and an invented figure whom Swinburne depicts elsewhere as a son

of Apollo and symbol of the inspired poet. When he encounters the god, Thalassius is somehow immune to Pan's power
to terrify. One of the difficulties of the poem as a whole, as
the very presence of Thalassius suggests, is Swinburne's idiosyncratic use of mythology, such as the mysterious claim that
Urania (the muse of music and dance) gave Pan 'kingdom
and glory', restoring 'grace' to him and 'life' to his 'leaves'
– unless this is a roundabout way of affirming the power of
Pan's music.[68] More recognizable is the command Pan gives
to Thalassius that he 'Hold fast to the green world's pleasance:
/ For I that am lord of it am / All.' This revelation or reminder
leaves Thalassius curiously nonplussed; he responds by
claiming that 'woods may be walked in of mortal / Man's
thought, where never thy feet / Trod.' The interiority of
human thought somehow lies outside the 'all' claimed by
Pan. Thalassius concludes the dialogue by acknowledging
that Pan rules over 'All secrets of birth and growth' and 'All
glories of flower and tree', while reserving for himself 'The
words of the spell of the sea' – like human thought, conceived
of as being outside Pan's jurisdiction, perhaps a metaphor
for poetry itself, the artifice of which endures like the ocean
beyond the biological cycles of birth and death.

In 'A Nympholept', Swinburne takes on the persona of
one who is possessed by the nymphs. The ancient Greeks
believed that this condition, designated 'nympholepsy', was
marked by religious devotion to the nymphs and a kind of
religious ecstasy.[69] In common with many other nineteenth-
century poems, Swinburne's 'A Nympholept' gestures
towards an experience of the ineffable. Pan is both alluded
to and addressed directly, and this god is very much the
Orphic Pan. The speaker of the poem identifies him as a
source of elemental power:

The word of the wind and the leaves that the light
    winds fan
As the word that quickened at first into flame,
    and ran,
Creative and subtle and fierce with invasive power,
Through darkness and cloud, from the breath of
    the one God, Pan.[70]

The primordial 'word' breathed by Pan ignites and spreads through the cosmos, echoed distantly by the 'word of the wind' that rustles through the leaves. Although he experiences a kind of ecstasy induced by the power of nature, the Nympholept cannot decide if it is 'rapture or terror' that seizes him, torn between the two states Pan inspires. He suggests that the breath of Pan might be felt in the fear we experience in the woods or the 'stress' induced by the sun. Our senses are unable to apprehend the ineffable directly. The Great God is immanent in 'the semblance of things that are', a presence revealed by the sun, but also hidden by it – perhaps because Pan is present in the darkness also.

The Nympholept recognizes that Pan is present 'in all things evil and fearful' as well as 'all things good'. This ability of Pan to combine light and dark, and good and evil, mirrors his half-human, half-goat appearance. The Nympholept goes on to celebrate Pan in a lengthy prayer-like reverie that affords Swinburne the opportunity to allude to some of Pan's less commonly celebrated achievements, such as his helping Zeus to recover his tendons from Typhon. He returns to the Orphic sense of the god's identity with the cosmos itself, noting ironically that the very stars appear to scorn humanity, 'Whose souls have strength to conceive and perceive thee, Pan, / With sense more subtle than senses that hear and see'. The Nympholept is one gifted with spiritual senses that offer an intuitive apprehension of Pan's reality. By the end of the poem he recognizes that he himself is 'but a dream' of Pan's, reversing his earlier claim that it is we who 'conceive and perceive' the god.

'The Palace of Pan' is really a hymn to the woods, which Swinburne imagines as a pagan temple in which the changing times of day preserve the mysteries of Pan and his followers. To discern Pan's presence, we must approach him with 'rapture too sacred for fear' and 'passionate awe that is deeper than panic'; 'rapture' and 'awe' counter the 'panic' that the god induces.[71] Swinburne's poem suggests that all we need to experience nature as sacred is to cultivate a sense of wonder and reverence. Doing so will allow us to encounter the living Pan as he slumbers in the woodland.

Pan appeared in two important works of fiction in 1894, Arthur Machen's *The Great God Pan* (which will be discussed in detail in Chapter Five) and *Pan* by the Norwegian novelist Knut Hamsun (1859–1952). Hamsun won the Nobel Prize in Literature in 1920, but ended his life in poverty and disgrace after supporting the Nazis during their wartime occupation of Norway. *Pan* centres on the figure of Thomas Glahn, who lives a marginal existence on the outskirts of the northern wilderness. Like Pan, Glahn is driven by sexual passion to break his solitude, but is frustrated in his pursuit of the woman he most desires, Edvarda. Although present symbolically and thematically, the god does not make an actual appearance. Glahn is happiest alone in the woods, where he is 'filled with joy and gratitude at the fragrance of the roots and leaves and the fatty odor of the pine, reminiscent of the smell of marrow'.[72] His affection for pine in particular is a strong Pan association, echoing as it does the god's pursuit of the nymph Pitys. Early in the novel, we have Hamsun's one explicit image of Pan, when the Doctor notices Glahn's 'powder horn, with a figurine of Pan on it' and starts 'to explain the myth of Pan'.[73] What his explanation is, however, we do not discover. At the beginning of Chapter viii Glahn is out at night at a time of year when the northern sun barely sets. He claims to have met with 'strange adventures' that no one would believe:

> Wasn't Pan sitting in a tree watching to see how I would comport myself, and wasn't he hunched over so that he seemed to be drinking from his own belly? But all this he did so that he could cock his eye and watch me, and the whole tree shook with his silent laughter when he saw that my thoughts were running away with me.[74]

This Pan is both ridiculous and sinister, voyeuristically watching Glahn and somehow monitoring his thoughts. It is an idiosyncratic vision of the god, revealing more about Glahn's unstable mental state (as isolation and romantic frustration take their toll) than about Pan himself.

LATE NINETEENTH-CENTURY ART AND MUSIC

The late nineteenth century also brought a greater interest in depicting Pan in visual art. In England, *Pan and Psyche* (1872–4) by Edward Burne-Jones (1833–1898) portrays a concerned Pan placing a hand on Psyche's head as she emerges naked from the river, in a scene from the myth as told by Apuleius; his head is lean and human, apart from his long, pointed ears. While we see his furry legs (they are not quite 'shaggy'), his cloven hooves are tucked away neatly behind a rock. Pan's connection to the wilderness is suggested by the wreath of ivy encircling his unkempt hair, as well as the rocky terrain in the background.[75] More mysterious is Burne-Jones's *The Garden of Pan* (1886–7), which depicts three naked youths. A young man and woman crouch on the grass, the woman's arms around the man, gazing up at the third figure, who is looking at the viewer and playing a reed pipe. The pipe is the only suggestion that we are looking at Pan, although his unkempt hair (reminiscent of *Pan and Psyche*) and wild eyes distinguish him from the couple. In the background, a round hill surrounds Pan's head, providing just the subtlest hint of a nimbus. The setting is a river landscape with wild rushes, green hills and forest. After returning from a trip to Italy, Burne-Jones had planned a painting on an epic scale, depicting the origins of the world and peopled with a panoply of mythical figures, but he eventually decided on this more modest scene.[76] Who the youthful couple represent is uncertain, although they seem to embody an innocent sexuality under Pan's enchantment.

Completely opposite to Burne-Jones's delicate, fine-boned Pans are those depicted by the Swiss symbolist painter Arnold Böcklin (1827–1901). Böcklin earned fame in the

Arnold Böcklin, *Spring Evening*, 1858, oil on panel. A reclining Pan plays his pipes while two female figures (possibly Persephone, goddess of Spring, and her mother, Demeter) listen in the shadows.

German-speaking countries for his symbolic explorations of mortality and death in a variety of classical settings. Several of his portrayals of Pan are goatish and sensual – one can almost smell the rankness of the god's animality – but the better of his Pan paintings are partial exceptions. *Spring Evening* (1858) depicts a mellow-looking Pan making music as he is secretly watched by two female figures, perhaps the harvest goddess Demeter and her daughter Persephone, goddess of spring. *Pan in the Reeds* (*Pan im Schilf*; 1858) depicts a sad-looking god half-hidden by reeds, playing on his pipe – presumably the aftermath of his unsuccessful pursuit of Syrinx.[77] He is depicted in a similar pose, although more goatish and sitting atop a hill, in *Pan and the Dryads* (*Pan und Dryaden*; 1897).[78] *Pan Terrifies a Shepherd* (*Pan erschreckt einen Hirten*; 1860) depicts a frightened shepherd running down a mountain, accompanied by an equally frightened goat. Just over the mountaintop, a mischievous Pan looks over his shoulder with amusement.[79] In *Pan (or Faun) Whistling at a Blackbird* (*Faun einer Amsel zupfeifend*; 1863), Böcklin includes the incongruous details of a modern flute and sheet music, in an otherwise rather charming image of Pan entrancing, and entranced by, a little bird.[80] *Idyll*, or *Pan Amidst Columns*, presents a series of ruined columns with a large Pan emerging from the wilderness beyond.[81] This Pan is ruddy-faced (a detail taken from Virgil) and narrow-eyed, with white hair and beard suggesting great age; the pipes he plays are enormous. Unlike Burne-Jones, Böcklin doesn't shy away from depicting Pan's cloven feet, and in this painting they are almost cartoonishly large; the god seems to lumber towards us as he plays. The impression is that of some ancient supernatural presence enduring long after the demise of classical civilization. Looking at this painting, one can't be sure whether Böcklin is trying to express the numinous quality of a god or depicting Pan as

Arnold Böcklin, *Idyll (Pan Amidst Columns)*, 1875, oil on canvas. Böcklin's Pan seems to emerge from a world more ancient than the crumbling ruins that surround him.

a semi-comical bumpkin. The portrayal may reflect that very discomfort about Pan's status that goes back to the ancient world. He is a god who has variously provoked fear, awe and laughter.

The English illustrator most closely connected to the literary *fin de siècle*, Aubrey Beardsley (1872–1898), drew three remarkable Pans, and was himself caricatured as Pan in *Punch*. The image *Pan Asleep* from 1893 depicts the shaggy head of the god, with a bestial face, resting against a tree.[82] A hairy hand rests in the crook of his arm, holding his pipes. Beardsley's other portrayals are much more in the Burne-Jones style, depicting a svelte youth with stylized horns and goat legs. He appears this way in the ornamental frontispiece Beardsley made for Arthur Machen's *The Great God Pan*, where he looks back at us over his shoulder.[83] Pan's pointed ears are visible through his long tresses, and his head is surmounted by large curling horns. In his right hand he holds a staff from which his pipes hang by a strap. In 1896 Beardsley drew a self-portrait for *The Savoy* magazine depicting himself

Aubrey Beardsley, *Pan Reading to a Woman by a Brook*, 1898, ink on paper. The leading artist of the Decadence in England, Beardsley produced several images of Pan. Here, the god appears more captivated by his book than by the fashionable young woman accompanying him.

tethered to a statue of Pan.[84] The statue of the god faces away but clearly still holds the artist under his spell, even at a distance. One of the most surprising depictions of Pan in Western art, Beardsley's drawing known as 'Pan Reading to a Woman', portrays an earnest-looking Pan, his head covered with grapes, reading a book to an attentive woman, fully clothed in a ballooning dress, her hair tied primly with a bow.[85] In his story of Venus and Tannhaüser from 1895 Beardsley describes a ballet set in ancient Arcadia that features an altar to Pan prominently displayed centre stage.[86]

By the late nineteenth century Britain had expanded its empire around the globe, and Pan could appear in places far from his European homelands. The Australian painter Sydney Long (1871–1955) produced an Art Nouveau masterpiece in *Pan* (1898), which depicts the god playing for a group of dancing nymphs and satyrs beneath Antipodean gum trees.[87] His painting thus combines classical myth, international artistic style and local landscape. Long translates Pan into an Australian setting, a quietly subversive move against the dominance of European subject-matter in colonial painting, and a theme that is also illustrated in his *Faun and Nymph* (1910).[88] He returned to the same subject-matter as *Pan* in a more stylized manner in *Fantasy* in 1916–17.[89]

Pan's appeal as a subject for painters would decline dramatically as the nineteenth century came to an end, but the god's modern musical career was only just beginning. He is a character in the operetta *Daphnis et Chloé* (1860) by Jacques Offenbach (1819–1880), and was played by the acclaimed actor Léonce (Édouard Théodore Nicole; 1823–1900) at the Théâtre des Bouffes-Parisiens.[90] His successor in the role was the famous Austrian playwright Johann Nestroy (1801–1862), who was so wildly popular as Pan that he inspired prints and even statuettes depicting himself in the role. Although not

H. Sophie Loury (1858–1915), cover art (colour lithograph)
for the American magazine *The Echo* (1895). Playing on Pan's mythological
connection with Echo, this Chicago-based publication included Pan
on several covers.

about Pan himself, the *Prélude à l'après-midi d'un faune* (Prelude to the Afternoon of a Faun; 1894) by Claude Debussy, a symphonic poem based on *L'après-midi d'un faune* (1876) by the poet Stéphane Mallarmé, would inspire many Pan-themed compositions in the early twentieth century.

The magnificent third symphony of Gustav Mahler begins with a movement that the composer originally entitled 'Pan Awakes, Summer Marches In', distinguishing between two sections and identifying the second as a 'Bacchic Procession' in a letter to his friend the critic Max Marschalk.[91] The symphony opens with trumpets, drums and a crashing cymbal,

Johann Nestroy as Pan in the operetta *Daphnis et Chloé* by Jacques Offenbach. Nestroy made the role of Pan hugely popular with audiences.

and has a tense, rather sinister feeling that suggests the awakening of an elemental power. Woven throughout the first movement is a 'Pan tune' that evokes the god in his pastoral character. Mahler himself expressed fascination with the duality of Pan's identity as pastoral god and as 'all', noting that the god's name could serve as a title for the symphony as a whole. When the symphony was published in 1898, however, Mahler dropped the titles of the various movements. Recalling the first time he heard Mahler play the complete symphony for him on the piano, his friend Bruno Walter wrote, 'I saw him and I saw Pan within him.'[92] This would not be the last time that Pan inspired the composer. According to his biographer Henry-Louis de La Grange, in the summer of 1904, probably while composing the finale of his sixth symphony, Mahler arrived home in a breathless panic to tell his wife, Alma, that he had felt the eye of Pan watching him as he worked.[93]

NIGHT TERRORS

As the nineteenth century closed, a major work of scholarship explored Pan's identity as the cause of nightmares, prefiguring his later associations with the power of the irrational. *Ephialtes* (1900) was the first modern study of Pan. It was written by the German classical scholar Wilhelm Heinrich Roscher (1845–1923), an expert in comparative Greek and Roman mythology. *Ephialtes* would shape modern perceptions of Pan by scholars and influence the tradition of depth psychology pioneered by Carl Jung. Roscher adds a new dimension to our understanding of Pan by focusing on his 'function' as 'the demon or evil spirit of nightmares', whom the Greeks named 'Ephialtes' (leaper).[94] While classical sources consistently identify Pan as the cause of that sudden terror we call 'panic', the god's connection to nightmare is less immediately obvious and requires investigation. Although in modern English the word 'nightmare' is used informally to designate any bad dream, Roscher is interested in the experience we usually designate 'night terror', where the bad dream is accompanied by a sense of being suffocated. Such suffocating dreams may involve the vividly experienced presence of a sinister figure applying pressure to the chest, accompanied by an inability to move one's muscles. *Ephialtes* argues that for the ancient Greeks, Pan was just such a figure. Roscher expresses particular interest in the many hybrid creatures reported by dreamers, from those that combine different animals to those combining animal with human, including a bizarre figure whose features include 'a goatbeard' and 'upright pointed ears – like Pan'.[95]

Much of Roscher's argument connecting Pan to the experience of dreaming hinges on his interpretation of an ancient Roman inscription from the second century. The inscription addresses an unspecified god as 'flute player', alluding to him as 'leader of the naiads' and thanking him for healing its author, Hyginus: 'For you have appeared to all my sheep, / Not as a dream vision but in the middle of the day.'[96] Roscher argues that the god being addressed is Pan, and cites the waking nightmare experienced by the pirates in *Daphnis and Chloe* as evidence to support this reading. He also provides a rationalizing explanation for the experiences of Hyginus that leads him to envision the original scenario. Roscher asks us to imagine that

a shepherd, Hyginus, is afflicted with a severe physical complaint and about midday lies down to rest among his flock. While he believes he is still awake, Pan-Ephialtes (the god of both shepherds and hunters) appears to him in an exceedingly vivid dream and by this apparition cures him.[97]

This sort of rationalist interpretation of Pan, which we have encountered before in the work of Francis Bacon and William Wordsworth, is necessary for Roscher to turn the experience of divine healing recounted by Hyginus into respectable modern evidence. Roscher's explanation soon acquires more fictional detail, as he imagines Hyginus experiencing the god's physical presence as his herd was panicked, and gratefully thanking the god for his cure. The problem with this kind of narrative explanation is that it tells a story that seems plausible even as it subtly distorts the scant details on which it is based. All the dedication of Hyginus tells us is that an unnamed god appeared to his sheep – he does not report seeing anything himself – and that through his presence, Hyginus was cured of his ailment. He does not reveal why he thinks his sheep saw a god. Perhaps they did suddenly panic at midday, and the shepherd attributed this to Pan's presence, a belief reinforced by his newly found health. We'll never know. As far as the god himself goes, the dedication mentions a flute and Naiads, whereas Pan traditionally plays a pipe and leads the nymphs – not quite the same, although the pastoral context perhaps suggests a local variation.

It is in his final chapter that Roscher makes his most persuasive argument for seeing in Pan an embodiment of the ancient figure of the nightmare demon. He defines Pan as 'the divine or demonic prototype of the old Greek shepherd and goat herdsman and as the incarnation of the ancient shepherds' life with all their experiences, customs, joys and sorrows'.[98] This chimes well with the earliest evidence we have for Pan's worship, statuettes of shepherds that bear the god's name. Roscher's survey of ancient references to Pan and dreaming reveals the ambiguity of ancient attitudes to Pan; he appears in waking visions and nocturnal dreams, and cures some diseases while causing others. More extensively, Pan was identified as the source of sudden terror in flocks as well as armies. Roscher argues that Pan's association with military panic derives from the panicky behaviour that sometimes overtakes herds of animals.

What are we to make of Roscher's argument that Pan is a nightmare demon? He offers not so much a linear argument as a constellation of examples and associations. Cumulatively, they tend to suggest that any experience of sudden terror in classical times came to be attributed to Pan, from panic to epilepsy and nightmare. As the first modern study of Pan, *Ephialtes* is a work of real importance, gathering evidence from archaeology and literature, and synthesizing the findings and theories of earlier scholars. At times, however, Roscher does distort or over-interpret some of his evidence, particularly the dedicatory epigram of Hyginus. Pan's complex and contradictory nature makes him a difficult god to fit neatly into any overarching theory. Roscher's interest in the subjective experience of Pan explains the enduring interest of his work for depth psychologists such as James Hillman, who includes a translation of Roscher's text in his book *Pan and the Nightmare* (1972). The sense of Pan expressing or embodying powers and experiences rooted deep within the human psyche would characterize many imaginative works in the early twentieth century, as the next chapter will show.

As you make your way through the gorge, the churning river rushes along on your left, while to your right a forest slopes up the cliffside. On such a day, with the warm sun shining down, it is easy to feel that a benign power animates all of nature and ministers to us in our sorrowful moments, as the poetry of Mr Wordsworth suggests. Yet as you behold the sublimity of the landscape around you, you cannot shake the feeling of being watched. Nor can you be certain that the sound of crunching leaves that has accompanied your journey these last few miles is really caused by some small animal burrowing or sparrows looking for food. At last you reach your destination, where a magnificent waterfall plunges down to the river, droplets of spray refracting the light into myriad colours. Looking up, you experience a moment of awe that makes your long trip from the city worthwhile. That sense of awe remains as you unpack bread and cheese and open up the latest issue of the 'Yellow Book' – not a publication you would be seen with at the bank. You linger over Mr Beardsley's drawings, especially the one of a young faun (or is it the god Pan himself?) who reminds you of that handsome clerk who joined your department last week. Should you ask him out for a drink after work?, you wonder. The long hike catches up with you, and you yawn and stretch before dozing off with your head resting on a convenient rock. In your dreams, you find yourself deep in the woods, and the feeling of awe inspired by the waterfall has become sinister. You are stalked by terror, and panic as you realize that there is no way out of the woods. You slip backwards on some wet leaves and lie staring up at the intersecting branches. Your breathing becomes more difficult as the branches take on the shape of horns and a goatish smell fills the air. Just as you feel an enormous weight settling on your chest, you awake with a start. A bleating laugh echoes through the gorge.

4

PAN IN THE TWENTIETH CENTURY

Beneficent god of nature, embodiment of sexual desire (especially in its socially forbidden forms), source of terror: by the dawn of the twentieth century, Pan had acquired the major characteristics that writers, artists and musicians would explore and develop over the next few decades. The Edwardian period was in many ways a mellower continuation of the *fin de siècle*, with Pan appearing in children's books and countless lyric poems, as well as musical compositions. When Pan appears in pre-war fiction for adults, however, he often has a darker character, not only in the work of James Stephens, E. M. Forster and D. H. Lawrence explored here, but in the occult-themed stories considered in the next chapter. The stylistic innovations of modernism marked a definite break with nineteenth-century precedents, and Lawrence brings to Pan a modernist sensibility that takes the god seriously as the embodiment of our deepest instincts and the inhuman powers of nature. Other writers, notably Stephen McKenna and Lord Dunsany, imagine what would happen if modern people really did come into contact with Pan. By the 1930s the magic spell Pan had cast on literature in English had been broken, and his occasional appearances are generally comedic. While he largely disappeared from painting, Pan found a new medium in book illustrations, especially for children.

In music, he enjoyed a vogue across Europe, where composers were particularly attracted to the possibilities for wind instruments suggested by the myth of Syrinx. For English composers of the early twentieth century, Pan inspired music ranging from the pastoral to the sinister, mirroring his portrayal in literature.

CHILDREN'S LITERATURE

The most famous modern version of Pan made his first appearance in J. M. Barrie's novel *The Little White Bird* of 1902. Barrie's Peter Pan stories had their origin in tales he told to the children of his close friend Sylvia Llewelyn Davies, one of whose sons was named Peter.[1] In *The Little White Bird*, Peter Pan is an infant, having been taken by the fairies when only a week old. He plays his pipes while riding on a goat, gathering up other lost infants and bringing them to a house built by fairies.[2] Barrie went on to revise the character into an older boy for his play of 1904, *Peter Pan; or, The Boy Who Wouldn't Grow Up*, subsequently published as the novel *Peter and Wendy* in 1911. The short book *Peter Pan in Kensington Gardens* of 1906 reprints chapters 11–13 of *The Little White Bird*, alongside illustrations by Arthur Rackham, who clearly shows Peter with a set of pan pipes. The success of the play and novel led to the Disney adaptation in 1953, and an American musical the following year. Many other versions have followed, notably *Hook* (1991) and *Return to Neverland* (2002), bringing Barrie's characters to a worldwide audience over several generations of children. Apart from his name, however, does Peter Pan really have any connection with the goat-footed god who is the subject of this book?

At first glance, Peter is about as far from Pan as we can imagine: an eternally pre-pubescent boy, sexually innocent and fully human in form. If we look more closely, though, we catch a few glimpses of the ancient god in Peter's character. He may lack horns and hooves, but the older version of Peter retains his pipes, which he plays for Wendy, sometimes dancing as he does so.³ The god Pan haunts forests and caverns, accompanied by satyrs and nymphs; Peter plays in the woods and lives in an underground home with his companions, the Lost Boys. Indeed, just as the satyrs are in a sense minor Pans, so are the Lost Boys minor Peter Pans, doomed like him to remain children forever. Pan's erotic pursuit of unwilling nymphs has a more innocent parallel in Wendy's voluntary journey with Peter, whose motives appear to be entirely non-sexual (although Wendy imagines kissing him). In Wilhelm Roscher's account, the satyrs are insatiable in their lust for women; in contrast, the Lost Boys simply want Wendy to be their mother. Peter Pan's torment of Captain Hook and the other pirates echoes Pan's torment of the pirates in *Daphnis and Chloe* – and Peter rescues Tiger Lily from their clutches by impersonating Captain Hook's voice, just as Pan rescues Chloe by creating the noisy illusion of an invading army. Barrie's work, I would suggest, revises a number of elements from the mythological and narrative traditions surrounding Pan, usually in a desexualizing way. Just as Pan traverses the human, animal and divine worlds, Peter shuttles between our ordinary world and Neverland, a world of pure imagination, while remaining forever on the border between childhood and early adolescence.

If Barrie transformed Pan in ways that render the original god nearly invisible, Kenneth Grahame added a dimension to Pan's character that would have a profound impact on how the god was imagined in the twentieth century and beyond: protector of wild animals. Grahame first wrote about Pan in 'The Rural Pan', a prose sketch included in *Pagan Papers* (1894),

in which the god provides a pointed contrast to more sophisticated deities such as Mercury and Apollo. Beyond the
busyness of Cheapside and Piccadilly, 'the rural Pan is hiding,
and piping the low, sweet strain that reaches only the ears of
a chosen few.'⁴ Grahame imagines Pan principally as a god
of rural solitude: 'In the hushed recesses of Hurley back-
water, where the canoe may be paddled almost under the
tumbling comb of the weir, he is to be looked for; there the
god pipes with freest abandonment.' Keeping well away from
London, enjoying the countryside near Dorchester or on the
Surrey Downs, Pan is a god who avoids society and the noise
of town life. It is in this brief sketch that Grahame first
imagines Pan as a friend to animals: 'Out of hearing of all the
clamour, the rural Pan may be found stretched on Ranmore
Common, loitering under Abinger pines, or prone by the
secluded stream of the sinuous Mole, abounding in friendly
greetings for his foster-brothers the dab-chick and water-rat.'
The Mole and his friend the Water Rat will reappear as
familiar characters in Grahame's best-known work, *The Wind
in the Willows* (1908).

Perhaps equally important is the way Grahame re-
imagines Pan as a god of the English countryside, one who
rejects the modern world of 'iron road and level highway' in
favour of 'the sheep-track on the limitless downs or the
thwart-leading footpath through copse and spinney, not without pleasant fellowship with feather and fur'. Pan's preference
for 'the sheep-track' recalls his origins as a god of flocks, but
his kinship with animals has been extended to the wild
inhabitants of the English woods. He may shun the flashier
Olympians, but 'he loveth the more unpretentious human-
kind' that works the soil – an association with farm labour
that would have surprised the ancients, who linked Pan with
the archaic, pre-agricultural world of early Arcadia.

Grahame nonetheless insists that Pan 'is only half a god after all, and the red earth in him is strong', suggesting that Pan is too much of the earth to qualify fully as a divinity. Indeed, he might be encountered in some country inn, disguised as 'hedger-and-ditcher or weather-beaten shepherd from the downs', sharing his mysterious wisdom in 'the musical Wessex or Mercian he has learned to speak so naturally'. After encountering such a figure, 'it may not be till many a mile away that you begin to suspect that you have unwittingly talked with him who chased the flying Syrinx in Arcady and turned the tide of fight at Marathon.' Grahame's imaginative transformation of Pan into an English rustic is among the most surprising we have yet encountered. Yet, in doing so, Grahame follows ancient tradition in assigning to Pan the values and traditions of the countryside in opposition to those of urban civilization. In the late nineteenth century the railway was bringing rural England into the modern world, something Grahame lamented: 'to-day the iron horse has searched the country through – east and west, north and south – bringing with it Commercialism, whose god is Jerry, and who studs the hills with stucco and garrotes the streams with the girder.' In opposition to modern commercial and technological values stands 'rural Pan and his followers', who hold out yet in the dwindling countryside. Grahame wonders where Pan will go once the last of the wild countryside has disappeared. This ecological vision of Pan looks back to John Gay in the eighteenth century, who seems to have been the first to imagine Pan as a guardian of the English woods, and forward to the environmentally based spirituality of the Findhorn community in Scotland (see Chapter Six).

Grahame's beloved classic for children, *The Wind in the Willows*, continues to explore the tension between modern urban values and those of the countryside, developing Pan's character as a guardian of the animals. On the one side we have Toad of Toad Hall, who embraces the modern world of cars and towns at the expense of his own animal nature; on the other, we have his friends the Mole and the Water Rat, who are content to live by the river and hope to save Toad from his own foolishness. Pan appears – although not by name – in Chapter Seven, 'The Piper at the Gates of Dawn'. Grahame added the chapter after finishing the rest of the book, and its self-contained narrative allows it to be dropped from abridged versions. Such abridgement is particularly common in American editions, suggesting a discomfort with Grahame's unapologetically pagan mysticism. The episode begins at night, as the Mole awaits the Rat's return from a visit to his friend Otter. Describing his visit, the Rat reveals that one of the young Otters, Portly, has disappeared, to the great distress of his family. Since it is a beautiful night, the two friends decide to take a boat out on the river and search for Portly. They hear a bird sing briefly, followed by the rustling of reeds and bulrushes. As the two animals listen intently, the Rat is suddenly overwhelmed with feeling. He describes the song as

> beautiful and strange and new. Since it was to end so soon, I almost wish I had never heard it. For it has roused a longing in me that is pain, and nothing seems worth while but just to hear that sound once more and go on listening to it for ever.[5]

When 'the thin, clear, happy call of the distant piping' returns, the Mole cannot at first hear it, but then he too is rapt 'as the liquid run of that glad piping broke on him like a wave, caught him up, and possessed him utterly. He saw the tears on his comrade's cheeks, and bowed his head and understood.' The animals are summoned by the mysterious music to an island. When they arrive, the Rat immediately knows they are in the right spot: '"This is the place of my song-dream, the place the music played to me," whispered the Rat, as if in a trance. "Here, in this holy place, here if anywhere, surely we shall find Him!"' The awe that suddenly seizes the Mole 'was no panic terror – indeed he felt wonderfully at peace and happy – but it was an awe that smote and held him and, without seeing, he knew it could only mean that some august Presence was very, very near.'

The piping and mention of 'panic terror' will have alerted us to the nature of this 'august Presence' that inspires such an intense experience of awe for the Mole:

Perhaps he would never have dared to raise his eyes, but that, though the piping was now hushed, the call and the summons seemed still dominant and imperious. He might not refuse, were Death himself waiting to strike him instantly, once he had looked with mortal eye on things rightly kept hidden. Trembling he obeyed, and raised his humble head; and then, in that utter clearness of the imminent dawn, while Nature, flushed with fullness of incredible colour, seemed to hold her breath for the event, he looked in the very eyes of the Friend and Helper; saw the backward sweep of the curved horns, gleaming in the growing daylight; saw the stern, hooked nose between the kindly eyes that were looking down on them humorously, while the bearded mouth broke into a half-smile at the corners; saw the rippling muscles on the arm that lay across the broad chest, the long supple hand still holding the pan-pipes only just fallen away from the parted lips; saw the splendid curves of the shaggy limbs disposed in majestic ease on the sward; saw, last of all, nestling between his very hooves, sleeping soundly in entire peace and contentment, the little, round, podgy, childish form of the baby otter. All this he saw, for one moment breathless and intense, vivid on the morning sky; and still, as he looked, he lived; and still, as he lived, he wondered.

This is Pan in all his wild physicality, yet he looks upon the animals with 'kindly eyes', and has summoned them to rescue the baby otter under his protection. The animals know him as 'the Friend and Helper'. From the earliest votive statues and inscriptions, Pan's ancient devotees regarded him as a helping god. In classical literature, Longus shows Pan rescuing the kidnapped Chloe, while Apuleius portrays a deeply caring Pan who comforts Psyche in her despair. Grahame's vision of Pan as guardian of the wild animals is original, extending Pan's ancient role of protector of flocks to the inhabitants of the wilderness he haunts. 'The Piper at the Gates of Dawn' is perhaps best understood as the development of those gentler aspects of Pan's character found in ancient tradition. It is also a profound expression of natural mysticism.

In Pan's presence, the animals experience longing, awe and a sense of reverence. These feelings are accompanied by fear, an emotion traditionally associated with Pan. When the Mole asks the Rat if he is afraid, his response reveals the contradictory feelings evoked by the god's presence: '"Afraid?" murmured the Rat, his eyes shining with unutterable love. "Afraid! Of HIM? O, never, never! And yet – and yet – O, Mole, I am afraid!"' Their direct apprehension of Pan's divinity inspires a moment of intense religious devotion: 'Then the two animals, crouching to the earth, bowed their heads and did worship.' When they open their eyes again, 'the kindly demi-god' has vanished, but he ensures that they forget what they have seen. This is itself a kindness to the animals, ensuring that the experience doesn't overwhelm their lives, so that 'they should be happy and lighthearted as before'. The Mole and the Rat wake into the ordinary world and rescue Portly. A large hoofprint puzzles the Rat, but also leaves him with a strange feeling. As they depart down the river, the animals hear faint traces of music. It is a song sung by Pan, pledging to help animals who are trapped or injured by hunters – but it soon fades, and the Rat falls asleep with a renewed sense of understanding. In his new role as protector of the wild animals, Grahame's Pan has left his ancient identity as a god of hunters far behind.

'The Piper at the Gates of Dawn' attracted the attention of the book's illustrators from the very beginning. W. Graham Robertson provided a frontispiece for the original edition of 1908, published by Methuen, and also designed an image of Pan for the book's cover.[6] The image depicts Pan with eyes closed, blowing fiercely on his pipes; below him are the Mole and the Rat bowing their heads in reverence, a portrayal that departs from the text by depicting the animals in their boat. Paul Bransom, best known as a wildlife artist, contributed the drawings for the first fully illustrated edition, published by Charles Scribner's Sons in America in 1913.[7] Bransom's illustration of 'The Piper at the Gates of Dawn' shows a realistic Mole and Rat on their hind legs, gazing up at Pan, who reclines leisurely against a rock, pipes in hand, gazing bemusedly at the animals. The most popular illustrations, which Grahame himself is known to have approved, are those created in 1931 by E. H. Shepard, who also illustrated *Winnie the Pooh*.[8] His ink drawing of Pan depicts the god with a look of benevolent concern, sitting with crossed shaggy legs, one

Charles van Sandwyk, 'The Piper at the Gates of Dawn', ink on paper, from *The Wind in the Willows*. Sandwyk's Piper, with his large eyes, conveys his compassion as 'Friend and Helper' of the animals.

hoof protecting the baby otter. If you don't recall this image from your childhood reading, that may be because it has been frequently expurgated in reprints. Were publishers concerned that Shepard's rather devilish-looking Pan would frighten children or offend Christian parents? Rackham created a series of full-colour plates for an edition of 1940, and his image of Pan is the first to portray the god staring straight at us.[9] His right leg bends protectively towards the sleeping otter, who is nestled in the grass between two hooves. Pan's gaze is unsettling, and, although he has a kindly expression, Rackham captures something of the god's danger. Among more recent illustrators, the Canadian artist Charles van Sandwyk creates an image of Pan that emphasizes both his benevolence and his non-human nature, as he smiles at us quizzically.[10] He stands over the sleeping Portly and carries a shepherd's crook, echoing his pastoral origin, from which sprouts new growth.

Grahame's vividly imagined Pan inspires the god's appearance as helper of the innocent in *Pan and the Twins* (1922), a novel for children by Eden Phillpotts (1862–1960). Set in the days following the death of the last pagan emperor, Julian, the story contrasts pagan and Christian values through the figures of the twins, one of whom is a gentle pagan, the other an austere Christian. Phillpotts's description of Pan as he first appears to the boy Arcadius emphasizes his connection to nature:

> It was, indeed, Pan himself – the Pasturer, son of Zeus and Callisto. He came, a stalwart shape with shaggy breast and arms, puck-nose, bright horns and genial countenance – man and animal one – with the all-seeing eyes of divinity. His syrinx hung over his shoulder and about his head there streamed a halo of adoring fire-flies, that moved as he moved.[11]

The 'halo of adoring fire-flies' is an original, if sentimental, touch, but this Pan is very much in the mould of Grahame's 'Piper at the Gates of Dawn'. Despite the novel being directed at children, Pan's main function is to offer an Epicurean philosophy of sensual delight as a counterweight to more austere forms of Christianity.

Early Twentieth-Century Literature

By 1900 Pan had become the presiding god of English literature, as though seeking to prove William Hazlitt's view 'that
the genius of our poetry has more of Pan than of Apollo'.[12]
Pan found himself presiding over an Edwardian idyll, a
golden summer in which youth relaxed and played by the
riverbank in a seemingly endless reverie. That dream would
be shattered forever by the Great War and the turn to modernism across the arts, but in the first decade or so of the
twentieth century Pan reigned supreme. Looking back from
the vantage point of 1930, Somerset Maugham reflected on
Pan's ubiquity in modern English culture:

> God went out (oddly enough with cricket and beer)
> and Pan came in. In a hundred novels his cloven hoof
> left its imprint on the sward; poets saw him lurking
> in the twilight on London commons, and literary
> ladies in Surrey, nymphs of an industrial age, mys-
> teriously surrendered their virginity to his rough
> embrace. Spiritually, they were never the same again.[13]

Maugham's observation registers the way that the return of
Pan corresponds with the waning of official Christianity as
a cultural force. The vision of divinity offered by Pan promised a restored connection with the natural world and our
instinctive life, both perceived as under threat by the modern
world of factories and railways. Declining alongside organ-
ized religion are 'cricket and beer', those cultural markers of
hearty English masculinity, showing that Maugham understands the close connection between Pan's revival and the
languorous Decadence of the 1890s. The rural fantasy that
characterizes so much Edwardian and Georgian verse also

seemed to invite Pan's presence. In her *Bibliography of Greek Myth in English Poetry*, published in 1932, Helen H. Law counted 106 references to Pan, one-third of which appeared between 1890 and 1930.[14] Although his role in poetry was typically that of the pastoral god, Pan's more disturbing side could be invoked as well.

The popular poet and children's author Walter de la Mare (1873–1956) included two closely related Pan poems in his first collection, *Poems* (1906), portraying the god as both sorrowful and terrifying. The first of these, 'They Told Me', opens by questioning the story of Pan's death:

> They told me Pan was dead, but I
> Oft marvelled who it was that sang
> Down the green valleys languidly
> Where the grey elder-thickets hang.[15]

The speaker initially wonders if the song might be that of 'a bird / My soul had charged with sorcery' – a sinister inversion of Keats's famous nightingale. He then speculates that he has not heard with the ear at all, but that his 'own heart heard / Inland the sorrow of the sea', the song embodying the inhuman sorrows of the natural world. (One also wonders if de la Mare was familiar with some of Pan's more obscure maritime associations in the classical sources.) The third stanza concludes the poem with evidence, perhaps, of the presence of a woodland god: 'I found amid the violets / Tears of an antique bitterness.' De la Mare succeeds in suggesting Pan's survival through traces of his sorrow and bitterness, clear allusions to the god's frustrations in love.

In 'Sorcery', the title of which borrows a word from 'They Told Me', de la Mare stages a dialogue about Pan between the anonymous speaker and a woodman. The figure of the woodman is part of the more sinister history of Pan; in Porphyry's ancient story, reported by Eusebius, it is wood-men who are struck dead when they see Pan in person. De la Mare draws on this Porphyrian background for the dramatic situation of the poem, which opens with the speaker asking whose voice he hears 'crying across the pool'.[16] He is told that 'It is the voice of Pan / Crying his sorceries shrill and clear.' Instead of Pan's pastoral music, de la Mare gives us a voice weaving dark magic through the air. When the speaker desires to know the song that Pan is singing, the woodman issues a stern warning that alludes to the Porphyrian tale:

> Seek not the face of Pan to see;
> Flee from his clear note summoning thee
> To darkness deep and black!

Whereas the tale told by Eusebius warns against the god's demonic powers of destruction, de la Mare's Pan threatens to lure us into his own darkness. This darkness may be literal, but it is also symbolic of the sadness alluded to in 'They Told Me':

> He dwells in thickest shade,
> Piping his notes forlorn
> Of sorrow never to be allayed;
> Turn from his coverts sad
> Of twilight unto morn!

Despite this warning, the speaker continues to listen to Pan's song as he 'dreamed his eyes to meet'. All he finds, however, is 'shadow', and he becomes engulfed in 'his woods' deep gloom', never again to see the dawn. As so often in de la Mare's poems, the nightmarish situations he creates have an emotional resonance that suggest they symbolize states of mind or feeling; in 'They Told Me' and 'Sorcery', Pan embodies melancholy in a way that is original and poetically effective.

De la Mare captures the eerie side of Pan's character, but other poets would explore the more philosophical side of the god as the poetic cult of Pan travelled far beyond the English countryside. In North America, for example, the Canadian poet Bliss Carman (1861–1929) gathered several volumes under the title *The Pipes of Pan* (1906). Carman lived most of his life in the United States, where his work was admired by a young Wallace Stevens; in Canadian literature, he is considered one of the 'Confederation Poets', and is best known for his poem 'Low Tide on Grand Pré' (1893). The first selection of poems included in *The Pipes of Pan* comes from *The Book of Myths*, originally published in 1902. It includes a long lyric poem, 'The Pipes of Pan', which acknowledges Pan as god of both nature and fertility, while hinting at his more philosophical identity. 'The Pipes of Pan' begins with the speaker hearing *'mysterious melodies / Such as those which filled the earth / When the elder gods had birth'*.[17] What follows is mainly spoken by Pan himself (who, somewhat confusingly, often refers to himself in the third person). Pan dreams of a lush Arcadian setting and recalls his pursuit of Syrinx, doomed to end in erotic disappointment:

> So the chase has always proved;
> And Pan never yet has loved,
> But the loved one all too soon
> Merged in music and was gone.[18]

Carman shows his familiarity with the myths associated with Pan, moving on to allude to the god's pursuit of Pitys ('All

that once was Pitys stirs / In the soft voice of the firs') and
Echo ('All that once was Echo still / Wandering from hill to
hill').[19] Pan's knowledge of loss and sorrow makes him well
disposed towards mankind, and he invites us to join him in
the woods. His music encompasses all the sounds and
beauties of nature. As a god of fertility, he presides over the
fecundity of the earth and its denizens:

> Here is Pan's green flower, the earth,
> He has tended without dearth,
> Brought to blossom, fruit, and seed
> By the sap's imperious need.[20]

Carman's four-beat couplets trot along as Pan's music
acquires ever more metaphorical power, eventually symbolizing a kind of cosmic love that binds the universe together,
a nod at the cosmic Pan familiar from the Orphic hymn,
bestowing love and happiness on all who hear it. More
specifically, Carman's vision of Pan reflects his commitment
to what the critic D.M.R. Bentley calls 'a strategy of mind-
body-spirit harmonization aimed at undoing the physical,
psychological, and spiritual damage caused by urban modernity'.[21] The Book of Myths also includes a poem titled 'Syrinx',
which reflects on wind instruments from around the world,
and 'A Young Pan's Prayer', where the speaker prays to Pan
to grant him manhood and 'The strength of the hills and the
strength of the sea'.[22] Carman's Pan has the power to imbue
us with the strength of the natural world.

That strength is not always enough to prevent a tragic
outcome. Pan is present both allusively and thematically as
the presiding god of homosexual love in a short novella of
1905 by Forrest Reid (1875–1947) named The Garden God,
which tells of an ill-fated love between two schoolboys. This

tale of blossoming homosexual attraction was particularly daring for its time, published a mere decade after the trial of Oscar Wilde. The deeply closeted Henry James was so shocked by Reid's dedication of *The Garden God* to him that he never spoke to his fellow writer again.[23] Its central character, Graham, is raised at home by his father, his mother having died in childbirth. Graham is educated in the Greek classics, and develops an intense inner life focused on an imaginary garden presided over by one of his father's statues. The statue is an antique reproduction of the Spinario, which depicts a boy pulling a thorn from his foot. When Graham is eventually sent to school, he initially recoils, yearning for the time spent in his inner world 'when Pan and his followers had been in every thicket by the way!'[24] Despite his reservations, Graham finds himself good at sports, and popular. He soon encounters a boy named Brocklehurst, whom he immediately recognizes from his father's statue. Blurring the lines between fantasy and reality, Graham tells him, 'you played on the flute of Pan; and you bathed in the streams . . . Do you remember?' Brocklehurst is intrigued, and the two soon become fast friends, although Graham's feelings are much more intense.

Graham's new experience of love opens up his imagination to the natural world, as he experiences at first hand feelings he has only read about in Greek:

That faculty for noting the listening soul, the spirit that is in leaf or plant, seemed to be a part of his very human nature, seemed as some ancient bond of relationship that bound him then, and would bind him for ever, to stiller and less perfect forms of life – to a whole world of pastoral divinities – the great god Pan himself; the Hamadryads, who inhabit the

forest trees; and Oreads, and Naiads, and Hyades –
the deities of water-springs, and streams, and showers
of summer rain.

He decides to read Plato's *Phaedrus*, and is immediately
captivated by Socrates' prayer to Pan: 'Beloved Pan, and all
ye other gods who haunt this place, give me beauty in the
inward soul; and may the outward and inward man be at
one.' This prayer also expresses the major theme of Reid's
story, as Graham attempts to live his innermost desires in the
outer world with Brocklehurst. After a beautiful afternoon
swimming together – at a place and in weather 'pleasant
enough for Pan' – a tragic accident occurs, forever dashing
Graham's dreams.

Other Edwardian writers take an even darker turn in
writing about Pan. E. F. Benson and Saki both write tales that
emphasize the danger humans face from direct contact with
Pan, a motif going back to Porphyry but given new currency
by Arthur Machen towards the end of the nineteenth century.
In his story 'The Man Who Went Too Far', published in 1912,
Benson (1867–1940) tells of a man destroyed by his fascination
with Pan's power. Its focus is a man named Frank Halton,
who is visited by a friend of the narrator's named Darcy.
What is likely to strike a twenty-first-century reader are the
homoerotic overtones of their friendship: the two men clasp
hands and Darcy looks upon Frank's strangely youthful face
with a rapturous gaze 'as of a lover listening to the voice of
his beloved'.[25] Frank's youthfulness increases with each passing day, accompanied by a surprising intimacy with the
natural world. He explains that three years earlier he heard
a mysterious piping among the reeds: 'It was, my dear Darcy,
as the Greeks would have said, it was Pan playing on his
pipes, the voice of Nature. It was the life-melody, the

world-melody.' Although his response is a feeling of panic terror, Frank is undeterred. After hearing the pipes again six months later, he develops a technique of passive receptivity that allows him to connect with this mysterious power. Darcy reminds him of the ancient tradition that to see Pan means death, but Frank seeks a more revelatory experience of the god. He has rejected Christianity altogether, enchanted by his new youthful vitality. Darcy warns Frank that the spirit of Nature necessarily includes suffering and death, but his pleas fall on deaf ears. One day, Darcy hears Frank crying out in agony, accompanied by 'a little mocking, bleating laugh'. He arrives in time to experience 'a sharp and acrid smell' and see a leaping 'black shadow' that 'seemed to jump into the air, then came down with tappings of hard hoofs on the brick path that ran down the pergola, and with frolicsome skippings galloped off into the bushes'. Darcy soon discovers the consequences of his friend's encounter with the supernatural – as well as physical proof. The story has little to say about Pan as such, and is not particularly frightening. Its barely sublimated homoeroticism and theme of divine punishment suggest that the story is a warning about openly following illicit desire – Frank, after all, is 'The Man Who Went Too Far'.

Like Benson, the short-story writer Hector Hugh Munro (best known by his pen name, 'Saki'; 1870–1916) also portrays a malevolent Pan in 'The Music on the Hill' (1911), but one whose hostility is clearly motivated by disbelief and an act of sacrilege. The story focuses on a newly married woman, Sylvia Setoun, who is frustrated with her husband, Mortimer, a man known for 'his unaffected indifference to women'.[26] When they move to Yessney, his manor farm, Sylvie observes that 'one could almost think that in such a place the worship of Pan had never quite died out.' Mortimer takes her flippant remark in earnest, warning her: 'The worship of Pan never has died out . . . Other newer gods have drawn aside his votaries from time to time, but he is the Nature-God to whom all must come back at last. He has been called the Father of all the Gods, but most of his children have been stillborn.' Sylvie is astonished at her husband's belief in the god, but he urges her not to announce her own disbelief 'too boastfully while you're in his country'.

Sylvie's dismissal of her husband's concern is consistent with her rationalizing of strange experiences. While retreating from an enormous sow, she is startled by 'the echo of a boy's laughter, golden and equivocal'. Although it confirms her sense that some strange presence haunts Yessney, she attributes the laughter to a young farmhand. She later discovers a bronze image of Pan deep in the woods, where someone has left a bunch of grapes. Disgusted, Sylvie takes the grapes, only to see that 'across a thick tangle of undergrowth a boy's face was scowling at her, brown and beautiful, with unutterably evil eyes.' She throws away the grapes. Mortimer is dismissive of her explanation that the boy must have been a gypsy, and cautions her to avoid the wilderness and any horned animals. Although Sylvie avoids both the wilderness and the farm, the story mounts to a chilling climax as she sees a great stag running down a hill to the accompaniment of 'wild music'. Saki's story is both suspenseful and eerie, dramatizing the terrible consequences of dismissing the supernatural. As a portrayal of Pan, 'The Music on the Hill' is original in imagining him as a sinister child, while retaining his traditional association with pipe music and horned animals. The special hostility he reserves for Sylvie is a reaction to her disbelief and her theft of a votive offering – something no pagan god would tolerate. Thematically, Pan's malign interest in Sylvie balances Mortimer's marital indifference;

the attention of the supernatural can be more harmful than the inattention of a mere mortal.

The threatening power of Pan also attracted the attention of a young E. M. Forster (1879–1970). Although he would later establish his reputation as a major modern novelist, in 1902 Forster was as caught up with Pan as any of his contemporaries as he wrote 'The Story of a Panic'. He later recalled his idea for the story: 'I would bring some middle-class Britishers to this remote spot, I would expose their vulgarity, I would cause them to be terribly frightened[,] they knew not why, and I would make it clear by subsequent events that they had offended the Great God Pan.'[27] The unnamed narrator and his wife are out for a picnic with a group of English tourists near Ravello. Among the company is a young boy named Eustace, who irritates the narrator with his reluctance to listen to adults or engage in physical exercise. In conversation with the artist Leyland, the narrator defends the rights of landowners to cut down trees for profit:

'I see no reason,' I observed politely, 'to despise the gifts of Nature, because they are of value.'

It did not stop him. 'It is no matter,' he went on, 'we are all hopelessly steeped in vulgarity. I do not except myself. It is through us, and to our shame, that the Nereids have left the waters and the Oreads the mountains, that the woods no longer give shelter to Pan.'

'Pan!' cried Mr Sandbach, his mellow voice filling the valley as if it had been a great green church, 'Pan is dead. That is why the woods do not shelter him.' And he began to tell the striking story of the mariners who were sailing near the coast at the time of the birth of Christ, and three times heard a loud voice saying:

'The great God Pan is dead.'

'Yes. The great God Pan is dead,' said Leyland. And he abandoned himself to that mock misery in which artistic people are so fond of indulging. His cigar went out, and he had to ask me for a match.[28]

Leyland's claim that it is we who are responsible for driving Pan away from the woods is answered by Sandbach's insistence on the traditional Christian interpretation of Pan's death. In retrospect, readers can recognize in this exchange the cause of what follows; the narrator's defence of profit-making forestry and the belief in Pan's death shared by Leyland and Sandbach are provocations of divine wrath. Forster (whose name is curiously apt in this context) seems to cast Pan as a god outraged by the destruction of forests by money-seeking aristocrats, much as John Gay did in the eighteenth century.

Soon after this conversational exchange, the party is startled by the shrill sound of Eustace's whistle. After a moment of eerie silence, the adults in the party find themselves seized by an inexplicable terror that drives them to run through the wooded landscape and into the valley below. The narrator attempts to describe the feeling:

It was not the spiritual fear that one has known at other times, but brutal overmastering physical fear, stopping up the ears, and dropping clouds before the eyes, and filling the mouth with foul tastes. And it was no ordinary humiliation that survived; for I had been afraid, not as a man, but as a beast.

Forster has ingeniously subjected his characters to the same kind of panic that the ancients believed herd animals experienced in Pan's presence. Their middle-class pretensions are

Mixing bowl (bell krater) by the Pan Painter, Athens, c. 470 BC, ceramic. The image depicts a shepherd (usually identified as Daphnis) fleeing in panic from the sexual pursuit of Pan. Behind Pan is a stone image of the phallic god Priapos in a rocky landscape.

Pan and the Nymphs (Pompeii, fresco, 1st century AD). This Roman fresco painting portrays a fully human-shaped Pan, apart from his small horns and ruddy-coloured skin. Pan's red skin is a detail mentioned by Virgil, who attributes it to berries smeared on the god's face. The nymphs in the fresco are portrayed as modest Roman maidens.

Annibale Carracci, *Pan and Diana*, 1597–1602, fresco. According to Virgil, Pan successfully seduced the moon goddess by offering her wool from his flock. Carracci painted the scene as part of *The Loves of the Gods* for the ceiling of the Palazzo Farnese in Rome.

Peter Paul Rubens and Jan Brueghel the Elder, *Pan and Syrinx*, c. 1617–19, oil on panel. Syrinx looks poised to turn into a reed as Pan grasps her garment.

Edward Burne-Jones, *Pan and Psyche*, 1872–4, oil on canvas.
In the legend related by Lucius Apuleius (*c*. AD 124–*c*. 170), Pan
persuades Psyche not to succumb to despair after losing her beloved Cupid.
Burne-Jones portrays Pan as compassionate and wise.

Arthur Rackham, 'Peter Pan is in the Fairies' Orchestra', ink and watercolour, from *Peter Pan in Kensington Gardens* by J. M. Barrie (1906). In his first published appearance, Peter Pan was an infant who played the panpipes and rode upon a goat while he searched for lost children to bring to the fairies.

Paul Bransom, 'The Piper at the Gates of Dawn', watercolour, from *The Wind in the Willows* by Kenneth Grahame (1913). Bransom, a wildlife artist, was the first illustrator of Grahame's novel. He emphasizes Pan's benevolent amusement at the Mole and the Water Rat.

Leon Bakst, 'Set Design for Act I from *Daphnis and Chloe*', 1912, watercolour on paper. Bakst's design presents a rocky and wooded landscape typical of Pan's habitation. In the centre are images of nymphs carved out of rock, below which two worshippers bow. Wreaths, possibly of pine, have been laid behind them.

Front cover of the English magazine *Pan*, 1/19 (1920). The self-described 'journal for saints and cynics' ran from 1919 to 1924, featuring images of fashionable modern women on its cover.

Francisco de Goya, *Witches' Sabbath*, 1798, oil on canvas.
Goya's painting depicts the Devil in the form of an upright goat surrounded
by a coven of witches. By the twentieth century, it was widely assumed
that the Church had assigned Pan's form to the Devil to discredit a popular
god of the pagan countryside.

Franz von Stuck, *Dissonance*, 1910, oil on cardboard. Inspired by Arnold Böcklin, Stuck made his reputation as a painter of mythological and allegorical subjects. Here, he offers a humorous allegory of 'dissonance', with Pan experiencing intense displeasure while a small faun attempts to learn the panpipes.

Thomas MacKenzie, 'A Swift Shadow Darkened the Passage', 1924, watercolour and body colour, illustration for *The Crock of Gold* by James Stephens, first published in 1912.

We Are All Pan's People by The Focus Group (2007), cover artwork by Julian House. The Focus Group (Julian House) and fellow Ghost Box artist Belbury Poly (Jim Jupp) have both invoked Pan in their eerie electronic soundscapes.

Ghost Box   08

We are all Pan's People
The Focus Group

overtaken by pure animal fear. Realizing that Eustace is not with them, the company hurry back to the hillside, where they find him lying unconscious. Ominously, the narrator discovers hoofprints in the nearby mud, which Eustace quickly erases upon waking. The boy is not the same, and the rest of the story explores the consequences of his strange transformation.

Eustace is no longer the sullen and inactive child who so annoyed the narrator; he moves constantly, and expresses a wish to see Gennaro, 'the new stop-gap waiter, a clumsy, impertinent fisher-lad'. When the party returns to the hotel, Eustace leaps joyfully into Gennaro's arms, much to the discomfiture of the narrator. Whatever transpires between them, Gennaro repeatedly says *Ho capito* – 'I have understood' – a remark that no one else can explain. He now addresses the boy using the familiar form *tu* instead of the more respectful *voi*. That night Eustace leaves his room and cannot be persuaded to return inside. When the narrator bribes Gennaro to trick Eustace by returning him to the English tourists, the unintended consequences of his actions produce a shocking conclusion to the story. Forster would allude briefly to Pan again in his novel of 1907, *The Longest Journey*, whose central character, Rickie, gathers a selection of his short fiction under the title 'The Pipes of Pan'.[29] In a wry comment in *A Room with a View* (1908), the narrator observes of his returning tourists that 'Pan had been amongst them – not the great god Pan, who has been buried these two thousand years, but the little god Pan, who presides over social contretemps and unsuccessful picnics.'[30]

Grahame, Benson and Forster all preferred the company of men, and all re-imagined Pan to meet their individual emotional and artistic needs. The Piper at the Gates of Dawn is radically different from the threatening Pans of Benson and

Forster. In terms of their sexuality, there are considerable differences as well among these writers. If Grahame was indeed a gay writer, as Peter Hunt argues in *The Making of the Wind in the Willows*, there is no unambiguous evidence that he was ever a practising homosexual.[31] Benson socialized openly in gay circles and lived with a man in Italy, but was discreet about his private life. Forster's sexuality was well-known in his own lifetime. The attraction Pan held for these men perhaps lay in his liminal status, his location outside the accepted limits of civilized behaviour. As classically educated men, they may have been aware of the early depictions of a phallic Pan pursuing the shepherd Daphnis, but would certainly have known the stories of his sexual frustration and solitude. At a time when homosexual acts were still a criminal offence, Pan may have seemed an apt symbol for the powers of nature manifesting in ways that troubled modern heterosexual culture. As we have seen, Oscar Wilde, who would famously be prosecuted for sodomy, celebrates Pan in his double villanelle in just this way (see Chapter Three).

Pan could also disrupt the social order with the threat of sensuality itself, as he does in the delightfully strange novel *The Crock of Gold* (1912) by Irish writer James Stephens (1880–1950). Among many other things, the book dramatizes human psychological development from adolescence into full adulthood. The different forces at work in the psyche are represented by different characters, which must be integrated and balanced; in this scheme, Pan embodies our instinctive life. His opponents are the Philosopher, who symbolizes the rational intellect, and the Irish god Angus Óg, who offers the possibility of a deeper love than the merely sensual. As the narrative unfolds, Caitlin, daughter of the farmer Meehawl MacMurrachu, encounters Pan as she awakens into adolescence. One day, while herding goats, she overhears beautiful and haunting music being played on pipes. Although she briefly glimpses the arms and shoulders of the player, it is not until the following day that she sees his face: 'His hair was a cluster of brown curls, his nose was little and straight, and his wide mouth drooped sadly at the corners. His eyes were wide and most mournful, and his forehead was very broad and white. His sad eyes and mouth almost made her weep.'[32] Unlike the smiling Piper at the Gates of Dawn, this is a deeply melancholic Pan. Caitlin is afraid when she sees the lower half of his body, but cannot bring herself to flee: 'His legs were crossed; they were shaggy and hoofed like the legs of a goat: but she would not look at these because of his wonderful, sad, grotesque face.' Pan is a stranger in Ireland, telling Caitlin that in his native country he is worshipped by all those who tend animals, but here he is very lonely. Seeing her fear at his half-bestial appearance, Pan counsels her to look and 'know that they are indeed the legs of a beast and then you will not be afraid anymore.' Pan attempts to woo her by arguing that the instincts lead to the 'Crown of Life', following the way of sensual love rather than spiritual wisdom. Yet it is not Pan's argument that persuades Caitlin to join him, but rather the fact that 'he was naked and unashamed.'

Concerned for his daughter, MacMurrachu turns to the Philosopher, who sends his children with a message to Pan. They are welcomed kindly, but the god rejects the Philosopher's accusation that he is doing something 'wrong' by 'keeping Caitlin Ni Murrachu away from her own place'. When they return, the Philosopher decides that he must take matters into his own hands, and sets out to persuade Pan to release Caitlin. In this initial contest between Thought and Instinct, Thought is utterly routed. Pan's sense of life is purely of the body: 'it is to be born and to die, and in the interval to

eat and drink, to dance and sing, to marry and beget children.'
Failing to convince Pan, the Philosopher vents his spleen on
Caitlin herself, dismissing her as a 'Hussy' as he petulantly
leaves their dwelling to the accompaniment of Pan's pipes.
The Philosopher is not done, however, and decides to seek
the assistance of Angus Óg, the Irish god of love.

Pan's victory over the Philosopher proves a hollow one,
as Caitlin's sense of dissatisfaction with the god intensifies.
She sits by herself in Pan's cave, reflecting on her disappointment as she discovers that on its own, bodily desire is merely
disturbing and unquenchable. Yet the Philosopher's alternative of abstract thought is no more satisfying. Pan arrives
home, and he and Caitlin suddenly hear beautiful singing
outside the cave. It is Angus Óg, who identifies himself as
Love, to which Pan responds that he is also called Love, as
well as Joy. After a brief argument, culminating in the appearance of Angus Óg's spear, the two gods agree to let Caitlin
choose between them; more precisely, she must choose 'the
greatest thing in the world', which will determine her choice
of god. Caitlin replies that Pan 'said it was Hunger and long
ago my father said that Commonsense was the greatest thing
in the world' – neither of which she finds ultimately satisfying. Angus Óg tells her that he believes the greatest thing is
'the Divine Imagination'. Caitlin, however, has her own ideas
and chooses happiness. In response, Angus Óg offers a
lengthy philosophical reflection, in which he identifies male
common sense with thought and female happiness with emotion, arguing that both are united in love. When he invites
Caitlin to join him, she is greatly distressed, as she has already
given herself to Pan. What persuades her to forsake Pan is
Angus Óg's plangent declaration of his need for her. He
describes his profound loneliness, saying that 'In all my
nation there is no remembrance of me. I, wandering the hills

of my country, am lonely indeed.' Hearing his speech, Caitlin frees herself from Pan's grip, which leaves her bruised, and the goat-footed god withdraws, conceding the victory to Angus Óg. In Stephens's allegory, Caitlin has been freed by her enthralment to bodily desire, integrating intellect and feeling in a higher form of love. Although Stephens's fable and characterization of Pan are both highly original, we might recognize in them a variation of the ancient contest between lust and love dramatized in Pan's defeat by Cupid, adapted to an Irish context, with Angus Óg taking the place of Cupid. Given the strong association between Pan and the English countryside in the work of Grahame, Benson and others, his defeat by Angus Óg may also have nationalist implications, as Mark Williams suggests in his recent book on the Irish gods.[33]

INTERWAR IMAGININGS

The modern writer who offers the most profound exploration of Pan's meaning is unquestionably D. H. Lawrence (1885–1930). In 1924 he published the essay 'Pan in America', and the following year his novella *St Mawr*. Both reflect on the endurance of Pan in the American landscape and the possibility of reconnecting with the god in the twentieth century. Lawrence's vision of Pan combines elements of both the pastoral and Orphic traditions in a daring and original synthesis. In 'Pan in America', Lawrence acknowledges the alleged death of Pan at the start of 'the Christian era', before asking who he really is: 'Down the long lanes and overgrown ridings of history, we catch odd glimpses of a lurking rustic god with a goat's white lightning in his eyes.'[34] Such a figure inspires fear more readily than love, and Lawrence notes the ancient belief that to see Pan was to be struck dead. Nonetheless, he

suggests that the god can be safely glimpsed at night, ener-
gizing the man fortunate enough to behold him: 'You might
dimly see him in the night, a dark body within the darkness.
And then, it was a vision filling the trunk and limbs of a man
with power, as with a new, strong-mounting sap. The Pan-
power!' Such power bestows on the male recipient the ability
to 'cast a spell' on others, particularly women.[35] Men were
not immune to the power of the wild, however, and Lawrence
notes the danger posed by Pan's companions, the nymphs,
who if glimpsed would cause men to pine away with
unfulfilled desire. In his brief overview of Pan's history,
Lawrence describes how men chose the city over the wilderness, pursuing power over each other. As a result, 'Pan
became grey-bearded and goat-legged, and his passion was
degraded with the lust of senility,' while the nymphs in turn
'became coarse and vulgar'. Finally, with the advent of
Christianity, Pan becomes the Devil.

Lawrence is struck by the incongruity between Pan's
ancient identity as god of 'All' and his diminished, almost
parodic role as Christianity's Devil, source and scapegoat of
all evil, 'especially our sensual excess'.[36] In Lawrence's myth-
ologizing, Pan seems to acquire his goatish lower half as a
result of this debasing change from Great God of All to Devil;
as we've seen, however, the tension between pastoral and
cosmic divinity in Pan's character has deep roots in antiquity.
Lawrence calls this diabolic transformation 'a most strange
ending for a god with such a name. Pan! All! That which is
everything has goat's feet and a tail! With a black face!' The
'black face' of the Devil replaces the ruddy complexion Pan
had in antiquity. As a final indignity, the nymphs themselves
become 'the nasty-smelling witches of a Walpurgis night',
while the satyrs turn into fairies or sorcerers. Nonetheless,
Lawrence argues that 'Pan keeps on being reborn,' pointing

to both his Renaissance and Romantic revivals. In spite of Wordsworth's pantheism, Lawrence regards the earlier writer's interest in Pan as particularly feeble, claiming that he chose to give the Great God the form of Lucy Gray (alluding to his poem 'Lucy Gray; or, Solitude' of 1798 with its famous opening line, 'Oft have I heard of Lucy Gray').[37] From England, Pan travels to America in the work of Ralph Waldo Emerson before he finds temporary expression in the poetry of Walt Whitman: 'To this new Lucifer Gray of a Pan, Whitman sings "I am All, and All is me." That is, "I am Pan, and Pan is me."'[38] Unfortunately, this American pantheism would not survive Whitman. Lawrence dismisses Pan's Victorian aftermath as so much self-indulgent play that quickly became boring. And yet Pan endures – in the American landscape.

Lawrence argues that Pan was at his most powerful when still 'nameless and unconceived.'[39] It was only when humanity imagined itself as in some way distinct from everything that it gave that everything a name: Pan. 'In the days before man got too much separated off from the universe,' Lawrence writes, 'he *was* Pan, along with everything else.' Self-consciousness is a form of separation: we know ourselves to be something apart from everything around us. Out of this division, humanity recognized a wholeness that seemed apart from ourselves as self-conscious creatures. Lawrence gives Pan an origin myth that is also a radically revised myth of the Fall; in place of 'original sin' leading to our expulsion from Eden, we have the development of self-awareness dividing us from the cosmos as a whole. That holistic cosmos is what humanity names 'Pan'. Unnamed and unrecognized, Pan in his oldest form endures in the New World.

At the heart of Lawrence's essay is a profound encounter with nature in the form of a single tree – fittingly enough, a pine tree, the tree sacred to Pan because of his love of the nymph Pitys, although Lawrence doesn't mention the myth directly. A tree, unlike us, is still an unselfconscious part of nature, yet for Lawrence it possesses its own will. Writing from New Mexico, he describes how 'on this little ranch under the Rocky Mountains, a big pine tree rises like a guardian spirit in front of the cabin where we live.' Marked by Indians and blasted by lightning, the pine endures – it is 'still within the allness of Pan'.[40] The lives of Lawrence and the tree interpenetrate each other. It is this sense of communion that brings Lawrence into contact with the Great God; he writes that the tree 'vibrates its presence into my soul, and I am with Pan'. In opening himself up to the being of the tree, Lawrence feels himself transformed, becoming 'more like unto the tree, more bristling and turpentiney, in Pan'.[41] Lawrence argues that it is we who choose to shut 'many doors of receptivity', ones that he prefers to keep open. He expresses the necessary attitude as 'Give me of your power, then, oh tree! And I will give you of mine.' It is this sacred bond with nature that Lawrence identifies as 'the oldest Pan'.

It is difficult to read very far in Lawrence without encountering attitudes that are deeply problematic for twenty-first-century readers, and 'Pan in America' is no exception. Like so many other non-Indigenous writers, Lawrence imagines Indigenous peoples who live within their traditional worldview as 'noble savages' whose relationship to nature serves as an example for modern Western readers alienated from the natural world. Presenting nameless Indigenous people as worshippers of the ancient Greek god Pan, ignoring their own mythologies and cultural traditions, Lawrence effectively co-opts them to make a rhetorical point about the modern West. For example, he imagines an old Indigenous man warming himself by a fire made from a tree he has felled, 'faintly smiling the inscrutable Pan-smile into the dark trees

surrounding'.[42] The man speaks to the burning logs 'in the
Pan voice', asserting his mastery over the tree and his absorp-
tion of its warmth. He prays silently for the fire to return
whence it came: 'Speech is the enemy of Pan, who can but
laugh and sound the reed flute.'[43] Language implies self-
consciousness, separating us from the undifferentiated
cosmos; the old man who 'sits stonily and inscrutably' (and
stereotypically, we might add) is imagined as retaining that
primordial unity. That unity is also present for the Indigenous
hunter, whose oneness with his prey causes the animal to
yield to him.[44]

Lawrence contrasts this experience of Pan with that of
modern Western men, 'who sit at home in their studies, and
drink hot milk, and have lamb's wool slippers on their feet,
and write anthropology'. This vision of an exceedingly pam-
pered academic is the culmination of a process whereby
humanity discovered the scientific laws enabling us to dom-
inate the world – it is this, and not Christianity, that for
Lawrence 'is the death of the great Pan'. Although he is critical
of this process, Lawrence accepts that there is no going back:
'The old connexion, the old Allness, was severed, and can
never be ideally restored. Great Pan is dead.'[45] To restore Pan
would be to renounce our conquest of nature and return to
a primordial world where men hunted to provide meat for
the women of their tribe. In such a world, everything is alive
and full of meaning. With his sense of the interconnectedness
of all living things, and his refusal to take anything in nature
for granted, Lawrence anticipates the ecological arguments
of later environmentalists. Yet he sees little ground for hope.
Despite his mainly positive, if largely imaginary, account of
Indigenous people earlier in the essay, he sees them as particularly vulnerable to the temptations of the modern West:
'It is useless to glorify the savage. For he will kill Pan with

his bare hands, for the sake of a motor-car. And a bored savage, for whom Pan is dead, is the stupefied image of all boredom.'[46] Such racist comments vitiate the serious and potentially fruitful points Lawrence wishes to make about the threat modernity poses to the Pan within. His concluding paragraphs offer us a choice 'between the living universe of Pan, and the mechanical conquered universe of modern humanity.' If we can see past some of Lawrence's more objectionable attitudes, his relationship with a single pine tree perhaps offers the clearest model of how we too might re-enter 'the living universe of Pan'.

In *St Mawr*, Lawrence explores the possibility of inhabiting that Pan universe in the twentieth century. One of his finest works of fiction (the critic F. R. Leavis regarded it as Lawrence's masterpiece), the novella contrasts the ennui of upper-class English life with the powerful vitality of a horse named St Mawr. The horse is bought by Lady Carrington, better known as Lou, the American wife of Rico, an Australian artist resident in England. Pan is the subject of a lively conversation early in the story. Accompanied by Lou's mother, Mrs DeWitt, the Carringtons are having dinner with a local clergyman, Dean Vyner. Lou comments that the Dean's face reminds her of 'the Great God Pan', which he dismisses by suggesting that he looks more like 'the Great Goat Pan'.[47] The Dean confesses to having trouble seeing 'the Great God Pan in that goat-legged old father of satyrs'. There follows a discussion about the original nature of Pan, with the most insightful comments being made by an artist named Cartwright:

I should say he was the God hidden in everything. In those days you saw the thing, you never saw the God hidden in it: I mean the tree, the fountain, or the animal. If you ever saw the God instead of the thing, you died. If you saw it with the naked eye, that is. But in the night you might see the God. And you knew it was there.[48]

Cartwright alludes to the story related by Porphyry of the woodsmen who died after seeing Pan in his divine form. Lou reasonably asks how the ancients could have conceived of Pan if they couldn't actually see him in anything. Cartwright answers,

> Pan was the hidden mystery – the hidden cause. That's how it was a great god. Pan wasn't *he* all: not even a great God! He was Pan, All: what you see when you see in full. In the daytime you see the thing. But if your third eye is open, which sees only the things that can't be seen, you may see Pan within the thing, hidden: you may see with your third eye, which is darkness.

As 'All', Pan is what cannot be apprehended by the physical eye – the totality of everything. Only the mysterious power of our 'third eye', which Cartwright identifies with 'darkness', can perceive Pan within things. When Lou asks if Pan could be seen 'in a horse, for example', Cartwright tells her, 'Easily. In St Mawr!' Lou's mother suggests that 'it would be difficult . . . to open the third eye and see Pan in a man.' Cartwright agrees, suggesting that in a man all that is visible is 'the old satyr: the fallen Pan'. His comments develop Lawrence's contrast between an original, formless Pan and his transformation into the goat-footed god.

In private, Mrs DeWitt expresses her frustration to Lou, who agrees that Pan is not to be found in modern men, picking up another theme from Lawrence's essay. Lou can find Pan easily enough in St Mawr, where he is a frightening presence for Mrs DeWitt, but confesses, 'When I look at men with my third eye, as you call it – I think I see – mostly – a sort of – pancake.'[49] Modern men are pancakes compared with the dangerous and primordial splendour of the living Pan. Mrs DeWitt despairs of finding 'the unfallen Pan' in any man she has met in the last fifteen years, including Cartwright: 'Isn't it extraordinary, the young man Cartwright talks about Pan, but he knows nothing of it at all. He knows nothing of the unfallen Pan: only the fallen Pan with goat legs and a leer – and that sort of power, don't you know.'[50] Modern men can be lecherous seducers, but such sexual power is merely the fallen form of the deeper and more authentic power to enchant that Lawrence identifies in his earlier essay.

For the rest of *St Mawr*, Pan is evoked symbolically rather than directly. His most powerful symbol is the horse itself, which nearly kills Rico on an expedition to a Shropshire land-mark called the Devil's Chair, suggesting the Christian conflation of Pan with the Devil. Lawrence describes it as 'one of those places where the spirit of aboriginal England still lingers, the old savage England, whose last blood still flows in a few Welshmen, Englishmen, Cornishmen'.[51] None of the characters is able fully to inhabit 'the living universe of Pan', although Lewis, the Welsh groom, and Phoenix, Mrs DeWitt's half-Mexican, half-Navajo servant, come closest.[52] As in 'Pan in America', Indigenous people are more symbolic than real for Lawrence in *St Mawr*, and his portrayal of Phoenix is marred by the racialized thinking typical of early twentieth-century writers. Both Phoenix and Lewis embody Lawrence's idea of 'aboriginal' races, being darker and closer to the earth, and therefore to Pan. Lewis, for example, is described as 'walking his horse alongside in the shadow of the wood's-edge, the darkness of the old Pan, that kept our artificially lit world at bay'.[53] They have an innate understanding of the 'Pan-power' embodied by St Mawr, who ultimately finds freedom of a kind on a ranch in the American Southwest, where he is brought by Lou and Mrs DeWitt. In contrast, Rico identifies jokingly with the phallic god Priapus, whose image adorns a ring he has received while convalescing; he embodies a kind of promiscuous male sexuality detached from its primal sources of power.[54] At the end of the novella, Mrs DeWitt tries and fails to live alone on a remote ranch over-run by rats, in a landscape pregnant with Pan symbolism in the form of goats and pine trees. The name of the ranch, significantly, is 'Las Chivas', Spanish for 'the goats'. Pan endures in America, but remains elusive to modern Western consciousness.

Lawrence's story 'The Overtone' is an elegy to Pan that also meditates on the relationship between Pan and Christ. It was published posthumously, and was formerly assumed to belong to the same period as 'Pan in America' and *St Mawr*, but is now dated to 1913.[55] Whereas Lawrence's later writings on Pan focus on the possibility of the god's rebirth in modern times, 'The Overtone' is more interested in balancing pagan with Christian attitudes. The central character, Mr Renshaw, is attracted to a young woman named Elsa Laskell, whom he meets at a dinner party. Stepping outside, he sees her approaching in the darkness, and attempts to allay her fears by assuring her that Pan is dead. Her reaction is to fight back her tears: 'For when he said "Pan is dead," he meant Pan was dead in his own loose, long Dane's body. Yet she was a nymph still, and if Pan were dead, she ought to die.'[56] When Elsa asks Renshaw what he would do if the moon approached in the form of 'a naked woman', he answers that he would 'Fetch a wrap, probably.'[57] Renshaw's response alludes playfully to Pan's seduction of the moon goddess Selene, whom he woos with a gift of wool. The point of the ironic allusion is that

Renshaw is no Pan, at least not any more. They are soon joined by the hostess and Mrs Renshaw, and the conversation turns to the relationship between Pan and Christ. Elsa rejects Renshaw's bitter comment that 'Christ was woman, Pan was man,' offering instead her own more nuanced reflections on the meaning of the two gods.[58] She combines pagan and Christian views, allocating to Christ the daytime world of ethical exchange and to Pan the night-time realm of love and sex. She explains that 'love is no deal, no merchant's bargaining, and Christ neither spoke of it nor forbade it.'[59] The cross, for her, symbolizes the promise of men not to cheat women in their business dealings, but when she is a 'nymph', Elsa belongs to the wildwood. Her reflections become an incantatory chant, affirming her dual identity as woman and nymph, and her dual loyalty to Christ and Pan: 'Both moving over me, so when I am in sunshine I go in my robes among my neighbours, I am Christian. But when I run robeless through the dark-scented woods alone, I am Pan's nymph.'[60] Elsa's Pan is the god of nature, darkness and the life of the senses, anticipating Lawrence's view of the god in 'Pan in America'. She is relieved when her older, embittered companions return to the house.

Lawrence wrote 'The Last Laugh' in 1924, so it belongs to the same time as 'Pan in America' and St Mawr, but it has a very different feeling, that of an old-fashioned horror story where Pan is the cause of sudden terror. Set in Hampstead, 'The Last Laugh' explores how the return of Pan would be experienced by modern Londoners. As in his other Pan writings, Lawrence presents him as a god of sensory experience, but in this story, that experience is often unshared and a source of confusion. The story opens on a winter night, as Miss James and Mr Marchbanks depart from their friend Lorenzo. Marchbanks has a face with 'beautiful lines, like a faun, and a doubtful martyred expression. A sort of faun on the Cross, with all the malice of that complication.'[61] For her part, Miss James possesses 'an odd, nymph-like inquisitiveness'. As they walk along, Marchbanks suddenly asks her if she can hear someone laughing. Miss James has impaired hearing, and sets up her elaborate hearing aid, but the only laughter she can hear is from Marchbanks himself. They are soon joined by a police constable who, like Miss James, hears only Marchbanks's laughter. Soon, however, Miss James herself perceives something no one else can, glimpsing a figure concealed amid holly trees and elms. To the astonishment of Miss James and the constable, Marchbanks leaves them to enter the house of an unknown woman who has emerged from her door. An enormous gust of wind begins to blow, and the two remaining companions hear mysterious laughter from within a church accompanied by 'gay, trilling music', the sound of the wind 'running over the organ pipes like pan-pipes, quickly up and down'.[62] Miss James and the constable feel the stirrings of sexual attraction, but she will only allow him to rest on her sofa. In the morning, Marchbanks arrives and they make a shocking discovery about the constable, one with dire consequences.

Despite the apparent failure of Pan to regenerate the modern world, Lawrence still hopes for a kind of pagan revival among ordinary people, if we can identify his perspective with that of the gamekeeper Mellors in *Lady Chatterley's Lover* (1928). Mellors writes to Connie that 'the mass of people' should be content in their devotion to Pan: 'They should be alive and frisky, and acknowledge the great god Pan. He's the only god for the masses, forever. The few can go in for higher cults if they like. But let the mass be forever pagan.'[63] Lawrence's ideal is that 'the mass' of people reconnect with the instinctual sources of desire and joy.

Aldous Huxley (1894–1963), Lawrence's friend and fellow modernist, takes a lighter view of Pan in his short story 'Cynthia', published in his collection *Limbo* in 1920, offering a modern take on the myth of Pan and Selene. Huxley's narrator recounts the story as an anecdote from his pre-war days at Oxford. The story focuses on a friend of the narrator named Lykeham, who has returned from London with the extraordinary story that he has spent the night with a goddess. Lykeham encountered her at the theatre, describing her appearance as 'quite incredibly beautiful – rather pale and virginal and slim, and at the same time very stately'.[64] These lunar qualities prompt him to recognize her as a goddess at once and, to his astonishment, she in turn acknowledges him as a god. The narrator is dismissive, and mocks Lykeham's suggestion that he might be Apollo. He describes Lykeham's appearance as 'repulsive at first sight, but [he] had, when you looked again, a certain strange and fascinating ugly beauty'. A fortnight later the two students go for a late-night walk, when Lykeham suddenly sees the moon over the crest of a hill and begins to run towards it, crying 'It's she!' As they approach Witham Wood a beautiful, pale woman emerges, and the narrator returns to his rooms to leave the couple in privacy. As he looks up which gods had been the moon's lovers, he suddenly realizes which god his ugly friend most closely resembles, teasing Lykeham as 'GOAT-FOOT' when he returns from his assignation in the woods.

The return of Pan and its consequences are explored in two novels of the 1920s, *The Oldest God* by Stephen McKenna (1888–1967) and *The Blessing of Pan* by Lord Dunsany (1878–1957). Despite their shared themes, they are radically different in tone. McKenna's novel is earnest and moralizing, while Lord Dunsany's is light-hearted and satirical. Although McKenna is largely forgotten today, he was a prolific writer who published 47 novels and 6 non-fiction works in his lifetime. *The Oldest God* (1926) asks what would happen to polite society if modern people followed their desires uninhibitedly, succumbing to the influence of Pan. McKenna recounts the strange events that take place during a Christmas gathering at Nateby Castle in Northumbria, former seat of the Dennisons but now the home of a wealthy American named Mrs Reid. The unnamed narrator, an old family friend of the Dennisons, travels to Nateby with his wife, Enid. On the train, they are reunited with several friends from before the war, all scarred in different ways by the conflict. They are joined at the castle by Professor Shapland and his wife, who side with them during a fateful conversation. After viewing a religious painting in the gallery, the elderly professor wonders aloud why the Devil has a cloven hoof, which leads to a more specific question: why did Christians assign to the Devil the traditional image of Pan? He suggests that after the early Christian missionaries had dealt with the Egyptian and Olympian gods, 'they had to wrestle with something older and stronger still, the spirit of wild nature, which simple folk had personified as Pan. He was the oldest god.'[65] Because of the difficulty the missionaries had weaning the populace away from Pan, they identified him with Satan – such, anyway, is the professor's theory. The topic of conversation shifts to whether or not it would be better to abandon modern social conventions and live according to nature, and the majority of guests choose nature. At this very moment, the rotund figure of Punch Escott arrives, drunk as usual, and accompanied by a mysterious guest, Mr Stranger.

Hovering over the novel is the question of whether Stranger is really 'the oldest god', Pan. Through the narrator's account, McKenna makes a circumstantial case that remains ambiguous at least until the end of the novel. Most of the guests – those who voted for nature – begin to succumb to their natural inclinations, whether it be engaging in extra-marital affairs, fighting or simply falling asleep in a chair after dinner. The narrator and Professor Shapland strongly suspect that Stranger's presence is to blame, despite his refined manners and appearance. Enid faints after glimpsing Stranger's unusual foot. As readers, we never directly see a cloven hoof, nor does Stranger admit to being Pan when confronted by the narrator. Although he increasingly inspires fear in the narrator and the professor, Stranger remains unfailingly gracious and rather shy. He is even glimpsed in the chapel on Christmas morning.

After he departs, the narrator finds a note, in which Stranger defends himself:

> You are so unlikely to have had the experience that I must ask you to consider what your own attitude and conduct in a party of strangers would be if one section declared that you were the reincarnation of the nature-spirit, while another proclaimed that your hat concealed the horns, your boot the cloven hoof, of the traditional devil.[66]

While suggesting that neither Christ nor Pan can offer the modern world a practical model, Stranger also accuses the party-goers of leaving the possibility of the divine out of their calculations altogether. He ultimately endorses Professor Shapland's theory: 'The rule of Pan came to an end on the day when a fanatic preached that kindly, joyous, savage Pan was in truth the embodiment of original sin!'[67] McKenna's novel here offers an original explanation for the end of Pan's reign, while rejecting the idea that the god died. His rule ends not with the birth or death of Christ, but with the later linking of Pan and the Devil by Christian zealots. This falsification, Stranger suggests, has left modern men and women peculiarly unable to come to terms with their instinctual life, able neither to follow it joyfully nor to repress it successfully in service of spiritual ideals.

Instinctual life and a return to paganism gradually overtake a small village in Lord Dunsany's novel *The Blessing of Pan* (1928). The fantasy writer Edward Plunkett was also an Irish aristocrat – the 18th Baron of Dunsany, near Tara. As Lord Dunsany, he published numerous works of fantasy, including *The King of Elfland's Daughter* (1924) and tales set in his fictional kingdom of Pegana. The god Pan first appears in Dunsany's writing in three of his *Fifty-one Tales* (1915), where he is initially perceived as dead but subsequently undergoes a resurrection. Most of the 'tales' read more like prose poems with just a hint of plot. 'The Death of Pan' briefly narrates how some Londoners venture out to Arcady lamenting the god's death, only to discover his body lying on the ground: 'Horned Pan was still and the dew was on his fur; he had not the look of a live animal. And then they said, "It is true that Pan is dead."'[68] That evening, however, a star appears and a group of 'Arcadian maidens' come dancing from the forests. Seeing the recumbent Pan, they burst into laughter, at which the god awakes: 'And, for as long as the travellers stood and listened, the crags and the hill-tops of Arcady rang with the sounds of pursuit.' Pan responds to laughter and joy, not the sounds of mourning. In 'The Prayer of the Flowers', a group of flowers grieve over the transformation of the countryside by modern industry, and offer up a prayer to Pan:

> Great engines rush over the beautiful fields, their ways lie hard and terrible up and down the land.
>
> The cancrous cities spread over the grass, they clatter in their lairs continually, they glitter about us blemishing the night.

The woods are gone, O Pan, the woods, the woods.
And thou art far, O Pan, and far away.[69]

Dunsany's language reveals an attitude to modern industrial England consistent with that of Kenneth Grahame and Oscar Wilde; the railway tracks are 'hard and terrible' while the cities are 'cancrous'. As the narrator stands waiting on a station platform, he hears Pan's musical voice respond, telling the flowers, '"Be patient a little, these things are not for long."' The English countryside endures; modern civilization will not. Another story, 'The Tomb of Pan', tells of the building of 'a white and mighty tomb of marble' for Pan, and the disputes that ensue over whether the god should be honoured in this way.[70] The last word, however, goes to Pan himself: 'But at evening as he stole out of the forest, and slipped like a shadow softly along the hills, Pan saw the tomb and laughed.' One year after the Great War began, Lord Dunsany reaffirms what Pan's nineteenth-century followers claimed: that rumours of Pan's death were greatly exaggerated.

Both Pan and literary interest in him survived the Great War, but he was no longer the god of English pastoral retreat. In *The Blessing of Pan* Dunsany imagines the god's return, but takes a more sceptical (though humorous) view of what that would mean than in his earlier tales. The novel also introduces a theme that would haunt British popular culture later in the twentieth century: the disturbing revival of a pagan cult in the modern countryside. Pan himself does not appear in the novel, at least not directly. The main character is the Reverend Elderick Anwrel, who takes over as parson in the small English village of Wolding, only to discover that there are strange goings-on. His first clue is the sound of hauntingly beautiful music on the outskirts of the village. Writing to the Bishop, Anwrel insists 'that tune is no common melody, but is something I never have known to come out of music, and has some power I never dreamed possible, and I need your help in this trouble as I never needed it yet.'[71] When he hears it next, the music 'thrilled the clergyman's heart with awful longings, which he could no more tell of in words than he could have put words to that tune'.[72] Dunsany's language here echoes that of 'The Piper at the Gates of Dawn' in *The Wind in the Willows*; like the Water Rat, Anwrel struggles with the emotions evoked by this otherworldly music. The villagers are powerless to resist its summons.

Anwrel traces the outbreak of pagan feeling to one of his predecessors, the Reverend Arthur Davidson. Seeking information about him, Anwrel consults an elderly parishioner, Mrs Tichener. She describes seeing him dance one night in the rectory garden, and noticing some anatomical peculiarities, notably an extra joint above his habitual spats:

> 'And his knees, Mrs Tichener?' he said.
> 'I couldn't be sure, sir. They didn't look right as he danced, and he always walked very stiff, but I couldn't be sure. But the joints at each end of his spats, I saw them clear, sir. He was dancing high in the moonlight. Very short boots he always used to wear: neat and small.'[73]

When Anwrel speaks to the parents of Tommy Duffin, whose playing on a mysterious set of pipes summons the village to dance, they tell him that when they were married by Reverend Davidson, he spoke a blessing over them in an unknown tongue that touched Mrs Duffin's heart deeply. Much of the humour in the novel derives from Anwrel's total inability to convince anyone else that something is amiss in the village; neither the Bishop nor Mr Duffin will listen.

When he visits Snichester to see the Bishop, Anwrel gazes up at the cathedral and sees something unexpected among the carvings of angels: 'the conqueror of Wolding, goat-hooved Pan'.[74] He encounters a wanderer named Perkins, who claims to have seen through the illusions of the world and counsels the vicar to abandon his struggle against Pan, who, he says, 'was always friendly to Man'.[75] In Wolding, Pan's grip over the people continues to increase. By the time Anwrel returns, Mrs Tichener is teaching her Sunday school pupils a chant in Greek: 'I Pan, of all the Arcadian valleys, King.'[76] Although he is fearful of being sacrificed in honour of the god, by the end of the novel Anwrel discovers that the villagers need his priestly services to perform the rites that are due to Pan. After the triumph of paganism, Wolding becomes a notably shabby village whose inhabitants seem content to let things return to nature. Like McKenna's *The Oldest God*, Dunsany's *The Blessing of Pan* questions whether abandoning the values of modern life would lead to something better. Although his younger self was whole-heartedly committed to the pastoral cult of Pan, a decade later Lord Dunsany satirizes its naively romantic attitude to nature. This satirical approach aligns *The Blessing of Pan* more closely with James Stephens's *The Crock of Gold*, suggesting a distinctly Irish revision of modern English pastoral.

The English writer Sylvia Townsend Warner (1893–1978) offers a revision of her own in her novel of 1929, *The True Heart*, a modern retelling of Apuleius' tale of Cupid and Psyche set in nineteenth-century Essex. Warner was the niece of Arthur Machen, and her writings formed the basis of several works by the Pan-inspired composer John Ireland. Her first novel, *Lolly Willowes; or, The Loving Huntsman* (1926), tells the story of a spinster who decides to become a witch. It features a Devil who, like Pan, leads forest revels, and who later disguises himself as a gardener. Although a 'huntsman' of souls, Warner's Devil has affinities with Arcadian Pan, who was also the god of hunters. The protagonist of *The True Heart* is Sukey, who despairs of being reunited with a beautiful (though dim-witted) young man named Eric. In Apuleius' version, Pan rescues the despondent Psyche after she throws herself in the river. Warner revises this, with Sukey wandering sad and lost in the countryside before encountering a mysterious tramp. He is concerned about her and offers to walk her to the village of Southend. As they make their way down the wet road, surrounded by hedges and forest, Sukey realizes that her companion is playing on a mouth organ:

> The soft rambling sound was like no music she had heard before; it had none of the vigour of a hymn. Continuous and indefinite, it was noise to hear rather than listen to. It lulled her, it persuaded her along as though it were gently gathering her up like silk on a reel. She was conscious no longer of the heavy walking rhythm at her side. The man had now become a music.[77]

Warner subtly evokes the magical powers of Pan's music, identifying it completely with the one who plays it. The two characters rest in a shed, and when the man strikes a match to light his pipe, Sukey sees 'his red, wet, and hairy hand' in the glow.[78] He reveals that he has worked as a sailor and cattleman, but now wanders from farm to farm as a casual labourer. Sukey falls asleep, and when she awakens she finds the man gone, but he has left her the gift of a painted box inscribed with the message 'Friendship endears.'[79] Warner's warm and affectionate revision of Pan's character is entirely consistent with his helpful role in Apuleius' story. In spite of the many clues she provides about her characters (such as Pan's music and hairiness), Warner notes in her preface to the Virago reprint in 1978 that when the novel first appeared, only her mother recognized that she was retelling the story of Cupid and Psyche.[80]

In an entirely different revisiting of the literary past, the American fiction writer William Faulkner (1897–1962) offers a satirical revision of the early twentieth-century Pan horror story in 'Black Music', published in 1933. Its narrator is visiting Rincón, a town in Puerto Rico, and becomes curious about a peculiar old man named Wilfred Midgleston, who arrived from the continental United Stated decades earlier and lives alone in poverty. Rumour has it that he committed robbery and had to flee the country, but when the narrator meets him, he has a much stranger tale to tell. Midgleston reveals that he once spent a day as a 'farn'.[81] In his version of ancient history, he explains that wealthy Greeks and Romans would retreat to the country to engage in their wild parties, angering the gods. When Midgleston can't remember the name of the woodland god, the narrator suggests 'Pan':

> 'That's it. Pan. And he would send them little fellows
> that was half a goat to scare them out –'
>   'Oh,' I said. 'A faun.'
>   'That's it. A farn. That's what I was once.'

Midgleston's tale begins in New York, where he worked as a draughtsman for an architect named Middleton. The wife of one of his clients, Mr Van Dyming, has bought a rural property where wild grapes grow, and where the former owners have met with violent accidents. After Mrs Van Dyming has moved into her new house, Midgleston is sent to bring her the portfolio for a theatre she hopes to build on the property. As he sits in the train sipping iced water, the world begins to swirl around him, and he sees a mysterious face through the window: 'It was not a man's face, because it had horns, and it was not a goat's face because it had a beard and it was looking at me with eyes like a man and its mouth was open like it was saying something to me when it exploded inside my head.'[82] The nature of what really happens is left ambiguous; when a doctor on the train attempts to revive him, Midgleston, a temperance man, realizes he is drinking whisky. When they arrive at the railway station, Midgleston purchases a tin whistle and continues drinking in the wagon that takes him to the Van Dyming estate.

At this point in telling his tale, Midgleston pulls out a newspaper cutting that serves to explain what happened next. The newspaper quotes Mrs Van Dyming's account of seeing a naked man in her garden who wields a blade that shines in the moonlight, and who makes a strange whistling sound as she flees. She is pursued by a local bull, which she escapes by pressing her body against a tree as the bull circles her. So ends Midgleston's brief career as a faun. He reveals to the narrator that he fled the United States in embarrassment, leaving his wife to collect on a large insurance policy, and she has subsequently remarried. Faulkner concludes his story with a sense of ambivalence over Midgleston's true identity, as well as over the precise nature of what happened. Did a man who had never drunk alcohol before simply lose control, or was he visited by the woodland god who always protects his mysterious vineyard hidden deep in the Virginia mountains?

Modern poetry

In 1912 the modernist poet and impresario Ezra Pound published his poem 'Pan Is Dead' in *Ripostes*.[83] Being dead, Pan
himself does not appear in the poem, but the work shows
that his death has had devastating consequences for the natural word. Despite Pound's proclaiming the new modernist
style of 'Imagism' in the same volume, 'Pan Is Dead' is very
much a poem under the influence of nineteenth-century language. Partly an elegy for Pan, it opens with an announcement
of his death: 'Pan is dead. Great Pan is dead. / Ah! bow your
heads, ye maidens all, / And weave ye him his coronal.' The
maidens respond to this plea by pointing out that nature itself
has died, and so nothing remains with which to weave Pan
his coronal. To this objection, the speaker has nothing to say,
only asking, 'How should he show a reason, / That he has
taken our Lord away / Upon such hollow season?' 'He' is
Death, within the poem a more powerful force than nature
itself, symbolized by the dead god Pan.

Pound's fellow American, the poet Robert Frost (1874–
1963), included the poem 'Pan with Us' in his first collection,
A Boy's Will (1913).[84] In the table of contents, the poem is
described as 'about art (his own)'. In it, Frost imagines Pan
transplanted to the New World, pleased by the wilderness
he finds there while realizing that his music and ordinary
pursuits are out of place. The opening stanza conveys a sense
of the god's great age by emphasizing the greyness of his
appearance: 'Pan came out of the woods one day, – / His skin
and his hair and his eyes were gray, / The gray of the moss
of walls were they.' The god is pleased as he stands 'pipes in
hand', surveying a landscape without sign of human habitation – so pleased that he gleefully 'stamped a hoof'. The
absence of people, apart from a handful of occasional rural

visitors, brings calm to his heart. Nonetheless, the New World landscape is also a location where his traditional piping has no place:

> He tossed his pipes, too hard to teach
> A new-world song, far out of reach,
> For a sylvan sign that the blue jay's screech
>   And the whimper of hawks beside the sun
>   Were music enough for him, for one.

A musical instrument belonging to the Old World, like Pan's pipes, is difficult to make play 'A new-world song'; here, in North America, 'the blue jay's screech' and 'the whimper of hawks' are 'music enough', at least for Pan. In any case, Pan's pipes are powerless to move New World flora, such as the juniper. He is not just in the wrong place spatially; the 'pagan mirth' of Pan's music has given way to 'new terms of worth' that leave him uncertain what to do: 'Play? Play? What should he play?' If we consider Frost as a poet steeped in the tradition of English poetry, 'Pan with Us' can be read as an expression of his own early dilemma over how to give expression to North American experience using language and forms brought over from Europe.

Patricia Merivale argues that the Great War put an end to what she terms the 'public myth' of Pan, although the god would endure for some as a private symbol.[85] When he does appear, he is glimpsed only briefly, and the two most famous Pan poems from the 1920s and '30s are both by non-English writers. In the poem '[in Just-]', composed by the American E. E. Cummings (1894–1962) in 1920, we meet 'the // goat-footed // balloonMan' as a herald of spring, but this Pan 'whistles' rather than pipes.[86] The Irish poet W. B. Yeats (1865–1939) presents a fragmented vision of the god (or the god's followers) in the final section of his late poem 'News for the Delphic Oracle'.[87] The first section presents two lovers from Irish mythology, Oisin and Niamh, alongside two mystical Greek philosophers, Pythagoras and Plotinus, lying down and sighing beside the ocean; in the second part, each rides on 'a dolphin's back', re-experiencing their deaths until they arrive 'in some cliff-sheltered bay / Where wades the choir of love'. The kind of love celebrated by the choir turns out to be something much more earthy than the romantic love of Oisin and Niamh, or the philosophical love espoused by Pythagoras and Plotinus:

> From where Pan's cavern is
> Intolerable music falls.
> Foul goat-head, brutal arm appear,
> Belly, shoulder, bum,
> Flash fishlike; nymphs and satyrs
> Copulate in the foam.

If the god himself doesn't appear directly, the orgiastic experience of the satyrs and nymphs is clearly inspired by Pan's music. There is some ambiguity in Yeats's catalogue of body parts, which could describe the satyrs and nymphs, but could equally apply to the god Pan himself. The sexual power of the god manifests itself in the copulating nymphs and satyrs, who teach a lesson about love very different from that of Celtic romance or Greek philosophy.

PAN IN EARLY TWENTIETH-CENTURY MUSIC

The music of Pan that so enchanted Yeats's nymphs and satyrs was also a potent source of inspiration for several composers in the early decades of the twentieth century. On the continent, Jules Mouquet (1867–1946) wrote 'La Flûte de Pan', a sonata for flute and piano that evokes different aspects of Pan's character across its three movements, and which was prefaced by a short poem.[88] The first movement, 'Pan et les shepherds' (Pan and the Shepherds), creates a suitably mellow, pastoral mood, while the second, 'Pan et les oiseaux' (Pan and the Birds), is melancholy, suggesting a lonely god who echoes the trilling sound of birdsong on his pipes. The final movement, 'Pan et les nymphes', is lively and playful; listening, you can imagine Pan and his nymphs stepping lightly through the woods. The Finnish composer Jean Sibelius (1865–1957) composed a short dance intermezzo called *Pan och Echo* (Pan and Echo) in 1906, music for a tableau of Pan, Echo and a troop of nymphs.[89] It opens in a calm mood, suggesting Pan and Echo cavorting on a hill, and concludes with the frenetic energy of the nymphs' dance. *Syrinx* by Claude Debussy (1862–1918) is a three-minute composition for solo flute. Originally entitled *Flûte de Pan*, it was composed as incidental music for the poetic drama *Psyché*, written by Debussy's friend Gabriel Mourey.[90] Alternately languorous and lilting, *Syrinx* is an eerie evocation of the god through an allusion to his most famous myth. The French composer Albert Roussel (1869–1937) similarly evokes Pan through flute and piano in the first of his three *Joueurs de flûte* (Flute Players; 1925), simply called 'Pan'.[91] Although only just over three minutes long, the piece combines the joy and melancholy we associate with the god's moods.

Pan is an important presence in the one-act ballet *Daphnis et Chloé* by Maurice Ravel (1875–1937), commissioned by Sergei Diaghilev and first performed by his Ballets Russes in 1912. Adapting the ancient Greek novel by Longus, Ravel invokes Pan at several key moments in the ballet, beginning at the end of Part I, where the nymphs lead Daphnis to a great rock and summon the Great God. As his shape appears, Daphnis bows down before him. The form of Pan appears again at the end of Part II, after throwing the pirates who have kidnapped Chloé into a panic that forces them to release her. The third part opens with the most famous music from the ballet, 'Lever du jour' (Sunrise), which unites Daphnis and Chloé. In honour of Pan, the lovers stage a pantomime of the myth of Syrinx, which includes what one conductor, Gerard Schwarz, has described as 'the greatest flute solo probably ever written', a haunting and melodic interpretation of Pan's music.[92] As the pantomime comes to a close, the flute playing becomes increasingly melancholic, suggesting Pan's feelings of frustration and loss over Syrinx.

The Polish composer Karol Szymanowski (1882–1937) concluded his work *Myths* (1915) for violin and piano with a section called 'Dryades and Pan'. In a letter to the American violinist Robert Imandt, he describes how the music is meant to create a narrative of 'the murmuring of the forest on a hot summer's night, thousands of mysterious voices, all over-lapping in the darkness – the fun and dancing of the Dryads. Suddenly the sound of Pan's pipe'.[93] An anxious quiet follows, then the god himself appears. After inspiring both amorous desire and fear in the dryads, 'Pan skips away – the dance begins anew – then everything calms down in the freshness and silence of the breaking dawn.' Among Szymanowski's most popular and influential compositions, *Myths* introduced a new style of playing the violin, and would directly inspire later composers such as Béla Bartók and Sergei Prokofiev.[94] 'Dryades and Pan' encompasses a wide range of moods associated with the god, from an eerie sense of his hidden presence, to fear and confusion, to the ecstasy of frenetic dancing. At once daringly modern and deeply suggestive of the mysteries of the ancient world,

Szymanowski's invocation of Pan in *Myths* expresses the emotions the god inspires.

The Norwegian composer Carl Nielsen (1865–1931) wrote his *Pan og Syrinx* for a retrospective performance of his work in 1918. This symphonic poem is a musical retelling of the classical myth, with woodwinds suggesting the innocent play of Syrinx and rather sinister strings heralding the arrival of Pan. Much of the composition suggests Pan's pursuit of Syrinx, and Nielsen creates dramatic tension in the chase. As the piece comes to an end, we experience Pan's sorrowful disappointment at Syrinx's transformation. The work concludes with Pan's lonely piping, followed by a tense and melancholy cello line that echoes his arrival.

As these examples show, the musical fascination with Pan was a Europe-wide phenomenon, but as we might expect, given his many literary appearances, the god was particularly alluring to English composers. Edward Elgar (1857–1934) made his first foray into Pan music with a setting in 1899 of a poem by 'Adrian Ross' (Arthur Reed Ropes), 'The Pipes of Pan', essentially a catalogue of the god's major qualities and associations.[95] In 1902 Elgar composed *Five Partsongs from the Greek Anthology*, including 'After Many a Dusty Road', a translation by Edmund Gosse that he subsequently published under the title 'To a Traveller'. The poem is Pan's advice to a traveller, urging him to 'linger here a while' and relax in the shade before continuing his journey.[96] Although Elgar's scoring of these two songs doesn't evoke Pan directly, both suggest a gentle, pastoral mood. His single-act ballet of 1917, *The Sanguine Fan*, took its inspiration from an actual fan, on which the Victorian artist Charles Conder had drawn the myth of Pan and Echo. Elgar wrote the piece to support charities in wartime. Set in eighteenth-century France, the ballet tells the story of a couple whose courtship is tragically interrupted by Pan and Echo.[97] Pan appears on stage, his presence suggested musically by the clarinet, while the flute is reserved for Echo. The Elgar scholar Matthew Riley suggests that Elgar's First Symphony uses flutes to evoke the sound of wind blowing through reeds, creating a similar experience to that of the animals in Kenneth Grahame's 'The Piper at the Gates of Dawn'.[98] In 1921 Elgar linked his vocation as composer to a childhood spent listening to the sound of reeds by the river, writing to the critic Sidney Colvin, 'I am still at heart the dreamy child who used to be found in the reeds by Severn side with a sheet of paper trying to fix the sounds and longing for something very great – source, texture and all else unknown.'[99] His experience of yearning 'for something very great' deep in the natural world is shared by all artists who have found inspiration in Pan.

Elgar's turn to Pan was echoed in the work of numerous other English composers, and in popular music. In 1904 Gustav Holst (1874–1934) and Ralph Vaughan Williams (1872–1958) collaborated on settings of the folk songs and dances from Ben Jonson's masque *Pan's Anniversary*.[100] Holst set the dances to traditional Elizabethan folk tunes, while Vaughan Williams composed the hymns and fanfares. The entire masque was performed in Stratford-upon-Avon in April 1905 for a celebration of Shakespeare's birthday.[101] The music makes for pleasant listening and has a courtly, Renaissance feeling, but is not especially suggestive of Pan. The Edwardian musical comedy *The Arcadians*, with a book by Mark Ambient and Alexander M. Thompson, made its debut in 1907 and ran for more than eight hundred shows, eventually making its way from London's West End to Broadway. Set in modern London, the story concerns the arrival of a group of Arcadians, who wish to return the city to simpler ways. The score, by Arthur Wimperis, Lionel Monckton and Howard

Talbot, included a hit song, 'The Merry, Merry Pipes of Pan', celebrating the pristine glory of Arcadian life.[102]

Among more serious composers, Arnold Bax (1883–1953) and Arthur Bliss (1891–1975) both wrote music directly or indirectly inspired by the god. Bax, regarded in the early twentieth century as Britain's most accomplished symphonist, is perhaps best remembered today for his symphonic poem *Tintagel* (1917–19). His orchestral work *Enchanted Summer* (1912) included a quotation from Shelley's 'Hymn of Pan'.[103] This was followed by three compositions evoking the woodland world of Pan and his followers. *Nympholept*, a tone poem, was published with a quotation from George Meredith's poem 'The Woods of Westermain', but also gestures to Swinburne's poem 'A Nympholept' (see Chapter Three) in suggesting the experience of possession by the nymphs.[104] The fourth movement of *Spring Fires*, based on Swinburne's 'Atalanta in Calydon', is called 'Maenads'. In his programme note, Bax alludes directly to Pan: 'The dryads, maenads and bassarids fly dancing and screaming through the woods, pursued relentlessly by Bacchus and Pan and their hordes of goat-footed and ivy-crowned revellers.'[105] *Happy Forest* of 1914 (which Bax rewrote for orchestra in 1922) takes its title from a prose poem by Herbert Farjeon, evoking a more pastoral and idyllic world of shepherds and satyrs.[106]

Arthur Bliss invokes Pan throughout *Pastoral: 'Lie Strewn the White Flocks'* (1928), which includes settings of John Fletcher's 'Hymn to Pan' and Poliziano's 'Pan and Echo' alongside poems by Robert Nichols and Theocritus. Bliss also composed a musical interlude for the work, 'Pan's Sarabande.' Among other English composers, Alec Rowley (1892–1958) wrote a piano suite called 'Festival of Pan' in 1919, while 'Pan's Holiday' by Frank Bridge (1879–1941) appeared in 1922.[107] Even Benjamin Britten (1913–1976) contributed to the

English tradition of Pan music, opening his 1951 composition *Six Metamorphoses after Ovid* with 'Pan.'[108]

While many English composers occasionally wrote pieces connected with the god, John Ireland (1879–1962) was fascinated throughout his life by Pan and the musical possibilities suggested by pagan worship, despite also being a devout Anglican. For many years a statue of Pan stood on his piano for inspiration.[109] Unlike his musical contemporaries, however, Ireland was drawn to both the pastoral aspect of the god and his darker side, as explored in fiction by Arthur Machen, E. F. Benson and Saki. According to his biographer Fiona Richards, Pan was the inspiration behind two works Ireland composed in 1913, 'The Scarlet Ceremonies', one of three piano pieces he grouped as *Decorations*, and an orchestral work, *The Forgotten Rite*.[110] The title of the former was taken from a story by Machen, 'The White People', which tells of a young girl's induction into a witch cult. Its mysterious ending was understood by many readers as implying that the girl died after an encounter with Pan. Ireland claimed in a letter that Machen had told him something about the story known only to himself, and it is possible that he intended the story to be understood this way.[111] 'The Scarlet Ceremonies' opens frenetically, evoking a wild dance rising to a pitch of excitement, then descends into a more mellow mood before rising again towards a conclusion that variously suggests incantation and the sound of a harp. *The Forgotten Rite* was inspired by Ireland's time on the island of Jersey, where he sensed a spiritual reality behind its natural beauty. Richards notes that two pagan ritual sites were being excavated at the time of Ireland's visit.[112] She describes *The Forgotten Rite* as 'essentially an invocation of Pan', while acknowledging the composer's less specific reference to it as a 'pagan ceremony'.[113] Ireland's ceremonial music belongs to the pastoral and sensuous side of the Pan tradition, with lush strings creating an idyllic mood, and a flute suggesting pan pipes. The movements of the piece suggest different aspects of Pan's character, but they avoid his darker side, which Ireland explored later in 'Le Catioroc' from his piano suite *Sarnia: An Island Sequence* (1940–41).

In 1939 Ireland had moved to Guernsey, fascinated by its mixture of pagan and Christian sites. Le Catioroc is a headland on the island at the south end of Perelle Bay, where a megalithic site known as Le Trepied Dolmen is traditionally associated with witchcraft and pagan rites. Ireland wrote to the pianist Clifford Curzon that 'there can be no doubt that Pan was worshipped there.' For Ireland, 'the essence underlying Pan, the Satyrs, the Fauns, is a world of hidden, forbidden beauty connected with Nature.'[114] He found literary inspiration in Machen's *The Great God Pan*, and included lines from Pomponius Mela, alluded to by Machen, as a headnote to the music. Mela describes a bacchic revel at which 'the chorus of aegipans resounds on every side; the shrilling of flutes and the clash of cymbals re-echo by the waste shores of the sea.'[115] Ireland originally planned to call this movement 'Ægipans' Headlands'.[116] The movement begins and ends with a calm but slightly sinister evocation of the landscape, and at its centre is the wild dance of the aegipans in their worship of Pan. The goat-footed god would continue to figure in Ireland's imagination, if not directly in his music. As late as 1952, he wrote about Pan in terms that oppose him to the modern world in ways familiar since the nineteenth century: 'The Great God Pan has departed from this planet, driven hence by the mastery of the material & the machine over mankind.'[117] Ireland's three compositions can be understood as an attempt to invoke Pan musically in a world that has driven the god out.

The culmination of English Pan music might have been *The Great God Pan*, an ambitious choral opera by Granville Bantock (1868–1946), but only the first part was completed, and no recording has ever been made. Its premiere in Sheffield in 1915 was cancelled because of the war. The fullest account of the work is given by H. Orsmond Anderton in his book on Bantock, published in that year.[118] The musicologist Eric Saylor notes that the text of the opera was written by Bantock's wife, Helena, and 'is much more passionate and erotic than most Arcadian texts, presenting a vision of Pan that is almost Wagnerian in its Romantic grandeur: this is the sensual Dionysian deity, not the mysterious Piper at the Gates of Dawn.'[119] The first part of *The Great God Pan*, 'Pan in Arcady', begins with an invocation of the god as 'God of forests, god of liberty' and 'God of the unfettered mind' – a view of Pan consistent with the Edwardian view of Pan as god of rural escape.[120] The narrative focus is the myth of Pan and Echo, who sings from within a glowing rock.[121] Thinking he has caught a glimpse of Echo, Pan asks the nymphs and dryads if they have seen her, but they only echo his final word. After venting his frustration, Pan vows that he 'will seek the light divine' as he aspires to

> Clasp the whole world's completeness,
> And, filled with love's immortal ecstasy,
> Drain to the full the cup of love's desire.[122]

Bantock's language suggests that Pan is anticipating his own transformation from the pastoral god who is disappointed in love into the god who encompasses all things ('the whole world's completeness'). In the pastoral present of 'Pan in Arcady', however, he returns to his traditional role as he initiates two dances, 'The Revelry of Pan and the Fauns' and

'The Dance of Pan and the Satyrs'. After a final dance, 'The Wounded Faun', in which a faun succumbs to a hunter's arrow, Pan is left alone.[123] Bantock concludes this first part of his choral opera with an adaptation of the myth of Selene's seduction by Pan, a consummation celebrated by the fauns, satyrs, dryads and nymphs.[124]

The second, fragmentary part of *The Great God Pan* is even stranger. Set at the court of the Roman emperor Elagabalus, 'The Festival of Pan' opens at a banquet being given in Pan's honour, as a chorus chants 'Io Pan! Evoë, Evoë!' – an ecstatic chant associated with Dionysian rites, adapted for the goat-footed god.[125] After some seductive banter between the emperor and a Syrian maiden, a monk named Gregory appears to denounce the lasciviousness of the banquet. He cries out, 'Great Pan is Dead!', then smashes a statue of the god.[126] A curtain descends over the alcove where the statue had been, and a red light glows behind it. When the curtain opens, the figure of Youthful Pan has taken the place of the smashed image. The god condemns the life-denying faith of Gregory, urging the revellers to celebrate life itself.[127]

Bantock has come full circle, echoing the opening of 'Pan in Arcady', with its invocation of Pan as 'god of liberty'. Pan concludes his address with a declaration of his own divinity: 'I, Pan, am the embodied mystery of the world. Hearken, O men! Attune your ears to me. Lo! I am Pan!'[128] 'The Festival of Pan' ends with a hymn of praise sung by the chorus. Bantock later incorporated some of his musical sketches for this second, incomplete part into his Pagan Symphony of 1927 (first performed in 1936), and set two Pan-themed pieces in *Three Songs from the Greek Anthology*, 'Pan's Piping' and 'The Garden of Pan'.

You recall those golden afternoons of your youth, picnicking by the river with your friends and, on occasion, their lovely sisters as well. After a morning of leisurely rowing, the beer and sandwiches or tea and biscuits tasted wonderful. On one occasion, nodding off in the tall grass, you could swear you heard the haunting sound of pipes echoing through the reeds, and cannot be sure you were dreaming when you saw the figure of Pan himself sitting nearby, goat legs crossed while he played. All you know for certain is the feeling of calm and well-being that swept over you as he smiled benignly at all those gathered by the river, including the otters and other creatures splashing in the water.

Those days have vanished forever, along with so many of your friends killed in the war. You have not seen or dreamed of Pan since, but once felt his presence when walking back to the village as the shadows lengthened. That time it was different; there was no piping, melancholy or cheerful, just an intuition that he was there in the darkness. The stronger the feeling became, the more frightening it seemed, so much so that you broke into a run as the lights from the village appeared down the road. Although you have never shared this experience with another – what could you possibly say about it? – you cannot read a poem or story that mentions the god without a shiver running down your spine.

5

PAN AS OCCULT POWER

With sources deep in antiquity, the magical arts flow like an underground stream beneath Western culture. In the ancient world, Pan and other gods were publicly worshipped with sacrifices, petitioned with prayer and thanked with votive offerings. Alongside these recognizably religious practices, there developed rituals designed to bring the worshipper into direct contact with the gods, invoking their presence to achieve spiritual union, or for more practical ends. As we saw in Chapter One, the Orphic hymns appear to have been composed with a ritual context in mind, invoking the various gods to obtain blessings and power. This magical practice, known as 'theurgy' (from the Greek for 'divine working'), was closely entwined with the philosophy known as Neoplatonism, a religious development of Platonic thought. Although they differed in details, Neoplatonists (such as Plotinus, Porphyry and the Syrian Iamblichus) viewed the universe as emanating from an absolute divinity through layers of universal and personal consciousness, culminating in the physical world. The absolute deity (referred to as the One or the Good) was beyond human comprehension, but could be approached through the traces it left in slightly lower forms of consciousness, identified by Iamblichus and others with the pagan gods.[1] Neoplatonism

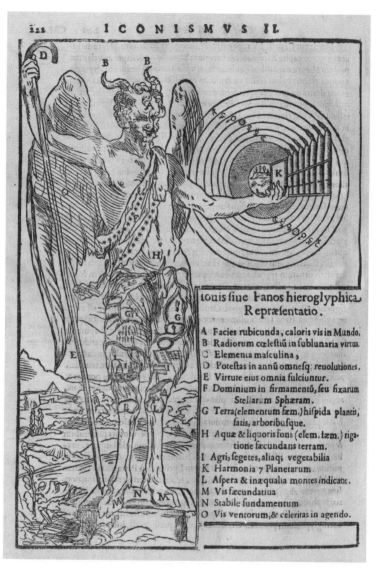

Athanasius Kircher, 'Iouis siue Panos Hieroglyphica repraesentatio,' from *Obeliscus Pamphilius* (1650). Kircher's illustration of Pan offers a visual interpretation of the correspondences between Pan and aspects of the physical universe.

would influence the development of Christian mysticism, Jewish Kabbalah and Islamic Sufism; it would surface again during the Renaissance, shaping the revival of High Magic.

A tradition of learned magic survived from the ancient world through the Middle Ages, centred on magical books known as 'grimoires'. These books, often attributed to the biblical King Solomon, provide directions for ritually summoning demons and angels to do the magician's bidding. The medieval grimoires include demonic names that appear to be those of ancient Near Eastern deities, albeit in garbled form. Ronald Hutton has recently argued that some of the spells may even be of Egyptian origin.[2] It was not until the Renaissance, however, that the pagan gods in their original forms returned to Western spiritual and magical practice, often in Neoplatonic allegories of the soul, such as those depicted in Botticelli's *Birth of Venus* and *Primavera*.[3] Pan is an occasional presence in these allegories (as we saw in Signorelli's *School of Pan*; see Chapter Two). He also appears in the work of the seventeenth-century polymath Athanasius Kircher (1602–1680). In his *Obeliscus Pamphilius* (1650), an attempt to decipher Egyptian hieroglyphics, Kircher includes his own 'hieroglyph' of Pan, uniquely depicted with wings.[4] As with earlier Renaissance allegories and emblems, this hieroglyph presents correspondences between parts of Pan's body and aspects of the universe. For example, the ruddiness of Pan's face symbolizes cosmic heat, and his pipes correspond to the harmony of the planets. Although not designed for specifically magical ends, Kircher's hieroglyph demonstrates a typically magical perspective on the world, seeing symbolic correspondences that can be invoked to obtain knowledge of the occult (literally 'hidden') powers governing the cosmos. The hieroglyph anticipates the Pan-inspired image of Baphomet designed in the nineteenth century by Éliphas Lévi.

The scientific revolution and rationalism of the eighteenth-century Enlightenment led to a decline in magic as an explanatory model of the world, but with the rise of Romanticism and its interest in the supernatural, magic underwent a gradual revival in the nineteenth century. In England, serious students of magic formed the Hermetic Order of the Golden Dawn, a hierarchical organization devoted to ritual magic. Several members of the Order, including Arthur Machen, Aleister Crowley and Dion Fortune, had a particular interest in the powers embodied by the god Pan. While Machen clearly feared those powers, Crowley and Fortune made the god central to their magical practice. The rise of modern witchcraft, with its reverence for the Horned God, brought Pan within its orbit, from the early scholarship of Margaret Murray to the art and magic of the Australian witch Rosaleen Norton.

THE OCCULT REVIVAL

Central to the nineteenth-century occult revival was the work of the French ceremonial magician Éliphas Lévi (1810–1875), who created what is perhaps the most famous emblem of occult knowledge ever produced. In his *Dogme et rituel de la haute magie* (Dogma and Ritual of High Magic), Lévi included an illustration and written account of the figure he described variously as 'The Sabbatic Goat', 'The Baphomet of Mendes' and 'Pantheos'.[5] The last name means 'god of all', which is to say Pan in his cosmic aspect. 'The Sabbatic Goat' refers to the beast (really the Devil in disguise) that witches were believed to venerate at their assemblies (or 'sabbats'); Francisco de Goya's painting *Witches' Sabbath* (1798) depicts this scene.[6] 'Baphomet' was the name of the idol that the Inquisition accused the Knights Templar of worshipping;

Éliphas Lévi, illustration of the figure he referred to as
'the Baphomet of Mendes', 'the Sabbatic Goat' or 'Pantheos', from *Dogme
et rituel de la haute magie* (1854–6). Lévi's image, though symbolically
complex, would help link Pan with Satan in the popular imagination.

several admitted – under torture – to doing so. (Scholars now
believe that 'Baphomet' is simply an Old French corruption
of the name Mohammed, but this was not clear in the nineteenth century.[7]) With the phrase 'The Baphomet of Mendes',
Lévi conflates the alleged Templar idol with 'The Goat of
Mendes', a ram-headed Egyptian god described by Herodotus.
In Lévi's view, they are all forms of the same being, understood
by his worshippers as Pan:

Yes, in our profound conviction, the Grand Masters
of the Order of Templars worshipped the Baphomet,
and caused it to be worshipped by their initiates; yes,
there existed in the past, and there may be still in the
present, assemblies which are presided over by this
figure, seated on a throne and having a flaming torch
between the horns. But the adorers of this sign do not
consider, as do we, that it is a representation of the
devil; on the contrary, for them it is that of the god
Pan, the god of our modern schools of philosophy,
the god of the Alexandrian theurgic school and of our
own mystical Neoplatonists, the god of Lamartine
and Victor Cousin, the god of Spinoza and Plato, the
god of the primitive Gnostic schools; the Christ also
of the dissident priesthood.[8]

Although we may, as Lévi acknowledges, regard the form of
this entity as diabolical, for believers 'it is that of the god Pan'
– and several other gods besides, including a version of Christ.
Whereas for Rabelais Pan was the Christ accepted by orthodox believers, Lévi's Pan-Christ is heterodox, the god of 'the
dissident priesthood'. Lévi imagines a continuous tradition
of Pan worship from Plato and the ancient theurgists to
contemporary French thinkers.

Given that Lévi explicitly identifies this figure of
Baphomet with Pan, it is worth looking at his explanation of
its symbolism in some detail:

A pantheistic and magical figure of the Absolute. The
torch placed between the two horns represents the
equilibrating intelligence of the triad. The goat's head,
which is synthetic, and unites some characteristics of
the dog, bull, and ass, represents the exclusive

responsibility of matter and the expiation of bodily sins in the body. The hands are human, to exhibit the sanctity of labour; they make the sign of esotericism above and below, to impress mystery on initiates, and they point at two lunar crescents, the upper being white and the lower black, to explain the correspondences of good and evil, mercy and justice. The lower part of the body is veiled, portraying the mysteries of universal generation, which is expressed solely by the symbol of the caduceus. The belly of the goat is scaled, and should be coloured green; the semi-circle above should be blue; the plumage, reaching to the breast, should be of various hues. The goat has female breasts, and thus its only human characteristics are those of maternity and toil, otherwise the signs of redemption. On its forehead, between the horns and beneath the torch, is the sign of the microcosm, or the pentagram with one beam in the ascendant, symbol of human intelligence, which, placed thus below the torch, makes the flame of the latter an image of divine revelation. This Pantheos should be seated on a cube, and its footstool should be a single ball, or a ball and a triangular stool.[9]

Taken altogether, Lévi's image balances the Absolute and the human, the human and the animal, mind and body, male and female – all under the sign of 'divine revelation'. It is a cosmic image with a symbolic complexity to rival that of any Renaissance emblem or Baroque hieroglyph. Despite the rich complexity of Lévi's image of Pantheos, many viewers over the last century or so have seen in it a representation of the Devil. Such associations persist to our own time. In 2018, for example, the Satanic Temple attempted to install a sculpture of 'Baphomet', flanked by two children, beside the Ten

Commandments outside a courthouse in Little Rock, Arkansas. The attempt was met with outrage by American Christians and was ultimately unsuccessful, although newspapers such as the *Washington Post* accurately reported on its symbolic meaning.[10]

Why is Pan's image so persistently identified with the Devil in modern culture? One common answer is that given by Professor Shapland in Stephen McKenna's *The Oldest God* (see Chapter Four): early Christians, horrified by Pan's associations with nature and sex, identified him with Satan in an attempt to persuade his followers to reject the flesh and seek a more spiritual path. D. H. Lawrence says much the same thing in 'Pan in America'. This explanation seems to make sense, until we look at medieval and early modern representations of the Devil. He is typically portrayed as a kind of monstrous assemblage of animal parts, with horns, reptilian scales and bat wings being particularly common. He is occasionally depicted with the legs of a goat, but reptilian claws are much more common than cloven hooves. In the eighteenth century, when he does appear with beard, horns and goat legs, the Devil typically has bat wings or a long, pointed tail.

Ronald Hutton suggests that the identification of Pan with the Devil may date only to the nineteenth century.[11] My own view is not only that Hutton is correct, but also that the identification can be traced directly to Lévi's image and another it inspired, the goat pentagram included in Stanislas de Guaita's tome *La Clef de la Magie Noire* (The Key to Black Magic; 1897).[12] Reproduced countless times in occult-themed books, horror films and television programmes, these two images have accumulated all kinds of demonic association for modern audiences. As just one example, the Hammer horror film *The Devil Rides Out* (1968; released in the United States as *The Devil's Bride*), directed by Terence Fisher and based on a novel by

Dennis Wheatley, opens with an image of the goat pentagram that morphs into Lévi's Baphomet. During the film, we repeatedly see the goat pentagram painted on the wall where the Satanists hold their indoor rites; when the goat-headed Devil appears in person at an outdoor ceremony, he is identified by the Duke de Richleau (played by Christopher Lee) as 'the Goat of Mendes'.[13] These images in turn respond to a long tradition of European iconography connecting goats with witchcraft. Goya's *Witches' Sabbath* is perhaps the most famous example, but as early as 1500, Albrecht Dürer (1471–1528) depicted a witch riding backwards on a goat.[14] In Christian tradition, the goat symbolized the sin of lust, but the pagan world also viewed the goat as a symbol of excessive sexual desire, sacred to Aphrodite as well as to Dionysus and Pan. Two of Goya's witchcraft paintings, *Witches' Sabbath* (1798) and *Witches' Sabbath* (or *The Great He-Goat*) (1821–3), depict the Devil in beast form as a goat standing on its hind legs. It is true that the earliest bronze sculptures of Pan also depict him as a goat standing on his hind legs (though with a human torso and arms), but these were not familiar to nineteenth-century Europeans. We will consider Pan's relationship to modern witchcraft in more detail later in this chapter.

Through the figure of Baphomet, Lévi's writings brought Pan into the mainstream of the late nineteenth- and early twentieth-century occult revival. They were studied carefully by members of the Hermetic Order of the Golden Dawn. One of its early members, Arthur Edward Waite, translated several of Lévi's books, including *Dogme et ritual de la haute magie* in 1896 (as *Transcendental Magic*). The Golden Dawn was founded in 1888 by William Wynn Westcott, Samuel Liddell MacGregor Mathers and William Robert Woodman, after Westcott claimed to have found manuscripts written by a German occultist named Anna Sprengel, who had received

Albrecht Dürer, *Witch Riding on a Goat*, c. 1500, engraving. Christians
in the Middle Ages regarded the goat as a symbol of lust
and an animal associated with witchcraft.

instruction from 'Secret Chiefs'.[15] Sprengel appears to have been invented by Westcott, and scholars today regard his narrative as a founding myth rather than a factual account.[16] Imaginative power is as central to modern magical practice as it is to literary art, which may explain why many writers – among them the poet W. B. Yeats, the horror writers Arthur Machen and Algernon Henry Blackwood, and the occult authors Aleister Crowley and Dion Fortune, all Golden Dawn members – found the prospect of magic so appealing. All explored the nature of Pan in their writings, and Crowley and Fortune made him central to their magical practice as well. Their work emerges from the literary culture of late Victorian and Edwardian England, and their Pan-inspired fiction, poetry and rituals are shaped by it.

ARTHUR MACHEN

The portrayal of Pan by the Welsh writer Arthur Machen (1863–1947) combines sheer terror with the threat of insanity, and sexual licence with an abyss of meaninglessness. Machen's vision of Pan was shaped by his deep involvement in the occult. As a young man in Wales, he also had an uncanny experience that sheds light on his peculiar understanding of the god. Climbing among the hills, he found in the 'grey limestone rocks something threatening, Druidical'.[17] As each hill gave way to yet a higher hill, 'with no end or limit that the eye could see', Machen recalled the words of the *Gloria Patri*: 'For ever and ever. Amen.' Years later he would learn of the Welsh equivalent, '*ac yn y wastad* – and into the waste, the waste of time being understood'.[18] Machen's response to the experience registers an acute horror of limitlessness and of 'waste' in the sense of 'void', both qualities associated with his later portrayal of Pan.

Although Machen did not join the Golden Dawn until 1900, and would later be dismissive of the group, he was familiar with occult literature from the 1880s onwards. In 1885 he was employed as a subeditor by the publisher George Redway, whose firm published work by Samuel Mathers, one of the Golden Dawn founders.[19] In 1896 Redway published *The Mysteries of Magic: A Digest of the Writings of Éliphas Lévi*, translated by Waite, who would later become one of Machen's closest friends. The volume included the description of Baphomet quoted above, although not the illustration. (Machen was fluent in French, and may well have read Lévi's original text.) Lévi's vision of Pan as an absolute power combining male and female attributes anticipates Machen's own version of the Great God, although the latter was more directly influenced by the seventeenth-century Welsh mystic and alchemist Thomas Vaughan, who believed that the original stuff of life was bisexual in nature.[20] Machen also catalogued a large library of esoteric literature for a bookseller, a collection he later described as evidence of 'that inclination of the human mind which may be a survival from the rites of the black swamp and the cave or – an anticipation of a wisdom and knowledge that are to come, transcending all the science of our day'.[21] He began publishing sections of *The Great God Pan* in 1890, and it was brought out in book form along with his short novel *The Inmost Light* by the Bodley Head in 1894. The book featured a frontispiece designed by Aubrey Beardsley, creating a visual link between Machen's work and the Decadent movement. Despite Machen's later dismissal of this connection, several themes explored in *The Great God Pan*, such as degeneracy and the fascination of evil, are typical of the Decadent movement. The Bodley Head was also the publisher of the *Yellow Book*, a periodical that featured illustrations by Beardsley and the work of major writers of the 1890s.[22]

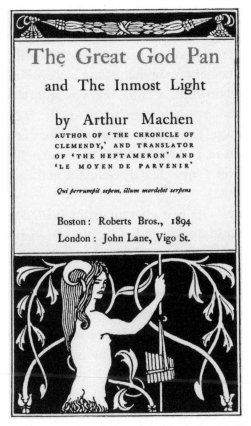

The Great God Pan

and The Inmost Light

by Arthur Machen

AUTHOR OF 'THE CHRONICLE OF
CLEMENDY,' AND TRANSLATOR
OF 'THE HEPTAMERON' AND
'LE MOYEN DE PARVENIR'

Qui perrumpit sepem, illum mordebit serpens

Boston: Roberts Bros., 1894
London: John Lane, Vigo St.

Title page of *The Great God Pan* (1894) by Arthur Machen,
with a pen and ink illustration by Aubrey Beardsley. Machen's portrayal
of the god would shape future perceptions of him as a dark power
threatening to human beings.

The Great God Pan considers what would happen if the forces embodied by the god erupted into our world by combining with the human. The novella opens with an account of a strange medical experiment gone terribly wrong, as a character named Dr Raymond seeks to expose his subject to a vision of Pan. A gentleman named Mr Clarke is assisting Raymond with a procedure that will enable a young woman to see reality directly:

There *is* a real world, but it is beyond this glamour and this vision, beyond these 'chases in Arras, dreams in a career', beyond them all as beyond a veil. I do not know whether any human being has ever lifted that veil; but I do know, Clarke, that you and I shall see it lifted this very night from before another's eyes. You may think all this strange nonsense; it may be strange, but it is true, and the ancients knew what lifting the veil means. They called it seeing the god Pan.[23]

The notion of a more authentic reality 'veiled' by the phenomenal world apprehended by our senses is found in a variety of religious and esoteric traditions, including Neoplatonism. For the ancients, seeing any god directly would destroy mere mortals, as in the story related by Porphyry, where the woodcutters who saw Pan died instantly. Raymond assures his assistant of the results he can obtain by slicing into a particular area of his subject's brain: 'Clarke, Mary will see the god Pan!'

As he enters Raymond's laboratory, Clarke finds himself overwhelmed by a sleepiness caused by fumes, experiencing a reverie in which he encounters 'a presence, that was neither man nor beast, neither the living nor the dead, but all things mingled, the form of all but devoid of all form'. The phrase 'neither man nor beast' is an apt description of Pan's traditional form, while the repetition of 'all' reminds us of his other cosmic identity as god of everything. This paradoxical being seems to separate Clarke's body and soul. Raymond and Clarke perform the operation, but whatever it is Mary has seen as a result, the procedure leaves her bereft of speech and reason. Although he expresses pity for Mary, the doctor claims 'it could not be helped; and, after all, she has seen the Great God Pan.'

Pan next makes his presence felt in a narrative told by one Dr Phillips, a friend of Clarke, concerning a young woman named Helen V., who was sent to live in the Welsh country-side by her adoptive parents. One day, a local boy is found screaming in terror after going to pick some flowers in the woods by a Roman road and falling asleep: 'He was suddenly awakened, as he stated, by a peculiar noise, a sort of singing he called it, and on peeping through the branches he saw Helen V. playing on the grass with a "strange naked man," whom he seemed unable to describe further.' In the weeks that follow, the boy wakes in the night screaming about 'the man in the wood!' When his father brings him to the house of a local gentleman to wait while he works, the boy again falls into a fit of screaming. A local doctor is called, but the boy falls into a state of terror, pointing at an object on the wall and again crying about 'the man in the wood'. The object in question is 'a curious head, evidently of the Roman period, which had been placed in the manner described. The head is pronounced by the most experienced archaeologists of the district to be that of a faun or satyr.' Has the boy seen Pan? Helen then strikes up a friendship with a young woman named Rachel, who takes her on excursions into the forest; after one such excursion, Rachel is strangely altered, and dis-covered in a dishevelled state on her bed, asking 'Ah, mother, mother, why did you let me go to the forest with Helen?' After this episode, Helen mysteriously disappears. Clarke writes in his own hand on Phillips's manuscript, 'ET DIABOLUS INCARNATUS EST. ET HOMO FACTUS EST' ('And the Devil is incar-nated. And is made man'). Machen here explicitly plays with the nineteenth-century association between Pan and the Devil, rendering his version of Pan all the more terrifying.

The reach of Machen's Pan extends well beyond the Welsh countryside, working its way into the heart of the British capital. Beginning with the section entitled 'The City of Resurrections', *The Great God Pan* shifts its focus to the character of Villiers, a young gentleman who encounters an old friend, Herbert, who has been mysteriously ruined by his wife, Helen (née Vaughan). After reading in the newspapers that Herbert was discovered dead from starvation, Villiers visits his former home and is overcome with horror. Having received a letter from Herbert that also describes an experience of nameless terror, Villiers consults Clarke, Raymond's former assistant, who realizes that Herbert's wife was the same Helen V. described by Phillips. Clarke shares a book of drawings by his late friend Meyrick, a painter who died in South America. They are prefaced by a Latin inscription describing the bacchic revels of satyrs and aegipans – the same passage quoted by John Ireland as a preface to 'Le Catioroc' from his piano suite *Sarnia* (see Chapter Four). As Villiers looks over Meyrick's drawings, he is terrified by what he sees: 'The figures of Fauns, and Satyrs, and Ægipans danced before his eyes, the darkness of the thicket, the dance on the mountain-top, the scenes by lonely shores, in green vineyards, by rocks and desert places, passed before him; a world before which the human soul seemed to shrink back and shudder.' At the very end of the notebook, Villiers recognizes the woman depicted in the final drawing as Herbert's wife.

The investigation turns to a number of suicides linked to one Mrs Beaumont, and their connection to her apparent revival of ancient rites in honour of Pan. Villiers and his companion Austin discover a written account of the revels that she 'provided for her choicer guests'. Machen leaves the details to our imagination, but Villiers provides a suggestive description:

Yes; it is horrible enough; but after all, it is an old story, an old mystery played in our day, and in dim London streets instead of amidst the vineyards and the olive gardens. We know what happened to those who chanced to meet the Great God Pan, and those who are wise know that all symbols are symbols of something, not of nothing.

Villiers sees in the revels a modern repetition of the ancient rites in honour of Pan. He alludes to the destruction of the woodcutters narrated by Eusebius and Porphyry. His faith in the reality behind symbols is a tenet not only of occult practice, but of the cultural movement known as Symbolism, which flourished alongside the Decadence of the 1890s. Its greatest practitioner was the French poet Stéphane Mallarmé, whose masterpiece *L'après-midi d'un faune* (Afternoon of a Faun) lies just beyond our scope. Villiers's reflections on Pan's symbolism point to the meaning of the god for Machen's story, without stating it directly:

It was, indeed, an exquisite symbol beneath which men long ago veiled their knowledge of the most awful, most secret forces which lie at the heart of all things; forces before which the souls of men must wither and die and blacken, as their bodies blacken under the electric current. Such forces cannot be named, cannot be spoken, cannot be imagined except under a veil and a symbol, a symbol to the most of us appearing a quaint, poetic fancy, to some a foolish, silly tale. But you and I, at all events, have known something of the terror that may dwell in the secret place of life, manifested under human flesh; that which is without form taking to itself a form.

Such an attitude echoes that of Éliphas Lévi in his description of the symbol he labelled Baphomet or Pantheos. The symbol of Pan gestures towards 'the most awful, most secret forces', which must be symbolized because they cannot be named or experienced directly without destroying the human soul. These are the forces that have apparently incarnated themselves in the person known as Helen Vaughan or, more recently, Mrs Beaumont. Villiers's language also suggests a horror of sexuality, particularly female sexuality, finding 'terror' within 'the secret place of life, manifested under human flesh'. This sexual horror is also what is experienced by Rachel in her fateful walk with Helen earlier in the story.

Not wishing to spoil the story for readers who have not yet read it, I will avoid giving any more plot details, as hair-raising as they are. The final section is presented as a series of fragments, the first of which is taken from the papers of one Dr Robert Matheson. It includes his own account of witnessing 'a Form, shaped in dimness before me, which I will not further describe. But the symbol of this form may be seen in ancient sculptures, and in paintings which survived beneath the lava, too foul to be spoken of.' As we might guess, this 'Form' has 'a horrible and unspeakable shape, neither man nor beast' – but perhaps a combination? We learn in the remaining fragments of an ancient temple near the Welsh village of Caermaen, where Helen Vaughan was sent as a girl. A Latin inscription carries a dedication: 'To the great god Nodens (the god of the Great Deep or Abyss) Flavius Senilis has erected this pillar on account of the marriage which he saw beneath the shade.' Nodens (the name of a real Celtic deity, about whom little is known) is here presented as a native British equivalent of Pan. In an inversion of his traditional cosmic associations, this Nodens-Pan is the god not of 'all' but of nothingness – 'the Great Deep or Abyss'.

This is the terrible power that has manifested itself in the human world. Machen's Pan departs significantly from both the pastoral and Orphic traditions concerning the god, expanding the panic terror he causes into a kind of existential horror in the face of the abyss. The association between Pan's capacity to instil terror and his sexuality is an ancient one, seen in depictions of his attempted rape of Daphnis, as well as in the myth of Syrinx. As with so many versions of Pan, Machen's portrayal develops some aspects of the mythological and Orphic traditions, while ignoring others. In depicting Pan as a nebulous occult power, Machen seizes on the darker, more threatening aspects of the god, magnifying them until his positive aspects disappear altogether. His version would influence those modern writers who were wary of Pan's power, including E. M. Forster, Saki and E. F. Benson.

ALEISTER CROWLEY AND VICTOR NEUBURG

The most notorious occultist of the twentieth century, Aleister Crowley (1875–1947), self-styled 'Beast', was also particularly fascinated with Pan. At the end of the nineteenth century Crowley was an aspiring poet with a penchant for sexual experimentation and drug use. These habits intertwined with an interest in magic, and his later writings on the subject have had more influence on later magical practice than those of any other modern occultist. He entered the Golden Dawn as an acolyte of Mathers, who granted him authority over the London branch, but he was eventually expelled at the insistence of other members who disapproved of his authoritarian attitudes and his sexual proclivities. In one memorable incident, Yeats barred Crowley from entering the Golden Dawn's Temple of Isis until a police constable could be summoned.[24] Undaunted, Crowley went on to found his own magical

Aleister Crowley making the 'Horns of Pan' gesture. Pan was a central figure in Crowley's occult thought and practice.

orders and develop a philosophy rooted in his aphorism 'Do what thou wilt shall be the whole of the law.'[25]

Crowley's 'Hymn to Pan' was composed in 1913 but not published until 1919, when it appeared in *The Equinox*, the official magazine of the magical order Argenteum Astrum, which he founded in 1907 after leaving the Golden Dawn.[26] He had published a poem entitled 'Pan to Artemis' in the magazine ten years earlier, but this invocation of the goddess has little to do with Pan beyond the title. Unlike Shelley's 'Hymn of Pan', Crowley's hymn is intended as an actual summons of the god, although at times it reads like an onanistic fantasy. The hymn's opening lines are an invocation as much of the lust the god inspires as of the god himself:

> Thrill with lissome lust of the light,
> O man! My man!
> Come careering out of the night
> Of Pan! Io Pan!
> Io Pan! Io Pan! Come over the sea
> From Sicily and from Arcady![27]

Crowley identifies Pan with Bacchus, requesting him to come accompanied by fauns, leopards, nymphs and satyrs. One of the more startling lines appears to ask Pan to 'Come with Apollo in bridal dress,' although this line is followed by '(Shepherdess and Pythoness)', so it is at first reading not entirely clear if the god is being asked to arrive in drag, or if the Shepherdess and Pythoness are the brides of Pan and Apollo, respectively. Crowley also plays with Pan's Satanic associations, describing him as 'Devil or man' and claiming to be 'numb / With the lonely lust of devildom'.[28] The hymn shifts from a summons to a plea to be ravished by the god, asking to be given 'the token erect of thorny thigh': 'I am a man: / Do as thou wilt, as a great god can.' By the end of the hymn, the speaker's invocation is successful and he has been possessed by the god:

> I am Pan! Io Pan! Io Pan Pan! Pan!
> I am thy mate, I am thy man . . .
> And I rave; and I rape and I rip and I rend

Everlasting, world without end,
Mannikin, maiden, Maenad, man,
In the might of Pan.
Io Pan! Io Pan Pan! Pan! Io Pan![29]

In becoming Pan, the speaker of the hymn is transformed from ravished to ravisher in an ecstasy of sexualized violence directed against beings of both genders.

'Hymn to Pan' was written in response to the Pan poetry composed by Crowley's lover and magical acolyte, Victor Neuburg (1883–1940). Neuburg had founded the Pan Society while an undergraduate at Cambridge, which briefly became a source of controversy in 1908, when the university attempted to ban Crowley from attending a meeting.[30] Neuburg's collection of poems *The Triumph of Pan* was published in 1910 by Crowley's Equinox Press. Among its extensive prefatory material is a lengthy quotation from Éliphas Lévi, further evidence of his influence in British occult circles. In the strange and fascinating title poem, Neuburg claims a kind of divinity: 'I am grown a god, a sinewy token / Of Pan's most ardent strife.'[31] This is the cosmic rather than pastoral god, who 'is spinning thoughts of form and sense / Out of the formless void, stark, cold and dense'. Where Machen's Pan embodies the power of the void, Neuburg's version of the god more positively transforms that 'formlessness' into 'form and sense'. Writing out of a sense of desolation, Neuburg imagines joining Pan's revels:

I seek the hidden grove
Where Pan plays to the trees,
The nymphs, the fauns, the breeze,
And the sick satyr with his syren-song
Makes the world ache with longing. I am strong.[32]

Neuburg is a better craftsman than Crowley, with a more certain command of metre and verse. When he attempts to convey ecstatic experience, his greater control paradoxically produces a more convincing expression of emotional transport. In an extraordinary passage that alludes to Pan's noonday rest, he imagines the god as an object of erotic desire:

> We found sleeping; yea, the Panic revel
> > Had drawn his spirit far;
> Asleep, he bore the aspect of a devil;
> > Awake, the morning star
> > Flashed in his eyes; oh, scan
> > The vision of great Pan;
> Thrust tongue and limbs against his pulsing side,
> And thou shalt know the dayspring as a bride![33]

Neuburg imagines the form of sleeping Pan as resembling a devil, while urging us to lick and embrace the god to arouse his sexual interest.

This fantasy of being ravished by Pan is also portrayed in a poem that appears later in the collection, 'The Lost Shepherd'. In it, the shepherd narrates his experience of being ravished by the god:

> And as he clasped me, slim and slight,
> > I roared with the pain he gave,
> And he cried, 'I will hold thee here all night,
> > My beautiful, dark-haired slave;
> > > Kiss my lips and laugh in my eyes,
> > > And I'll bring magic out of the skies,
> And thy flame shall yield to my eyes' fierce light
> Ere thine ashes are laid in the grave!['][34]

Ronald Hutton describes Neuburg's Pan as 'behaving more like rough trade' in this poem, where he demands both physical and spiritual surrender.[35] He offers in return 'magic out of the skies', perhaps a more meaningful phrase than at first appears, given Neuburg's occult interests.

In both poems, Neuburg reverses the traditional scenario of shepherd or nymph fleeing from Pan's sexual advances. In 'The Triumph of Pan', the god's body is imagined as both desirable and a source of spiritual renewal:

> The odour of thy hair,
> Thy feet, thy hands, shall bring
> Again the Pagan spring,
> And from our bodies' union men shall know
> To cast the veil from the sad face of woe.[36]

The 'Pagan spring' summoned by the speaker's sexual union with Pan is a season of liberated desire, at least for those 'men' veiled in the sorrow of unfulfilled desire. For them, 'There shall be no despair, / But Pan! Pan! Pan! and all the world shall be / Mingled in one wild burning ecstasy.'[37] The remaining sections of the poem explore the implications of this ecstasy, hailing the rebirth of Pan in the modern world. In doing so, Neuburg offers an ecstatically romantic response to Wilde's double villanelle of the previous century (see Chapter Three).

Seen in the context of Neuburg's Pan poems, Crowley's 'Hymn to Pan' can be read as a poetic response in which the speaker becomes the ravishing Pan ('I rave; and I rape and I rip and I rend') fantasized about by his lover. Yet to read Neuburg's poems and Crowley's 'Hymn' in exclusively personal terms is to miss the larger role played by Pan in the philosophical system Crowley developed, known as

'Thelema'. In 1907 he wrote *Liber vii*, the first of the Thelemic books that he claimed were revealed to him by the Egyptian spirit Aiwass. The book opens with a voice proclaiming the arrival of Pan:

1. Into my loneliness comes –
2. The sound of a flute in dim groves that haunt the uttermost hills.
3. Even from the brave river they reach to the edge of the wilderness.
4. And I behold Pan.[38]

Crowley's title page indicates that this 'Prologue of the Unborn' is spoken by an adept. The speaker imagines being surrounded by Pan, flooding his senses as he plunges into the 'abyss'.[39] He imagines this 'annihilation' as 'An end to loneliness, an end to all', before concluding with the chant 'Pan! Pan! Io Pan! Io Pan!'[40] Given its title, the poem appears to describe Pan's arrival and shepherding of the disembodied adept into a new incarnation.

In Crowley's Thelemic system of inner development and ritual practice, the 'Night of Pan' is the name he gives to the shattering of the ego. Crowley imagines the Night of Pan as being effected through the agency of an archetypal feminine power, 'the Great Sea whence all Life springs, and whose black womb reabsorbs all'.[41] Pan in this scheme embodies a fertilizing male power who is united with her: 'for is not Pan the All-Begetter in the heart of the Groves at high noon, and is not Her "hair the trees of Eternity" the filaments of All-Devouring Godhead "under the Night of Pan?"'[42] In *The Book of Lies* (1913), Crowley writes cryptically about his experience: 'O! the heart of N.O.X. the Night of Pan. / PAN: Duality: Energy: Death.'[43] The reference to 'Duality' suggests Levi's figure of

Baphomet, an association reinforced by the placement of these lines in a chapter called 'Sabbath of the Goat'. In his commentary, Crowley attaches esoteric significance to the three letters that make up Pan's name: 'The word Pan is then explained, Π, the letter of Mars, is a hieroglyph of two pillars, and therefore suggest duality; A, by its shape, is the pentagram, energy, and N, by its Tarot attribution, is death.'[44] This idiosyncratic interpretation of Pan's name requires a knowledge of the Golden Dawn correspondence of the Hebrew letter Nun with the Death card in the Tarot, as well as other occult symbolism. Elsewhere, Crowley connects the Night of Pan with the traditional Orphic or cosmic Pan: 'The reflection of All is Pan: the Night of Pan is the annihilation of All.'[45] If the Night of Pan is the destruction of both the individual ego and 'All', this implies an identification between the two, as though the 'All' we know and experience is really a projection of our own ego. To destroy both would imply a breakthrough in consciousness, a more authentic self-perceiving, a more authentic reality, perhaps symbolized by Pan himself. In any case, such transformations of consciousness were an integral part of Crowley's magical philosophy. His Thelemic adaptation of Pan is highly idiosyncratic, combining his experience of revelation with ancient Orphic tradition and nineteenth-century occultism.

ALGERNON BLACKWOOD

The supernatural fiction writer Algernon Henry Blackwood (1869–1951) was secretive about his many occult connections, but he is known to have joined the Golden Dawn in 1900, under the magical name *Umbram Fugat Veritas* (Truth makes shadows flee).[46] The motto's sense of commitment to truth is reflected in Blackwood's portrayal of Pan as a god who affirms the reality of deepest desires. Pan's power to connect us with our sexual instincts is his main attraction in Blackwood's story 'The Touch of Pan' (1917), in which the god is a powerful but unseen presence. Like Oscar Wilde's 'Pan', the story invokes the god as a necessary counterbalance to the modern world, rejecting the bourgeois social conventions that separate us from our authentically instinctive life. The central character, a man named Heber, has chosen poverty by marrying Elspeth, a young woman whom the narrator describes as 'an idiot', but one who 'certainly had the secret of some instinctual knowledge that was not only joy, but a kind of sheer natural joy'.[47] Blackwood's tale relates the supernatural experience that led to Heber's definitive rejection of a socially favourable marriage in order to be with the woman he loves. The evening begins at a party at the house of Elspeth's parents, where the guests evince 'a cynical disregard of the decent (not the stupid) conventions that savoured of abandon, perhaps of decadence'. They openly pursue adulterous liaisons, and even Heber's fiancée seeks out another lover. Disgusted with their modern mores and social artifice, Heber goes outside and encounters Elspeth in the garden. Unlike the women at the house party, Elspeth does nothing to appear fashionable or superficially attractive. Her words and actions are motivated by pure feeling. Heber adores her and responds willingly when she leads him into a pine grove, where he has already glimpsed mysterious figures dancing. 'In the heart of the wood dwell I,' she whispers to him. Elspeth agrees to meet him later that night.

At the appointed hour, Heber looks out of a window and hears a strange call like birdsong, 'soft and flutey, as though some one played two notes upon a reed, a piping sound'. He goes down to meet Elspeth, who kisses him and leads him dancing into the wood. As they race beneath the moonlight,

Heber realizes 'that she wore skins of tawny colour that clung to her body closely, that he wore them too, and that her skin, like his own, was of a sweet dusky brown'. Their transformation is even greater than it first appears, however, for Elspeth leaps into Heber's arms, but 'before he shook her free she had pulled and tweaked the two small horns that hid in the thick curly hair behind, and just above, the ears.' The revels continue into the night, when all of a sudden the dancers rise up and bow their heads: 'There was an instant's subtle panic, but it was the panic of reverent awe that preludes a descent of deity. For a wind passed through the branches with a sound that is the oldest in the world and so the youngest. Above it there rose the shrill, faint piping of a little reed.' While this moment resembles Kenneth Grahame's introduction of the Piper at the Gates of Dawn (see Chapter Four), Blackwood's Pan remains a powerful but invisible presence. The revellers hear his footprints and feel his touch, but do not see him. Pan brings them the gift of 'joy, the joy of abundant, natural life, pure as the sunlight and the wind'. He touches each of the dancers, and when he has passed by their celebration continues. In the final section of the story, Elspeth and Heber discover his fiancée and her lover escaping into the pine grove. An unseen presence intrudes upon their intimacy, spoiling their mood and sending them back to the house, but a sudden wind rushes through the wood, accompanied by the sound of familiar laughter. Blackwood's tale is both a satire on modern sexual mores (taking a dim view of flirting, make-up and backless dresses) and a powerful evocation of Pan as guardian of a more instinctive sexuality.

Dion Fortune

The relationship between magic, ritual and our instinctive life is also at the heart of Dion Fortune's form of magical working. Fortune (1890–1946) joined the Alpha et Omega lodge of the Golden Dawn in 1919, long after its heyday had passed, but her involvement launched a remarkable career that led to her founding the Fraternity (later, Society) of the Inner Light sometime in the early to mid-1920s.[48] In addition to teaching through esoteric societies, Fortune dramatized her ideas through occult-themed fiction, from her early *Stories of Doctor Taverner* (1926) to the posthumously published *Moon Magic* (1956). The latter was a sequel to her best-known novel, *The Sea Priestess* (1938), which served as a major inspiration for Marion Zimmer Bradley's *The Mists of Avalon* (1983), a feminist revision of Arthurian legend. Fortune's first fictional mention of Pan is in *The Winged Bull* (1935), when the god is briefly invoked in the British Museum.[49]

In *The Goat Foot God* (1936), Fortune explores the psychological implications of Christianity's fraught attitudes to human sexuality and our relationship to nature. The novel also presents, in fragmentary form, the 'Rite of Pan', a ritual invocation of the god created by Fortune and performed publicly on at least one occasion. At the centre of *The Goat Foot God* is the wealthy Hugh Paston, recently widowed when his wife was killed in a car accident alongside her lover. In his search for meaning, Hugh finds himself drawn to the satanic ambience of French Decadent novels, but is soon steered in a new direction by an antiquarian bookseller named Jelkes. Although he was once a Jesuit seminarian, Jelkes has a particular interest in pagan religion and encourages Hugh to reconnect with his instincts through a study of Pan. He introduces Hugh to his niece Mona, a young designer trying to make ends meet in London. As Hugh's interest in ancient magic grows, he decides to purchase Monk's Farm, built on the site of a medieval monastery, which he plans to restore as a temple to Pan. The monastery turns out to be the final resting place of a medieval monk named Brother Ambrosius, who was effectively buried alive for his attempt to revive the worship of Pan in the face of a hostile Church. Fortune's novel maintains an ambiguous attitude to Hugh's subsequent experience: is he possessed by Brother Ambrosius, or is he the monk's reincarnation? Or is he simply undergoing a profound psychological transformation as he rediscovers the passionate intensity of life? As the novel unfolds, Hugh finds himself falling in love with Mona, who is initially immune to his charms even as she works with him to realize his dream of restoring the monastery. For his part, Jelkes guides Hugh away from psychic danger and provides spiritual and practical counsel. The novel builds to a climactic ritual in which the boundaries between inner and outer worlds dissolve, completing Hugh's quest for psychological integration.

Pan is present thematically and allusively throughout the novel. Apart from the excerpts from Fortune's 'Rite of Pan', which we'll consider below, there are a number of references to the god that touch on the themes explored in this and the previous chapter. They shed light on Fortune's understanding of Pan as an archetypal power that connects us to nature through our instincts and passions. The novel suggests that the appeal of Pan for modern people is as a corrective to a civilization that represses those vital qualities he embodies. Human nature, Jelkes implies, is a mixture of fair and foul; too much sweetness and light requires its opposites. Dionysus, the Devil and Pan himself all embody those qualities rejected by civilized society. Jelkes's perspective echoes Carl Jung's idea of the Shadow, whose antithetical qualities must be acknowledged and worked through if the individual is to grow psychologically. A failure to do so, individually or collectively, produces a projection of those Shadow qualities on to others, demonizing them in the process. Fortune's novel mentions Jung several times, and he was a formative influence on her psychological approach to esoteric traditions. Hugh's intellect cannot make sense of his psychic ailment or explain what he means by 'Pan', yet his intuition and emotions drive him inexorably towards the god. As with other modern writers, most notably D. H. Lawrence, Fortune treats Pan as an irrational power that eludes our attempts to conceptualize him. He can be known only with our instincts. This explains the tendency of Fortune's novel to avoid discussing the god directly; he is beyond the capacity of discursive language to apprehend, like the Christian God in what is known as 'negative theology'.

If at first Hugh is unable to make contact with the god, he does manage to have a dream-vision of Pan's Arcadian setting, where he has a frightening experience. His initial attempt to summon Pan appears to begin successfully: 'He imagined the thin fluting pipe of the goatherd that at any moment might turn to the pipes of Pan; he smelt the smell of pines in the rare dry air; he felt the sun warm upon his skin; he heard the surf on the loud-sounding sea on the rocks far beneath.'[50] At this point, the vision dissolves as Hugh's intellect interrupts with a question about whether there are gulls in Greece. Frustrated, he begins to drift off, only to find himself returning in his imagination to the Arcadian world, where he follows a woman he initially mistakes for his wife deep into the forest. He loses sight of her as she enters 'a dense growth, dark with laurels. And through that darkness there came a curious cold exhilarating fear, a touch of panic.'[51] By creating a vision of Arcadia through an imaginative

'Composition of Place', Hugh has felt a moment of terror that is the archetypal experience of Pan.

As Hugh's interest in Pan gives way to a new obsession with Brother Ambrosius, interred beneath Monk's Farm, the novel begins to explore the connections between them. Hugh starts to feel the excitement Ambrosius must have felt during his medieval invocations of the god, and discovers that the monastery chapel is in reality a Temple to Pan. Hugh explains to Mona that Ambrosius sought to invoke Pan because he needed to reconnect with his instincts, but that his Christian contemporaries believed 'he was trying to raise the devil, and Pan and the devil were the same thing to their mediaeval minds.'[52] By now this is a familiar story, the major theme of Stephen McKenna's *The Oldest God* from the previous decade – but it is also one for which there is little evidence from the Middle Ages themselves. Jelkes has a more nuanced understanding of what we might call the psychodynamics of invoking Pan, recognizing that Hugh has already begun to break through many of his 'repressions'. This is, however, just the first step in a much deeper journey from the personal to the universal: 'Rouse the Pan Within and he makes contact with the Great God, the First-begotten Love, who is by no means merely a cosmic billy-goat.'[53] The language of 'the Pan Within' echoes that of D. H. Lawrence, who similarly sees Pan as opening the door to a deeper consciousness. As Hugh investigates the strange occult symbols and cubical altar in the chapel of Brother Ambrosius, he has a moment of sudden recognition: 'One of the charges made against the Knights Templar was that they had made cubical stone altars to the goat-god Baphomet, and concealed them under orthodox wood table-altars, made to open up like cupboard doors, so that the uninitiated suspected nothing.'[54] Hugh's intuitive leap from Pan to Baphomet takes us back to the territory first staked out by Éliphas Lévi, revealing Fortune's familiarity with, and debt to, the nineteenth-century French occultist.

As he prepares to receive 'the blessing of Pan', Hugh wonders what form the god will take during his invocation, if he might 'come crudely, as a materialising stench of goat', or 'more subtly in the soul'.[55] He realizes gradually that the mysterious woman he pursued in his early vision of Arcadia was in fact Mona, and the novel floats the possibility that they were lovers in a previous life when she confides that as a child she used to dream she was in ancient Greece clad only in fawn-skin. Mona has her own vision of the god, who appears in his classical form:

> And then there came to her the vision of Pan with his crook, Pan as the Shepherd; Pan with his pipes – the Nether Apollo – the harmoniser. She saw him, shaggy and wild and kind, leading the creatures of the flock of Ishmael down to the grey and barren shore that lay ahead. And he held out his crook towards her over the dark waters, and she waited, the creatures of the flock of Ishmael about his feet – creatures for whom there was no place in the world of towns and men.[56]

Pan imagined as Apollo's opposite ('the Nether Apollo') harks back to their musical contest judged by Midas (see Chapter One); in that story, Apollo with his lyre is the source of musical harmony, while Pan makes crude, rustic music on his pipes. Fortune here portrays Pan as 'the harmoniser', an image more consistent with Athanasius Kircher's 'hieroglyph' equating Pan's pipes with the music of the spheres. Fortune may well have been familiar with this image, which was reproduced in Manly P. Hall's esoteric classic *The Secret Teachings of All Ages* (1928). Mona feels that Pan will guide her safely through those waters. As her vision of Pan develops, she imagines him holding her in his friendly gaze.[57] Her experience of Pan is close to that of Mole and Water Rat in Grahame's 'The Piper at the Gates of Dawn', as she and Hugh join the wild things under the god's protection. This vivid reverie gives way to serious reflection on what it really means to invoke the Great God Pan. For Mona, it entails a return to our instinctual life that connects us to the rest of the natural world:

> This was the real invocation of Pan – the surrender to bed-rock natural fact, the return to Nature, the sinking back into the cosmic life after all the struggle to rise above it into an unnatural humanity. Animal is our beginning, and animal our end, and all our sophistications are carried on the back of the beast and we do ill to forget our humble brother. Uncared-for, collar-galled and filthy, he takes his revenge in the spread of disease.[58]

Mona's reflection chimes with Lawrence's observations in 'Pan in America' (see Chapter Four) about the way modern Western civilization has cut us off from 'the cosmic life' that he glimpsed among the Indigenous peoples of New Mexico. If an 'unnatural humanity' is one that tries to escape its animal roots, a 'natural humanity' is one that grows out of those roots and maintains its connection with our animal being. Thinking about our twenty-first-century COVID-19 pandemic, which may well have had its roots in the illicit trade in wild animals, Mona's final observation here seems especially poignant.

Despite the concrete vividness of Mona's visionary experience, Pan ironically becomes more metaphorical as the novel approaches its ritual conclusion. Although he thinks of Pan as a 'Presence' to be invoked, Hugh comes to understand the god in increasingly psychological terms. He asks himself, 'After all, what had his quest for Pan been save a hunger for the primitive and vital amid all the sophistication and devitalisation of his life?'[59] Hugh envisages his journey as a voyage into the darkness of his own subconscious mind. Reconnecting with his instincts, which have been repressed by the personal and cultural legacies of medieval Christianity, will allow Hugh to revitalize his own psyche, a renewed state symbolized by ancient Greece. Pagan vitality compensates Christian repression, in other words. In this scheme, Pan comes to symbolize an entire culture as well as the sources of life in the human psyche. The novel is not anti-Christian – Fortune herself remained a Christian her entire life – but it does suggest that asceticism produces a psychological and cultural imbalance that can be redressed by awakening our innate pagan energies. Thus Hugh finds that when he 'had asserted to himself the Divine Right of Nature, he had evoked Pan quite effectually. Each time he had renewed the assertion, Pan had answered. Each time he had doubted the natural divinity, the god had withdrawn.'[60] This assertion manifests in his behaviour towards Mona, and it is here that we see Fortune's old-fashioned understanding of heterosexual gender dynamics: 'When he had kissed Mona because he was man and she was woman, she had yielded as if something deep within her had acknowledged the right; but when he behaved towards her like a gentleman, she had kept him at arm's length and found nothing in him that attracted her.'[61] Mona responds to Hugh's assertive masculinity with a submissive acknowledgement of his right to kiss her, but resists his more solicitous behaviour. Connecting with the Pan within produces a corresponding reaction in Mona. Although Fortune's attitude to gender will probably raise eyebrows for twenty-first-century readers, it was typical of her generation; her other novels have strong female protagonists, but even here Mona is no push-over – she knows what she wants and makes her own decisions throughout *The Goat Foot God*.

In the end, Fortune's novel sidesteps the question of whether Pan has an objective existence outside the human psyche. Jelkes emphasizes that, practically speaking, it makes no difference, 'You got Pan at the first go-off; whether he is subjective or objective doesn't matter. You mean business, and that is an effectual invocation.'[62] This is a quintessentially 'magical' attitude, one we've seen, for example, in Crowley's interpretation of the letters of Pan's name. As Mona works to help Hugh set up his new home at Monk's Farm, she finds herself singing a song requesting Pan's blessing on the home, an excerpt from Fortune's 'Rite of Pan'. To perform the ritual invocation of the god, Hugh chooses a local stone circle that tradition associates with the Devil. He considers again the relationship between the Devil and Pan, noting that, despite their shared goatish attributes, 'there was a geniality and kindness about the celestial billy-goat that did not seem consonant with utter badness.'[63] On the evening of the invocation, Hugh and Mona go to the woods and undergo a shared mystical experience, culminating in the realization that Pan is one with the most powerful gods: 'The All-Father was celestial Zeus – and woodland Pan – and Helios the life-giver.'[64] In experiencing this knowledge at first hand, Hugh and Mona recover the insights of the ancient Orphic 'Hymn to Pan'.

In 1936, the year of the publication of *The Goat Foot God*, Fortune's magical order, the Fraternity of the Inner Light, acquired an abandoned church in Belgravia known as 'The Belfry' in which to perform their rituals. According to the occult writer Gareth Knight, Fortune staged the 'Rite of Isis' there and may also have performed the 'Rite of Pan'.[65] The three central figures of the Rite of Pan correspond to the main characters in Fortune's novel: the Priest (Hugh), Priestess (Mona) and High Priest (Jelkes). Fortune's novels offer 'exoteric' forms of teaching for a wide audience, while her rituals provide 'esoteric' experiences for initiates of her order.

The 'Rite of Pan' begins with a 'Doorkeeper' welcoming the participants and employing 'Composition of Place' to set the scene in ancient Arcadia, leaving civilization behind until we come to the woods, where 'the sound of the syrinx begins, faint and far, the pipe-call of Pan.'[66] After the Priestess ritually summons all those who would worship Pan, the Priest formulates Pan's Temple, a 'semi-circle of white columns supporting a plinth', in the middle of which is an altar bedecked with offerings to the god: 'honey, corn, and milk in earthen bowls, and wine in an earthen jar'.[67] The Priestess calls upon Pan's blessing in lines sung by Mona in *The Goat Foot God*:

> Come, Great Pan, and bless us all;
> Bless the corn and honey-bee.
> Bless the vine and bless the kine,
> Bless the vales of Arcady:
> Bless the nymphs that laugh and flee,
> God of all fertility.[68]

The Priest and Priestess then alternate parts as they vividly describe the Arcadian setting that awaits Pan's arrival, a place where 'goat-hoofs ring on the rocks above us,' 'music comes over the hill' and 'Syrinx calls from the distant river.'[69] Both then formally ask the god to return, and the Priestess declares herself Pan's bride. The High Priest declares: 'Within every man there is a hidden god of elemental power: this we name the Pan within. We call it forth to visible manifestation by the power of the name of the shepherd god of Arcady. Prepare ye now for the coming of the god!'[70] This declaration is followed by the Priest's invocation of Pan, to which the Priestess responds with a kind of hymn, which also provides the epigraph to *The Goat Foot God*. The hymn rehearses the story of the death of Pan, to which it adds the coming of the Iron Age as separating Golden Age humanity from the god. It also acknowledges the paradoxical nature of Pan, declaring, 'Pan is greatest, Pan is least!' After the invocation, the Priest identifies himself fully with Pan, and the Priestess with Venus (here called 'Kypris', after her Cyprian home). In the sexual polarity that energizes the ritual, the Priestess/Kypris stimulates the desire of the Priest/Pan: 'I awake the living Pan / In the heart of every man.' She welcomes the Priest/Pan, who pours wine for her from the altar, and she drinks. The ritual concludes with the High Priest affirming, 'The Great God Pan awakes in the heart.'[71] He then asks Pan to return to his proper place, and releases the participants to go. Fortune's 'Rite of Pan' creates a shared, vividly imagined experience that brings participants into contact with the Pan within. The High Priest's final words ask the witnesses of the Rite to meditate on the experience and 'send a record to the Temple of what they have perceived.'[72] The implication is that the Rite has awoken the subconscious minds of those who have participated, like Hugh's in the novel. Who knows what dreams and visions of Pan might follow?

MODERN WITCHCRAFT: THE HORNED GOD

Alongside the occult revival associated with ceremonial magic, the late nineteenth and early twentieth centuries brought a new interest in the origins of witchcraft. This interest by both scholars and practising occultists generated new ways of understanding Pan's identity. In 1899 the American folklorist Charles Godfrey Leland (1824–1903) published *Aradia; or, The Gospel of the Witches*, which purported to be a translation of an Italian manuscript given to him by a Tuscan informant named Maddalena.[73] Although Pan himself is not mentioned, the manuscript portrays a surviving pagan witch cult that worshipped the moon goddess Diana and her daughter Aradia, a figure derived from medieval legends of Herodias, the biblical queen who demanded the head of John the Baptist. In the foundational myth of *Aradia*, her father is identified as Lucifer. Mélusine Draco, a contemporary magical practitioner, notes that the pairing of Lucifer and Diana parallels that of Pan and Selene in classical mythology.[74] Ronald Hutton casts serious doubt on the authenticity of *Aradia*, but the book exerted a major influence on the development of Wicca and other modern Pagan movements.[75]

Leland's claim that witchcraft was a pagan survival would also be made by Margaret Murray (1863–1963), the most influential scholar of European witchcraft in the early twentieth century. Murray was an Egyptologist at Oxford whose research interests expanded to include a variety of ancient religions. As a pioneering feminist academic, she also actively campaigned for women's suffrage. During the First World War, when travel to Egypt was impossible, Murray developed an interest in the history and anthropology of witchcraft. This interest appears to have been personal as well as scholarly; she was later known to put curses on her academic rivals. In one case, Murray was observed cooking ingredients for a hex in a frying pan; coincidentally or otherwise, her intended victim became ill and left his position.[76] Her first book on the subject, *The Witch Cult in Western Europe* (1921), argued that the women and men executed as witches in early modern

Europe were members of a pagan fertility cult that had survived from Palaeolithic times.[77]

At the centre of Murray's witch cult was a Horned God, depicted in prehistoric cave art and surviving in various forms across Europe, including as the Greek god Pan. Murray explores the nature of the Horned God in greater detail in her second book, *The God of the Witches* (1931). In Hutton's view, 'The book represents the culmination of the cult of Pan in modern England, for it asserted the doctrine that the horned god of the greenwood had been the oldest male deity known to humans, and traced his worship across Europe and the Near East, from the Old Stone Age to the seventeenth century.'[78] Murray's arguments are rejected by scholars today, it must be said, but they were regarded as authoritative well into the 1960s and continue to enjoy a kind of half-life in popular culture. Hutton offers a persuasive summary of the case against Murray's scholarship, based on her highly select-ive use of evidence and habit of jumping to unwarranted conclusions. Reading Murray's book nonetheless remains a strangely compelling experience, in part because she imagines her alternative history with the vividness and attention to detail we find in the 'world-building' of fantasy writers such as J.R.R. Tolkien.

The first chapter of *The God of the Witches*, 'The Horned God', is framed with an unattributed epigraph (presumably composed by Murray herself) that neatly sums up the idea that Christians identified Pan with the Devil: 'The God of the old religion becomes the Devil of the new.'[79] Murray points to a variety of horned gods across the ancient world, of which Pan is the most familiar Greek example. For illustration, she includes an image of the vase depicting Pan's pursuit of the shepherd Daphnis, juxtaposed with an image of Theseus slaying the Minotaur – for Murray, yet another version of the

Horned God. She claims that Pan's 'universality is shown by his name, which points to a time when he was the only deity in his own locality'.[80] This statement is in many ways typical of the way Murray uses evidence. The ancient Greeks did believe that Pan's name meant 'all', a false derivation that Murray presents as accurate; she then infers from this false derivation that Pan's 'universality' actually meant that he was the sole god acknowledged by his original worshippers. This conclusion is really a leap in the dark, but it serves Murray's theory that the 'Old Religion' worshipped a single horned deity. To make her case that 'Pan' is but one name for the same Horned God found across cultures, she asks us to compare his appearance with 'the little dancing god of the Palaeolithic people . . . and also with the figure of Robin Goodfellow'.[81] Murray's association of these images here makes some intuitive sense (all three figures are semi-human with horns and hooves), but to suggest that a Palaeolithic cave painting, an ancient Greek vase and a seventeenth-century English woodcut all depict versions of the same Horned God fails to take into account their vastly different cultural contexts.

Murray's locating of Pan's ancient origins is, however, sound enough: 'Though our knowledge of him dates only to the late Iron Age, his worship is obviously of high antiquity, and he appears to be indigenous in Greece.'[82] Later in the book she offers her own interpretation of Pan's pipes that implies an identity between the god and ancient Egyptian iconography: 'The flute as an instrument for magical purposes occurs in Egypt at the very dawn of history, when a masked man plays on it in the midst of animals. The pan-pipes, as their name implies, belong specially to a god who was disguised as an animal.'[83] One might point out that Pan is not, strictly speaking, 'a god who was disguised as an animal,' but rather a god whose form is half-animal. Murray elides this distinction in order to suggest a link between Pan and this Egyptian 'masked man', who is not identified. Because of their traditional association with witches, goats also figure prominently in her discussion, although she does not connect them explicitly with Pan.

Through his association with Murray's Horned God, Pan was absorbed into the version of witchcraft promulgated by the man known as the 'Father of Wicca', Gerald Brousseau Gardner (1884–1964). Born in Lancashire, and having spent much of his childhood in Madeira, Gardner moved to Ceylon (now Sri Lanka) in 1900, eventually settling in what was then Malaya.[84] In Asia, Gardner worked as a tea and rubber planter, as well as a civil servant, developing a keen interest in local weaponry and magic.[85] When he returned to England in 1936, he settled near the New Forest and, he later claimed, was initiated into a local coven of witches a few years later. The truth of this claim has been widely disputed, and Hutton details the complex network of Gardner's occult connections before his publication of *Witchcraft Today* (1954), complete with a preface by Murray.[86] These connections included membership of the Rosicrucian Order Crotona Fellowship, an esoteric society founded in 1924. Gardner claimed that in 1939 some members of this fellowship introduced him to a local woman named Dorothy Clutterbuck, who allegedly initiated him into witchcraft.[87] In 1947 Gardner met Aleister Crowley, who appointed him to a high degree in the Ordo Templi Orientis. Despite regarding himself as head of the order in Europe, Gardner soon lost interest and began to promulgate the 'Old Religion', which he designated 'Wicca', adapted from an Old English word for witch. The repeal of the Witchcraft Act in 1951 provided an important context for the publication of *Witchcraft Today*, allowing Gardner to present Wicca as an ancient faith emerging from the shadows of centuries of persecution.[88] In its worship, Gardnerian Wicca (as it is now often called) balances the Horned God with a Moon Goddess, a pairing we have encountered before in the myth of Pan and Selene.

In *The Meaning of Witchcraft* (1959), Gardner makes several references to Pan that develop Murray's ideas from *The God of the Witches*. Responding to the claim that Christians had deliberately identified Pan with the Devil, Gardner insists that 'The Old Horned God of the witches is *not* the Satan of Christianity, and no amount of theological argument will make him so.'[89] He emphasizes the ancient provenance of the Horned God, referencing the same Palaeolithic cave painting as Murray, and insisting on the continuity of worship over time: 'He is the old phallic god of fertility who has come forth from the morning of the world, and who was already of immemorial antiquity before Egypt and Babylon, let alone before the Christian era. Nor did he perish at the cry that Great Pan was dead.'[90] Despite this persistence, however, in Gardner's account the Church deliberately chose Pan as the embodiment of evil:

> It was unfortunate that the god of the witches wore a helmet with horns, because when the Church began to proclaim the doctrine of the devil as God's adversary they made him in the image of the Greek and Roman god Pan. There were many statues of Pan surviving, half-man, half-goat, with horns upon his head.[91]

The 'helmet with horns' is apparently Gardner's own invention, but his language implies at least a subtle distinction between Pan in his classical form and 'the god of the witches', one that is elided by the Church in its eagerness to identify Pan with the Devil. He later acknowledges Pan's identity as god of fertility by describing a healthy and 'natural' sexuality as 'the Blessing of Pan', a phrase perhaps inspired by Lord Dunsany's novel (see Chapter Four).[92] Gardner also links Pan to the door god Janus, whose double-faced image is depicted with leaves on an ancient Roman bust:

> Closely akin to him are Sylvanus, Faunus, and Pan, who was hailed in Hellas as 'Pamphagë, Pangenetor,' 'All-Devourer and All-Begetter'; and as 'Chairë Soter Kosmou,' 'Beloved Saviour of the World,' yet from whose name was derived 'panic' as a term of terror. Priapus too was the Phallic God and the God of Gardens. The concept of fertility, of eternal, ever-renewing, upspringing life, is the basis of them all.[93]

Pan's titles are quoted by Gardner to suggest the veneration in which the Horned God was held in the classical world. Like him, the ancient Greeks saw affinities between Pan and Priapus, depicting both on the Attic vase painting of the attempted rape of Daphnis. Gardner's suggestion that both gods gave expression to the idea 'of eternal, ever-renewing, upspringing life' is surely right, although, as the vase image reminds us, this idea can also be accompanied by a sensation of primal terror.

On the other side of the globe, the visionary Australian artist Rosaleen Norton (1917–1979) developed her own version of witchcraft as a serious worshipper of Pan. Norton was born in Dunedin, New Zealand, and raised in a conventionally Anglican home with her two sisters. The family moved to Sydney to provide a more convenient base for her father, a master mariner who was often at sea.[94] As a child she enjoyed nature and drawing, but also began experiencing disturbing dreams and visions that increasingly drew her into an inner world. When she was seven, two blue marks appeared on her knee, which Norton later believed marked her as a witch.[95] She had a fraught relationship with her mother, and was often in trouble at school for frightening the other girls. As an adolescent, she rejected her parents' Christianity and began devising her own rituals to worship the nature god Pan.[96] This was not simply adolescent rebellion, but reflected a deepening spiritual awareness that is usually labelled 'mystical'.

In an interview with the *Australasian Post* in 1957, Norton explained that 'If the Kingdom of Pan had always been with me, it had been mostly in the background, overlaid by what was called reality: *Now it had begun to emerge and pervade the latter.*'[97] She describes a growing awareness of this 'Kingdom of Pan', experiencing it most vividly in solitude, at night and during storms. She felt a 'sense of some deep hidden knowledge stirring at the back of consciousness; and all about me the feeling of secret sentient life, that was in alliance with me, but that others were unaware, or afraid of, because it was unhuman'.[98] This 'hidden knowledge' and 'feeling of secret sentient life' is an emerging consciousness of the god Pan, who is present both in non-human nature and within our own unconscious minds. Her recognition of Pan's presence led the adolescent Norton to respond ritually: 'my first act of ceremonial magic was in honour of the horned god, whose pipes are symbol of magic and mystery, and whose horns and hooves stand for natural energies and fleet-footed freedom.'[99] In the tradition of a cosmic Pan that stretches back to Kircher, Bacon and the Orphic poet, Norton offers an allegorical reading of the god's pipes and physical appearance.

For her, this ceremony served as her 'oath of allegiance' to Pan and her 'confirmation as a witch'.[100] She did not shy away from the belief that Pan shared the Devil's form, claiming that at the time of her confirmation as a witch, she reflected that 'If Pan is the "Devil" (and the joyous goat-god probably is from the orthodox viewpoint) then I am indeed a "Devil" worshipper.'[101] Norton's visual representations of Pan frequently embrace these diabolical associations.

After studying art for two years at the East Sydney Technical School, Norton worked at a magazine called *Smith's Weekly*, where her writings and illustrations were encouraged but often deemed too strange for publication.[102] She found an outlet in the modernist magazine *Pertinent*, where she met her partner of several decades, the poet Gavin Greenlees.[103] In the 1940s Norton began painting images recording the visionary experiences she had while in a deep trance. These included encounters with beings that Norton regarded as having a real existence on the astral plane, in occult thought a subtler level of existence than our material world. Her portrayals of these entities, often highly sexualized human–animal hybrids, have a vaguely menacing appearance, but Norton experienced most as well-disposed towards her. Surpassing them all, however, was the figure of Pan. She described her idea of that god in the interview in 1957:

> I think the God Pan is the spirit whose body – or such of it as can be seen in these four dimensions (the fourth being time) – is the planet Earth, and who, therefore, in a very real sense, is the ruler and god of this world. Perhaps that is why he was given the name 'Pan', which in Greek means 'All', for he is the totality of lives, elements and forms of being – organic, 'inorganic' and otherwise, comprising the

planet as a whole: much as an animal body is a totality
of myriads of cells, bacteria, etc, in which ordered
whole these live and function, having their own forms
of 'intelligence' and perception, according to type.[104]

In Norton's spiritual and cosmological vision, Pan's spirit
animates the Earth, which is his body. Her account of Pan,
with its references to inorganic matter, cells and bacteria, is
in one sense an update of the Orphic tradition. What is original to Norton is her identification of Pan as the planetary
spirit of Earth, rather than god of the cosmos as a whole. This
Earth-centred vision of Pan has its roots in the god's ancient
ties to rock and forest, while anticipating the Gaia hypothesis
of James Lovelock and Lynn Margulis, which envisions the
Earth as self-regulating system. For Norton, however, the
spiritual dimension of our planet was an experiential reality.
Considering the Earth as Pan's body, she comments that *Such
a body would be the "world" to any of its micro-organisms,* and
the integrated consciousness of the body's owner would exist
in another "world", and on a different plane from theirs.'[105]
Pan is the macrocosm to our microcosm, just as our bodies
are 'the world' to a bacteria living inside us.

Norton's ideas about Pan informed her magical practice,
which occasionally got her into trouble in the puritanical
Australia of the 1950s. In 1955, for example, she and Greenlees
were arrested after photographs surfaced depicting the naked
couple performing a variety of sexual acts. She claimed in
court that they had been engaged in 'a sexual ritual dedicated
to Pan', part of her worship of the pagan gods, not witchcraft.[106] In her paintings that include Pan, Norton depicts the
god in a variety of ways, typically with horns curling back
on either side of his head. In the early but undated painting
Blueprint, his beardless and benign face looks down upon

Rosaleen Norton, Australian artist and witch, in front of her altar to Pan. The god played a major role in Norton's art and magical practice.

mysterious shapes and figures arranged around his torso. If this Pan's face is androgynous, his lower half is clearly sexed – an image of a magical cosmos poised between spirit and matter, perhaps. Like her magical practice, Norton's paintings belong to the 'dark' or 'left-hand' path, often depicting sinister or frightening figures with leering smiles. The image of

Pan she painted as a mural above her magical altar is no exception, and Norton plays with her viewers' association of Pan with the Devil in this and numerous other images.

For modern occultists, Pan is a source of danger and power that connects the cosmos and human sexuality, but their responses to his presence are startlingly diverse. Arthur Machen's Pan is a terrifying god of the abyss whose offspring manifests in our world with a voracious and perverse sexual appetite, destroying the objects of her desire. In contrast with this sexual horror, Algernon Henry Blackwood and Dion Fortune both celebrate Pan as the god of uninhibited hetero-sexual passion, a counterbalance to the repression and artifice of modern civilization. Their emphasis on normative hetero-sexuality elides some of the queerer aspects of the Pan cult at its height in the 1890s, when Pan was often a symbol of forbidden homosexual desire. Such aspects are developed by Aleister Crowley and his lover-disciple Victor Neuburg in their magical practice as well as their poetry. Crowley's Thelemic sex-magick would influence not just Fortune's ideas about 'sexual polarity', but also the witchcraft of Gerald Brousseau Gardner and Rosaleen Norton. Gardnerian Wicca drew on Margaret Murray's notion of a Horned God whose worship dates back to Palaeolithic times, of whom Pan is but one localized expression. By her own account, Norton was drawn to witchcraft because of her early sense of Pan's presence in the natural world and her own psyche. The god was at the centre of her pagan worship and magical practice, making many appearances in her visionary paintings. These various strands of modern occultism persist and develop into a more ecologically focused spirituality in the New Age of the late twentieth century, as we shall see in the next chapter.

The candles flicker on their stands as a gust blows through the makeshift temple. A strong scent of pine boughs suffuses the atmosphere as two green-robed figures, one male, one female, chant an ancient Greek hymn, with the male's arms raised in the shape of two horns. On the altar are offerings to Pan: pine cones, wine, the carved figure of a shepherd bearing a sheep. A piercing note from a reed pipe echoes through the room, and one by one the celebrants disrobe and begin to circle the altar. You can feel the energy generated by the dance, almost like an electrical current crackling through the close atmosphere. You get a sense of holy dread and foreboding. As you and the other celebrants dance to the sound of the pipes, the air above the altar seems to thicken visibly, and through the haze you begin to discern a dancing figure. The scent of pine now has a slightly goatish edge, and you can make out Pan's features more clearly – the cloven hooves and shaggy legs, a well-muscled torso and a face that combines elements of goat and man, surmounted by magnificent horns. You feel a surge of desire flood your body as you see the lithe limbs of the dancer in front of you. Pan's laughter – hearty, kind, life-affirming – fills all who have gathered to celebrate the god with an inexplicable sensation of pure joy.

6

CONTEMPORARY PAN

Pan's modern return demonstrates his persistence in Western culture as an image of our inescapable link with the natural world and a challenge to the repression of our instinctive life. Yet the places where Pan may be found have changed considerably in the hundred or so years that have passed since he was a major presence in the English cultural landscape. By the 1930s writers and artists had all but abandoned Pan, although he remained a central figure for some occultists, such as Aleister Crowley and Dion Fortune. In the decades after the Second World War, Pan nearly vanishes from the world of traditional high culture reflected in art, literature and music, while reappearing in more popular cultural forms. The Edwardian authors who had been devoted to him were largely the products of a male-dominated education system rooted in the classical languages. The certainties of their world were shattered by the Great War, and the modernists who followed saw themselves as heirs to a fragmented culture that could not be reassembled in its traditional forms. By the end of the Second World War this sense of separation from the pre-twentieth-century past had deepened. The postwar democratizing of education and rise of mass consumer culture diminished the authority of Greek and Latin, which had provided the basis of a classical education for generations of young men from the privileged classes. As more opportunities for publication opened up to men and women from different class backgrounds, English writing increasingly rejected the perceived elitism of both high modernism and the classics. A new realism in literature, and a turn to abstraction in the visual arts, left little room for Pan and the other gods. When we do catch a furtive glimpse of Pan in the contemporary scene, it is more likely to be in film, television or genre fiction, including comics and books for young adults. Pan also remains a strong presence in contemporary New Age and Pagan spirituality, the heirs of the occult revival that began in the nineteenth century. This spirituality informs many of Pan's recent appearances in popular music, as well.

RETELLING THE MYTHS

For most contemporary readers (including myself), access to the Greek myths and the classics generally is mediated through translations, retellings and modernizations. Among the most enduring retellings is *The Greek Myths* by the poet and novelist Robert Graves (1895–1985), first published in 1955 and still in print today. Graves's lucid prose style and inclusion of several versions of each myth make *The Greek Myths* particularly appealing to readers who want to know the stories in all their variety. In his brief chapter on Pan, Graves describes the god as 'a humble fellow, now dead', who 'was content to live on earth in rural Arcadia'.[1] As an example of Gravesian humour, we can consider his list of the various alleged parents of Pan, which concludes by suggesting that Zeus and Hybris are 'the least improbable' of all the options.[2] Who is this 'Hybris'?, you may well ask. Turning to the index, we find the name glossed as 'shamelessness', and the account of Pan's parentage its only appearance across the two volumes. Graves characterizes Pan as 'easy-going and lazy', aroused to anger only by those who disturb his noontime nap. He recounts the few myths associated with the god (which we explored in Chapter One), and concludes with an account of Pan's death, noting that 'Pan is the only god who died in our time.'[3]

Equally fascinating are Graves's notes to each myth, which identify sources but also offer interpretations of each story in light of his own mythology of the White Goddess. Graves believed that in prehistoric times a matriarchal religion that venerated a goddess of moon and Earth had been displaced by a patriarchal religion centred on a god of sun and sky, with disastrous consequences. Pan's marginal status in ancient Greek religion suggests to Graves that he was a survival from the older religion. Or perhaps we should just say 'the Old Religion', for Graves's interpretation of Pan is heavily indebted to Margaret Murray's ideas about witchcraft:

> Pan, whose name is usually derived from *paein*, 'to pasture', stands for the 'devil', or 'upright man', of the Arcadian fertility cult, which closely resembled the witch cult of North-western Europe. This man, dressed in a goat-skin, was the chosen lover of the Maenads during their drunken orgies on the high mountains, and sooner or later paid for his privilege with death.[4]

Graves's Pan is literally a man in a goatskin costume, the representative of the Horned God, who is killed after participating in erotic revelry with the Maenads – a name glossed as 'madwomen' in the index. His death is presumably to ensure the fertility of the herds and pastures.

In considering the mystery of Pan's parentage, Graves connects the multiplicity of accounts to the promiscuity of the 'orgies' held in the god's honour.[5] He offers several explanations for the puzzling claim that Pan's mother was Penelope, beginning with her name, which he glosses as 'with a web over her face', a detail that 'suggests that the Maenads wore some form of war paint for their orgies, recalling the stripes of the *penelope*, a variety of duck'.[6] Another explanation can be found in the animal disguise of one of Pan's purported fathers, Hermes:

> Hermes's visit to Penelope in the form of a ram – the ram devil is as common in the North-western witch cult as the goat – her impregnation by all the suitors ... and the claim that Pan had coupled with every one of the Maenads refers to the promiscuous nature of the revels in honour of the Fir-goddess Pitys or Elate.[7]

Like Murray, Graves doesn't hesitate to leap across historical eras, identifying the disguised Hermes with 'the ram devil' of later European witchcraft. Pitys, meanwhile, is elevated from the status of nymph to that of 'Fir-goddess', identified with Elate, whose name Graves glosses as 'fir-tree'. Orgiastic revels also provide an explanation for the myth of Pan and Selene, which 'must refer to a moonlit May eve orgy, in which the young Queen of the May rode upon her upright man's back before celebrating a greenwood marriage with him'. In Graves's imagination, the myths and cult of Pan are transformed into an ancient Arcadian version of Murray's witch cult. Graves's interpretation of Pan is entertaining and provocative, even if far removed from the more contemporary scholarship of, say, Philippe Borgeaud.

CONTEMPORARY POETRY, FICTION AND DRAMA

Aware of the deluge of Pan-inspired poetry and fiction that subsided only in the 1930s, the writers who have followed in its wake have tended to take an ironic or oblique approach to the god. When Pan appears in contemporary literature, he is often seen indirectly, through the eyes of Syrinx, or else invoked through allusions to earlier poetry. Just as ancient literary representations of Pan were the creation of town-dwelling Greeks and Romans, in the post-war decades he has had the strongest appeal to metropolitan poets. Three American poets of the so-called New York School, Frank O'Hara (1926–1966), John Ashbery (1927–2017) and Kenneth Koch (1925–2002), all wrote about Pan directly, allusively or through translation. The New York School poets rejected the high seriousness that characterized much mid-century poetry, finding equal inspiration in art, pop culture and daily life in the city. A *New York Times* review of O'Hara's *Collected Poems* (1971) was entitled 'A Pan Piping on the City Streets', which neatly captures the playful and more satyr-like aspects of this unfailingly urbane poet.[8]

O'Hara's Pan is an expression of the enduring power of sexual desire, and his poems also show an awareness of the modern tradition of Pan as a symbol of homoerotic love. His earliest Pan-themed poetry appears in 'Oranges: 12 Pastorals' (1949), a title that gestures to the ancient literary mode in which Pan frequently appears. In the second section, O'Hara's speaker addresses Pan directly, as the only one to be unaffected by the ravages of time: 'Pan, your flesh alone has escaped.'[9] The speaker asks Pan to remember him when he is nothing but a skeleton exposed to the elements, and asks the god to play his pipes so that the music fills his 'rain-sweet canals'.[10] O'Hara's tone is difficult to gauge. Is this a cry of anguish to the goat-foot god, or does the passage display a knowing awareness of its own absurdity? What does it mean to describe Pan as 'god of the attainable and always perfecting fruit'?[11] As with Rimbaud's poetry, which is a clear inspiration for these early pastorals, the poetic mystery resists and undermines our critical faculties.

As the sequence unfolds, Pan is treated both as a serious elemental force and more light-heartedly. In section 7, he is an earthy and sensual power, awakening the senses to receive the heavenly music of Orpheus.[12] O'Hara's tone is noticeably campier in the invocation of Pan dramatized in section 8, where he is described as 'god of our hearts', who bears the 'limp virgin' of summer in his arms, but who is also the 'beloved pimp of our hot flesh'. Pan's identification here with 'the fruits of the earth' envisions him as a god of nature, but this is undermined by the inclusion of the human-made 'fountains' (comically rhyming with 'mountains') and the jarringly modern 'flagpoles', a rather obvious phallic symbol in the immediate context of bearing 'seed'. The absurd list of epithets for Pan takes the god in a queer direction, labelling him 'disruptor of the sly, virtuous inseminator', presumably one who inseminates his (female) partner for the virtuous reason of fathering children. (Of course, we could also read O'Hara's ambiguous phrasing as calling Pan both 'disruptor of the sly' and 'virtuous inseminator', which would be ironic and camp in its own way.) In any case, the kinds of love that Pan has been imagined presiding over have been anything but conventionally procreative. Given the usually adversarial relationship between Christianity and paganism, it is telling that O'Hara imagines Pan 'seeking the salvation of souls', an activity usually attributed to Christ. The section concludes by portraying Pan in a more recognizable role, as a god who 'turns aside from the breathing limbs, Orpheus-over-the-hills, to play his pipes. / Everyone! Everywhere! Dance!'

O'Hara's ironically titled 'Ode for Saint Cecilia's Day' (1950) celebrates the music of Pan's pipes while rejecting the religious music associated with Cecilia, patron saint of hymns and the pipe organ. The title is taken from a poem by John Dryden that was set to music by Henry Purcell, and another musical composition by George Frideric Handel. O'Hara's poem opens in the dramatic moments after the transformation of Syrinx, when Pan swiftly binds the reeds. After his experience with Syrinx, Pan is concerned that they all might elude his grasp, fleeing into a lake, leaving him 'in idleness and lust / to polish the horns of his forehead!'[13] He cries as he binds the reeds together, fearful that his music will be lost if his 'desire' wains. Pan's music is inseparable from his erotic longing, and without it 'beauty might flee his new assault.' O'Hara presents Pan as the inventor of music, 'a final abstraction' of love. Those who are not interested in love may be content with knowing the martyrdom of St Cecilia, but those of us in thrall to love are 'seeking like Pan the pattern of our true desire' in music.[14] The poem questions whether a virgin such as Cecilia could really make music, so entangled is it with our own erotic desires. In the end, O'Hara rejects the pipe organ (Cecilia's instrument) as being too mechanical to express the bodily passions of 'war or love'.[15]

The third and final Pan poem O'Hara wrote, a sonnet called 'The Pipes of Pan' (1954), elegizes the Pan tradition in poetry. In it, he imagines being birthed by new flowers and identifies his will 'with the fresh green reeds' that grow in the wild. These reeds 'flay the air and do not break', but ultimately leave the earth behind, finding it 'mute and passionless'.[16] In contrast with O'Hara's two earlier Pan-themed poems, this sonnet avoids any expression of erotic desire and

instead expresses disillusionment, as though the ordinary
world of the senses is inadequate to the music of Pan. The
god himself is absent and his instrument is vanishing from
a world that is never passionate enough to be expressed in
his music.

In contrast with O'Hara, John Ashbery alludes to Pan only
indirectly in his poem 'Syringa' (1977), through an oblique
reference to the myth of Pan and Syrinx. Ashbery's poetry
foregrounds the way language mediates our conscious experience of the world. His poems can be simultaneously fun and
difficult, often avoiding the direct expression of situations or
feelings in favour of the suggestive power of language itself.
In 'Syringa', he contrasts Syrinx's story with that of Orpheus.
The title refers to the flowering plant more commonly known
as lilac, but it is also a near-homonym for the nymph's name
(the Latin *syringa* is derived from 'syrinx'.) Reflecting on the
transient nature of both music and memory, Ashbery's poem
insists that we must accept the flow of experience or risk
being transformed into 'the tossing reeds of that slow, /
Powerful stream'.[17] As an allusion to the transformation of
Syrinx into a reed, this is highly elliptical, and Pan himself is
nowhere to be found. These reeds are merely passive – they
are tossed about but do not act on their own. The same might
be said of Syrinx after Pan makes his pipes from her, but at
least those pipes offer the potential for music, unlike the other
reeds, which remain wholly part of the natural world,
separate from the world of art.

A poet who was part of O'Hara's and Ashbery's circle,
Kenneth Koch brings his comic sensibility to bear in his translation of Ovid's account of Pan and Syrinx. The story appears
in the myth of Io that Koch translated for the landmark
anthology *After Ovid: New Metamorphoses* (1994), edited by
Michael Hofmann and James Lasdun. Part of the comic effect

Koch creates is through his long fourteen-syllable couplets, the same metre chosen by Ovid's first English translator, Arthur Golding; they invariably sound over the top in English verse, which doesn't usually go beyond the roughly ten syllables in a line of iambic pentameter. The myth of Pan and Syrinx is told by Mercury to the hundred-eyed giant Argus, who falls asleep soon after the story begins. Mercury concludes his account by reflecting on the significance of Pan's failure, observing that 'To lose his girl was odious / But what those reeds made of his sigh was haunting and melodious.'[18] Koch's American idiom serves his comic purposes, but he is also capable of evoking real pathos in describing Pan's marvel at the reeds' music: 'Touched by the wonder of the reeds, enchanted by their tone, / Pan said, "In playing, thus, on thee, my dear, we shall be one."'[19]

The American poet James Merrill was not affiliated with the New York School, but, like O'Hara, was a gay writer who turned to the mythology of Pan to explore questions of gender and identity. Merrill's 'Syrinx' (1970) is a complex monologue spoken by the nymph, who describes herself as 'a thinking reed', presumably after her transformation.[20] Pan is alluded to in her observation that whoever plays her 'Draws out the scale of love and dread', a clear reference both to Pan's desire for Syrinx and to the 'dread' he causes – the nymph's fear of being raped, but also the more generalized panic associated with the god. She imagines herself as a mathematical formula that includes her addressee, until 'the great god Pain' suddenly arrives. Merrill has transformed Pan into 'the great god Pain', who reaches for the nymph and then abandons her. Whereas earlier gay writers identified with Pan as a symbol of male sexual transgression, Merrill speaks with the voice of Syrinx. His gender reversal is complicated by the origins of the poem in a letter written to his muse, Irma Brandeis, who was at the time suffering physical pain mirrored by Merrill's emotional pain over an unfaithful lover.[21]

On the other side of the world, the New Zealand poet Allen Curnow (1911–2001) ended his final collection, *The Bells of Saint Babel's* (2001), with 'Fantasia and Fugue for Pan-Pipe', a poem that is effectively an elegy for the whole Edwardian Pan tradition.[22] Curnow took his inspiration from two poems published in an anthology in 1906, *New Zealand Verse*, one by his father, Tremayne, and the other by Maud Goodenough Hayter.[23] Family rumour had it that these two had been engaged when young, but that Hayter had ended the relationship, and Curnow speculates that this circumstance is the biographical origin of these two poems.[24] He observes in the opening section that after the engagement ended, his father composed a poem entitled 'Pan', in which Tremayne was clearly in the role of the god, with Maud cast as Syrinx.[25] Although the poem hints at a passionate encounter, Tremayne is an unlikely Pan, concealing the 'feral horned / god's hinderparts' in 'clerical grey serge'.[26] The wildness suggested by Pan's form is hidden well by Tremayne's 'clerical grey' trousers, the adjective suggesting a Christian modesty at odds with the lustiness of the god. The second, more philosophical section expresses a kind of horror at Pan's music as a symbol of nothingness, 'black-hole tunes' with which 'Pan pistol-whips / the galaxies.'[27] Curnow hints at the cosmic Pan with his mention of 'galaxies', but this is no benevolent vision of galactic harmony. Confronted with the abyss, the 'Terrified mind' can only urge itself not to 'panic', an allusion to the dread that Pan traditionally inspires. The poet seeks refuge from the abyss in words, which name and give meaning to the world in which we find ourselves. In the third section, Curnow narrates a surprise visit from Maud sometime after the Second World War. She is now a 'fifty-something Syrinx' come to see a 'newly-wed son / of Pan'. It is clear that she has been crying, and Curnow recalls hearing that she worked as a fortune-teller; she soon leaves. The final section defines the present as two millennia since Christ, and since a voice announced 'GREAT / PAN IS DEAD' – words that Curnow imagines joining those written by Tremayne and Maud in a bottle cast out to sea.[28] He ends the poem with the lovely image of 'Hoofprints in soft / and softening sand' – a trace of Pan's presence that is also a metaphor for the writing of poetry itself.

The perspectives of these male poets finds a response, sometimes a direct one, in the work of the contemporary Welsh poet Zoë Brigley. Her recent poems can be read in the context of the resurgence of feminism in the twenty-first century, and the rise of the #MeToo movement. Brigley focuses on the sexual violence inherent in the myth of Pan and Syrinx. 'Dryad', from her collection *Hand & Skull* (2019), opens with an epigraph from Walter Savage Landor's 'Pan and Pitys', a poem we looked at in Chapter Three: 'I gave her what she asked: had she asked more / I would have given it.'[29] In Landor's poem, these lines are spoken rather defensively by Pan in response to Pitys' teasing about his seduction of the moon goddess Selene. Brigley's poem dramatizes the experience of an unnamed dryad as she is transformed into a tree to escape the assault of an unidentified aggressor. It thus presents an archetypal version of the sexual violence that occurs throughout classical mythology. Brigley brings the reader into this experience by addressing the dryad as 'you' throughout the poem. As the pursuer begins to grab his victim, the dryad recalls others who have suffered the same fate, including Syrinx, described as 'the reed-woman, transformed into / a mournful sound,' and Pitys, changed into a fir tree.[30] As in other classical myths of transformation, at the end of the poem the dryad finds herself becoming a tree at the precise moment she is about to be seized. Brigley also refers to the myth of Syrinx in another poem in the collection, 'Syringe'. The title plays on both the name of Syrinx and Ashbery's 'Syringa', which provides Brigley with her closing line, while her poem opens with a line from Merrill's 'Syrinx'. She thus positions the work in relation to these two precursors, which her own poem both follows and resists. At the centre of 'Syringe' is a memory of crossing a boardwalk over a marsh, which itself becomes a place of transformation: 'like Syrinx, the reed-woman / you make yourself spiked and narrow, speaking only when / the wind blows through you.'[31] In this radical revision of the myth, the 'you' of the poem transforms herself into a reed, and Pan is nowhere to be seen.

Although he is an enduring, if occasional, presence in contemporary poetry, Pan's fictional appearances are few and far between in recent decades. He lurks in the background of Stephen King's short story 'The Lawnmower Man' (1975) as the unseen owner of Pastoral Greenery, a lawn maintenance company that sends out a murderous satyr to cut the grass of the protagonist, Harold Parkette, with fatal consequences: Pan requires sacrifice.[32] King undermines the conventions of suburban life with Pan-inspired horror, and the story can be read as a distinctly American revision of such British subversions of village life as Lord Dunsany's *The Blessing of Pan*. A Marvel comic-book version of King's story by Walter Simonson was published in 1981 in the series *Bizarre Adventures*. (The film *The Lawnmower Man* of 1992 used King's title, but nothing else from his story.)

If King's story draws on the many Pan horror stories from the early twentieth century, Tom Robbins takes a comedic approach, portraying the god as a major aromatic force in his novel *Jitterbug Perfume* (1985). It is a rollicking, surreal tale that intertwines two storylines, one that begins in an eighth-century kingdom, the other in twentieth-century North America. When a king named Alobar flees from his would-be murderers, he encounters a rapidly diminishing Pan who is suffering the impact of Christianity's triumph, but who none-theless remains impressive: 'Despite Pan's bedraggled curls and matted wool, despite the drool in the goatee and the manure on his hooves, he was by far the most impressive being Alobar had ever met.'[33] He is distinguished by a goatish odour, and instils a feeling of panic as he leads Alobar up a mountain for an afternoon of sexual pleasure in a grotto full of nymphs. Despite the merry-making, the nymphs are dis-tressed by the gradual fading of Pan's potency. Pan urges Alobar eastwards to seek immortality. In India, Alobar meets a young woman named Kudra, who discovers him many years later in a lamasery. The couple fall madly in love, gain-ing immortality through bathing and making love in the caves of Bandaloop. They end up in seventeenth-century Paris as perfumiers, and, when their lives are threatened, decide to create a scent of Pan to bring him to North America. The two lovers become separated, each entering a different astral plane, but Pan assists Alobar in making the perfume, which he ends up losing in the New World. Meanwhile, in the present-day storyline, the Pan perfume is stolen from the aspiring perfumier Priscilla by the unscrupulous V'lu, whose partner is a washed-up perfumier named Madame Devalier.

Near the end of the story, all the characters gather in New Orleans and we learn, among other things, that Carnival was founded by Pan-worshipping shepherds.[34] In the section labelled 'Dannyboy's Theory', Dannyboy claims that 'Pan embodies mammalian consciousness, although there are aspects of reptilian consciousness in his personality as well.'[35] Dannyboy sees humanity as passing through these stages of consciousness as part of our evolutionary development, preparing the way for the next stage of 'floral consciousness', represented by Christ and the Buddha. The announcement of Pan's death was really signifying the subduing of animal consciousness by its floral successor, although neither Christ nor Buddha felt any hostility towards his predecessor.[36] Nonetheless, Pan will be missed by humanity because he 'is closer to our hearts and our genitals'. Although we will miss the way he drew us 'into the dance of lust and confusion', we must let him go: 'There is little place for Pan's great stink amidst the perfumed illumination of the flowers.'[37] In Dannyboy's vision, the scent of Pan must give way to the scent of flowers in order for humanity to move ahead in its evolutionary destiny.

More recently, Pan's mythology has been the subject of feminist scrutiny by Nina MacLaughlin. Her *Wake, Siren: Ovid Resung* (2019) retells Ovid's *Metamorphoses* from the perspective of the nymphs and goddesses who suffer from the predatory attention of male gods and heroes. 'Syrinx' is told from the point of view of the nymph's sisters, creating a collective female voice for the tale. Their view of Pan is that he is a

> Squalid god. Waist-up manhood, pumpkin-colored curls and his bushy beard, who knows what all lived in there, orange eyes, and his waist-down goathood with thick furred legs, leaving hoofprints on the forest floor, his fat animal hard-on leading the way.[38]

The 'pumpkin-colored curls' and 'orange eyes' are original to MacLaughlin, suggesting something autumnal about Pan's character, in contrast to his usual association with spring. His attention falls on Syrinx, a 'total virgin who planned on staying so', so beautiful that she is mistaken for the goddess Diana.[39] Pan begins harassing her as she makes her way through the forest, and the collective voice notes the feeling of being threatened: 'Am I about to be killed? Is this where my life ends? Sex and dread and threat.'[40] Here, the 'dread' that Pan traditionally inspires is intimately linked to the threat of sexual violence. As Pan pursues Syrinx through the woods, his sexual taunting becomes more lurid and degrading. When she reaches the river, the other nymphs reassure her: 'We've got you, sis. We've got your back.' Pan may be 'all friggin' woebegone because he missed his chance', but soon he is contentedly making music on his new pipes.[41] For the remaining nymphs, however, Pan remains a sexual nuisance. When they hear him play a haunting melody on the pipes, it sounds as 'if sad ghosts had voices, which is maybe exactly what it is'.[42] Pan may be a god, but from the perspective of the nymphs who are Syrinx's friends, he is little more than a lecherous old goat.

Pan returns to the stage, at least allusively, in the American playwright Amy Herzog's *The Great God Pan* (2014), which tells the story of a man's painful realization that he is a survivor of sexual abuse. When the freelance journalist Jamie is reunited with his childhood friend Frankie, he learns that Frankie was sexually abused by his father. As Jamie seeks the truth about himself, he goes to visit his former babysitter Polly, who is now in a nursing home. Jamie recalls that she used to take them to play by a creek near her house, a memory that prompts Polly to recite the opening lines of Elizabeth Barrett Browning's 'A Musical Instrument': 'That's what I used to recite to you, on our way down to the creek. "What was he doing, the Great God Pan, / Down in the reeds by the river? / Spreading ruin and" ... something, something, I don't remember, isn't that terrible.'[43] Polly's failure to remember what exactly Pan was doing down by the river mirrors Jamie's own inability to access his memory of being abused. In the final scene of the play, Jamie is reunited with Frankie, and the two begin to recite the Browning poem together, a symbol of their shared past and slow recovery of repressed memories.[44]

THE NEW AGE

If Pan is only sporadically present in contemporary literature, he has a much securer place in the esoteric and alternative spiritualities known as 'New Age'. From its beginnings in the early 1960s, the Findhorn community and foundation in Moray, northeastern Scotland, was in the vanguard of New Age spirituality in Britain. Today the Findhorn Foundation is a large spiritual community that provides a variety of educational programmes and supports an eco-village to promote sustainable living.[45] The community originated in 1962, when Eileen Caddy, Peter Caddy and Dorothy Maclean first moved into the caravan park in Findhorn village, after the Caddys had their positions eliminated at the hotel they managed, Cluny Hill.[46] All three were deeply immersed in various esoteric traditions. They were forced to grow their own food, and, following the guidance of Maclean's inner spiritual contacts, their fledgling garden began to produce vegetables of astonishing size. They attributed this success to the nature spirits Maclean had contacted, which she identified as 'devas', using an ancient Sanskrit word for divine being.[47] Robert Ogilvie Crombie (1899–1975), known as 'Roc', was a friend of Peter Caddy who became intrigued when he heard about the success of the garden. He would soon bring his own experience of the Great God Pan to enrich the spiritual life of the Findhorn community. Roc had been born into a middle-class family in Edinburgh, where he studied physics and chemistry at the university before a heart condition forced him to withdraw.[48] At the age of 33 he had a heart attack that forced him into retirement on his doctor's orders. In the 1920s and '30s Roc was active in Edinburgh's cultural life, particularly the theatre (he continued to act in small parts all his life), but at the beginning of the Second World War his doctor insisted that he leave for the country.[49] For ten years he lived in rural Perthshire, where his encounters with the natural world laid the groundwork for a series of extraordinary visions.

It was when he returned to Edinburgh that Roc experienced a visionary encounter that would prepare him for meeting Pan. Roc moved back in 1949, taking a one-bedroom flat where he would live for the remainder of his life.[50] He enjoyed visiting the Royal Botanic Garden, and on one such visit, in March 1966, was by his own account astonished to see an actual faun dancing around the trees.[51] Although he soon realized that he was seeing this creature with his inner eye rather than his physical senses, Roc felt certain of its reality.[52] The faun was as curious about human beings as Roc was about him. He learned that the faun was a nature spirit named Kurmos, and they enjoyed a pleasant conversation that continued in Roc's flat.[53] This encounter was, however, merely preparation for a much more significant one a few weeks later. Late one evening, as Roc was returning from visiting friends, he suddenly found himself walking through a spiritually charged atmosphere denser than air, and became aware of a powerful presence beside him in the shape of a faun, but larger.[54] As they walked together, his companion wanted to know if his presence inspired fear. Roc said it did not, and when asked to identify the one who walked beside him, said he was 'the great god Pan'.[55] Pan wished to see if

Roc viewed him as the Devil, or could accept his form as it was. Roc experienced Pan's presence as accompanied by 'a wonderful scent of pine woods, of damp leaves, of newly turned earth and woodland flowers'.[56] He found himself overwhelmed by feelings of awe and love.

Over the remaining nine years of his life, Roc's relationship with Pan and his nature spirits deepened. In May 1966, on a trip with Peter Caddy to the spiritual centre of Iona in the Inner Hebrides, Pan again appeared to Roc and revealed the reality concerning his form. According to Roc, Pan prefers not to take any form at all, but assumes the shape humans have given him. Roc describes Pan as 'beautiful' in appearance: 'Only the horns on the forehead, the cloven hooves and the fine silky hair on the legs suggest the animal part. The legs themselves are human, not animal.'[57] Such forms are taken by Pan and his nature-spirit subjects from those created by the human imagination; their 'natural' form is what Roc calls a 'light-body', made up of pure energy, but they adopt an 'etheric body' in order to work with the plants they nourish.[58] According to esoteric tradition, 'the etheric plane is made up of a fine energy substance from which is created the mould for every form we see manifest on the physical plane.'[59] The nature spirits Pan governs use their etheric bodies to develop plant life according to each species' archetypal pattern, imbuing them with spiritual vitality.

In his public writings and lectures, Roc makes it clear that he understood his communications with Pan and the nature spirits as being received by his unconscious mind through images and feelings, which his conscious mind translated for him into words. Through his visionary encounters with Pan, Roc developed a deeper spiritual understanding of the relationship between human beings and the world of plants and trees. This expanded awareness developed considerably when Pan integrated his consciousness with Roc's, allowing the latter to see nature from an even deeper perspective. Roc reported that Pan taught him of the existence of an 'Anti-Pan' who corresponds to the goatish, nymph-chasing version of himself, coarser in appearance and bringing negative, even dangerous energy to those who attempted to contact him.[60] Although Roc doesn't mention him by name, the Anti-Pan strongly suggests the kind of Pan invoked by Aleister Crowley in his notorious 'Hymn'. In contrast to the Anti-Pan, Roc's Pan is a servant of God; when Pan challenged Roc concerning his earliest ideas about him, Roc replied that he always imagined him as 'The Piper at the Gates of Dawn' from *The Wind in the Willows*. Whereas Kenneth Grahame's Piper was a protector of helpless animals, Roc's Pan is primarily a guardian of the plant kingdom and its attendant spirits. The teaching Roc received from Pan and his servants consistently emphasized the urgent need for human beings to cease their destructive behaviour towards nature, and instead learn to co-operate with the plants that sustain us. It is a message that resonates powerfully amid our twenty-first-century climate crisis.

What is a contemporary reader to make of Roc's account of his visionary experiences? The selections from his occult diaries published in 2011 make it clear that Roc was immersed in a variety of esoteric traditions and had many experiences that can only be described as 'mystical', including those he chose to share publicly. There is no question that he experienced his encounters with Pan's kingdom as the revelation of a deeper spiritual reality underlying the ordinary world of our senses. The journal entries, privately written for his own record, employ many technical esoteric concepts from theosophy and elsewhere, showing his familiarity with many spiritual traditions. They reveal that, far from embellishing his experiences, Roc omitted material from the accounts he presented to a wider audience, particularly material concerned with his own spiritual development and what he termed his 'Higher Self'. His visionary encounters with the world of nature spirits, for example, were much more extensive than he told his audiences through lectures and writings. The figure of Pan revealed in Roc's journals is a more testing figure, at one point physically embracing him to see if Roc was repulsed, and even sending a vividly experienced cobra that wrapped itself around Roc's body.[61] Although he publicly attributed his perceptual growth to an awareness of 'the cosmic Christ', his journal entries record a much deeper sense of reconciliation between those old rivals Pan and Christ.[62] On one occasion, while standing on the hill of Cluny near Findhorn, he had a simultaneous awareness of Pan behind him and a vision of Christ in front of him, and realized that the two shared a deep spiritual bond.[63] This reconciliation reflects the larger theme of integration that runs throughout Roc's writings, perhaps embodied most clearly in the figure of Pan himself, who from his Arcadian origins has brought together seeming opposites and confronted us with whatever we have deemed 'other'. A visionary in the tradition of Emanuel Swedenborg or William Blake, Roc is unique among modern mystics in experiencing Pan directly as a vital spiritual presence in the outer world of nature.

Inspired by Findhorn, Machaelle Small Wright founded the Perelandra Center for Nature Research in Jeffersonton, Virginia, in 1977, turning to Pan as ruler of the nature spirits. The name Perelandra comes from the fantasy novel of that name by C. S. Lewis, referring to the Garden of Eden on Venus. Wright's practice focuses on what she calls 'co-creative science', working with the spiritual intelligences of nature to achieve the balance necessary to produce optimal growth in plants. In addition to sustaining a remarkable garden, Wright has used this co-creative approach to develop a variety of flower essences and health programmes to promote well-being in people as well as plants. As at Findhorn, Wright works with both devas (the form-giving, architectural intelligences) and nature spirits (which bring balance and function to the devic forms). The nature spirits are presided over by Pan, whom Wright understands as 'the nature spirit level that oversees and co-ordinates the full nature spirit level', humorously describing him as 'the CEO of the nature spirit level'.[64] Pan acts as a bridge between the form-creating devic level and the implementation level of the nature spirits.[65] In the handbook for her Medical Assistance Plan, Wright explains that Pan 'is the only nature spirit element that does not have regional limitations. He is universal in dynamic. This means that everyone, no matter where they are positioned on the planet, can work with Pan.'[66] In emphasizing Pan's universality, Wright draws on the ancient tradition of the cosmic Pan who is god of all. As a universal intelligence within nature, Pan transcends our ordinary understanding of gender. Wright tells us, 'Pan is actually without, or beyond, gender. I refer to him as "him" because his energy feels masculine to me when I communicate with him.'[67] This is an original perspective on Pan's gender, the main precedent for which might be Lévi's bisexual image of Pan-Baphomet, although we may recall the female Pan figures from antiquity, which also raise the question of Pan's gender.

In the most recent edition of *The Perelandra Garden Workbook* (2020), Wright focuses on what she terms the 'Pan function', which 'operates as a switching station for various levels of nature intelligence to "meet and mix"'. This Pan function is uniquely accessible to humans, with whom it can communicate directly, 'hence, the experiences and the sightings people have had with the form they call "Pan".'[68] By bringing together the different levels of intelligence within nature, Pan maintains a balance between the spiritual energies and material forms of nature. In her own experience of Pan's presence, Wright says she has 'never felt anything that can even remotely be characterized as threatening or demonic – only a calm strength and power that is equally balanced by love and caring for me, Perelandra and planet earth'.[69] Her experience chimes with Roc's encounters with Pan, which were also characterized by a sense of love and power. Wright uses this connection to Pan in all of her gardening work. In words attributed to Pan, he counsels us that the nature spirit level has valuable lessons to teach us about the relationship between 'soul energy' and physical form.[70] Pan here reconciles matter and spirit in ways that echo the many ways writers and artists have imagined him reconciling other oppositions. Wright's point, however, is that matter and spirit are not opposites, but must work together if a balanced relationship with nature is to be achieved.

Like Roc, the mysterious esoteric writer Leo Vinci (surely a pseudonym) has left a record of his meeting with Pan, which took place on a journey through the inner worlds of spiritual exploration. His book *Pan: Great God of Nature* (1993) is difficult to obtain, but offers sustained and thoughtful reflection on Pan's role in Western culture and religion from an esoteric perspective.[71] The first part is an overview of the nature of Pan as revealed through ancient writers on religion and mythology, touching also on some of the art, literature and music the god has inspired. It lays the groundwork (for the writer, one suspects, as well as the reader) for the second part, which culminates in a record of Vinci's inner quest to meet Pan. This journey is mapped using the Tree of Life from the Jewish mystical tradition known as Kabbalah. What, we may reasonably ask, has Pan got to do with the Kabbalah? The answer involves the ways in which Kabbalah has been adapted (critics would say appropriated) by non-Jewish esoteric tradition. During the Renaissance, Christian humanists began to study Hebrew along with Greek, and eventually encountered Kabbalah, which they believed reflected the same philosophy they found in ancient Neoplatonism.[72] At the heart of Kabbalah is the diagram known as the Tree of Life, a spiritual map of the cosmos made up of ten spheres known as 'sephiroth', emanations from the Infinite leading down to our material world.[73] Each sphere presides over an aspect of reality and has a variety of correspondences – planets, colours, numbers and so on. Beginning with the Hermetic Order of the Golden Dawn, modern occultists have greatly expanded the correspondences to include other traditions, such as the Greek and other pagan gods – which brings us back to Pan. Vinci's journey to Pan is what practitioners call a 'pathworking', meditatively following the paths between the various spheres of the Tree of Life and opening the imagination to whatever it may find there. Like Roc with his visions, Vinci fully believes that he encountered another dimension of being through his pathworking, and insists on his scrupulous honesty in presenting these experiences.

Vinci experienced his Kabbalistic quest as a journey through a variety of landscapes, along pathways that connected the different sephiroth, each of which appeared to him as a kingdom with its own unique characteristics and inhabitants. Although he gathered esoteric lore as he travelled through the kingdoms, it was only when he arrived in the mysterious region known as Da'at that he found Pan. The nature of Da'at is an enormously complex subject in Kabbalistic tradition, but it can be thought of as either a spiritual state or a distinct sephirah encompassing all the others.

It stands before the Abyss at the upper end of the Tree, beyond which are the three sephiroth that are too close to divinity for human apprehension. When Vinci inwardly arrives in Da'at, he finds himself cutting several reeds that grow beside a river, then experiences a vision of elemental spirits dancing. He joins their chant of 'Io Pan' and soon hears the sound of hooves approaching from behind, accompanied by 'a faint smell of musk'.[74] Pan's presence evokes a feeling of warmth rather than panic.

As he did in his first meetings with Roc, Pan wants to know if Vinci regards him as the Devil; Vinci assures Pan that he approaches him with love. The god tells Vinci not to turn around and see him yet, lest he be frightened, but allows him to hold his pipes: 'Seven graduated reeds bound with thin leather thongs that look soft like chamois leather. Each pipe is held in place by the binding and the beeswax that fastens them.'[75] As in the illustration by Athanasius Kircher (a copy of which Vinci includes in his book), Vinci interprets the seven reeds as representing the seven traditional planets, but he adds to these the seven sephiroth on our side of the Abyss. He plays a few notes on the pipes before Pan invites him to turn around and see his form. Vinci's description of his vision is remarkably detailed:

> First you look into the face. It is a good face by any standards, strong and kind, but you are sure it could be very stern if the occasion demanded it. The head is covered with strong, curly brown hair that is tinged with red and gold at the ends. At times in the light it gives the impression of a soft fire. Rising from the hair above the forehead are two horns, they are deep brown in colour, tending towards black at the ends.[76]

Vinci goes on to describe Pan's hazel eyes as twinkling with wisdom and compassion. His ears 'seem pointed at the top, with a tuft of hair going backwards. There is a constant, though slight, movement of the ears, even when he is at rest.' He is bearded, with a muscular torso 'partially covered with the pelt of a lynx, spotted like a map of the heavens'. Whereas Roc's vision of Pan had legs that were human, though covered with fur, Vinci records Pan as having 'the hind legs of an animal that is used to running'.[77] Each terminates in a cloven hoof, which Vinci interprets as 'a token of the stability of the earth' as he reaches out to touch one.

Pan again asks Vinci whether he regards him as evil, revealing that while he responds to those who earnestly seek him out of love, he retreats if neglected – hence the repeated affirmations of his death. As Pan did with Roc, the god affirms that he is really a servant of God. He remains actively interested in humanity, waiting only to be called: 'I am close to the earth and if men call upon me I will be as good to them as I was to Athens.'[78] He and the other gods can be found where once they were worshipped, even if they are now neglected. Vinci briefly glimpses another form of Pan, which he describes only as 'Egyptian' in appearance, perhaps hinting at the equivalence the ancient Greeks saw between Pan and various Egyptian gods.[79] Their time together is cut short as Pan tells Vinci that he must depart, but before he does, he shares a secret word that Vinci can use to summon the god when he is needed. Pan warns Vinci that he will have to give him the gift of partial forgetfulness lest his pining for the experience makes ordinary life unbearable. Amid the smell 'either of cedar or of pine', Vinci gradually awakens in his own bed.[80] The parallels with Roc's visionary encounters with Pan are striking, and although Vinci makes no reference to the Scotsman or to the Findhorn community, some measure of influence cannot be ruled out. In both accounts, Pan wants to work with humanity but is concerned that he is either viewed as the Devil or not believed in at all. Vinci expresses great disappointment that his meeting with Pan was cut short after a brief introduction, so we'll never know if Pan would have communicated a message of ecological urgency to him as well. The presence of trees and elemental spirits in Vinci's inward journey suggests a Pan who is intimately linked with the powers of nature, as he was for Roc.

In the twenty-first century, the magical instructor Mélusine Draco explores Pan's legacy from the perspective of a modern Pagan in *Pan: Dark Lord of the Forest and Horned God of the Witches* (2016), part of the 'Pagan Portals' series from Moon Books.[81] As her title implies, Draco develops the identification of Pan with the Palaeolithic horned god argued for by Margaret Murray. She acknowledges that Murray's emphasis on a religious cult surviving for millennia led her scholarship astray, but questions more recent scholars' outright dismissal of Murray's notion of a horned god worshipped in various forms across Europe, including Pan. Draco notes in particular the role played by the Roman Empire in spreading the worship of Pan as far as Britain.[82] She also follows earlier writers in discussing the identification of Pan with the Devil by the Church, although, as we've seen, this may in fact be a much more recent phenomenon when it comes to the form of Pan. Like the other writers considered here, Draco relates some of her own experiences with Pan, whom she first encountered as a child in the forest, feeling his presence alongside her as she played, and hearing his hooves among the leaves.[83] Draco's Pan is well-disposed towards us, and also something of a mischievous practical joker. Her book includes several Pan-themed magical exercises, and for those seeking their own encounter with Pan, she recommends chanting the refrain from Crowley's 'Hymn to Pan'.

CONTEMPORARY MUSIC

Pan's appearance in contemporary music could be said to begin with an album title: *The Piper at the Gates of Dawn*, Pink Floyd's first full-length studio album, released in 1967. Like the chapter of that name in Kenneth Grahame's *The Wind in the Willows*, the album title was a last-minute addition by the band's lead singer, Syd Barrett; its original title was *Projection*.[84] Although none of the tracks makes direct reference to Pan, the album is infused with a visionary intensity that echoes that of Grahame's chapter. Andrew King, the band's manager at the time, recalled Barrett telling him of a mystical experience in which Pan showed him the secret workings of nature.[85] Most of the Pan visionaries we have met appear to have been able to cope with the demands of ordinary life, but Barrett suffered from serious mental illness, aggravated by his heavy use of psychedelic drugs, and was asked to leave the band the following year.

When Pan is suggested musically in the late 1960s and early 1970s, it tends to be through the haunting presence of the flute on albums recorded by such British bands as Traffic, Jethro Tull and Comus.[86] He doesn't emerge into contemporary music in his own right until the 1980s. In 1985 the Scottish-Irish band the Waterboys released their third studio album, *This Is the Sea*, featuring 'The Pan Within'. The band's lead singer and songwriter, Mike Scott, had previously explored pagan spirituality on the Waterboys' previous album, *A Pagan Place* (1984), but 'The Pan Within' was his first public expression of interest in the god. The song urges its listeners to seek out their inner Pan, to inhabit their bodies fully as they dance and breathe deeply as in meditation. Musically, the song suggests the god's presence through the wild fiddling of Steve Wickham. In his memoir *Adventures of a Waterboy* (2012; revised and reissued as *Adventures of a Waterboy Remastered* in 2017), Scott describes 'The Pan Within' as 'an occult love song, the premise and title of which come from Dion Fortune's writings'.[87] Just as Fortune does in *The Goat Foot God*, Scott's song encourages us to connect with our inner instinctive life. In 1986, shortly after the song was released, Scott had a personal experience of Pan as he was returning to the mainland from the Aran Islands. Walking up the stairs after a trip to the bathroom, Scott glimpsed a mysterious *'goat-like face in the mirror'*, which he at once recognized as Pan. At the same time, he realized the face was also his own.[88] Reflecting on the experience in his memoir, he describes a sudden understanding that *'Pan is an archetypal power deep inside all human beings,'* awakened during his time in the primeval atmosphere of Aran.[89] Scott's vision inspired 'The Return of Pan', the lead single from the Waterboys' album *Dream Harder* (1993). In it, Scott describes seeing Pan and looking into his eyes. The song refers to the ancient story of Pan's death, setting the event during a storm at sea at the time of Christ's birth, rather than the Crucifixion, but concludes by affirming the god's enduring presence on the Aran isle of Inisheer. Pan's return is evoked powerfully by the sound of clarinet balancing the hard-rocking guitar at the beginning of the song, as well as by the flute and drums at the end. In 1994 Scott's spiritual quest took him to the community at Findhorn, an involvement that would lead him to do archival research and write the introduction to *The Gentleman and the Faun* (2009), a collection of Robert Ogilvie Crombie's writings, talks and recollections.[90] On the Waterboys' album *An Appointment with Mr Yeats* (2011), Scott included a setting of Yeats's Pan poem 'News for the Delphic Oracle'. He wrote a brief introduction to the poem for the *Irish Times*, identifying it as his favourite Yeats poem and praising its 'visceral evocation of Pan'.[91] The Waterboys' album *Where the Action Is* (2019) includes a track called 'Piper at the Gates of Dawn', featuring Scott reading from *The Wind in the Willows* over evocative piano and drums.

Van Morrison and Paul Weller have written their own hymns to Pan. Van Morrison's 'Piper at the Gates of Dawn' from *The Healing Game* (1997) pays homage to *The Wind in the Willows*, repeating the title of both chapter and book amid a lyrical re-imagining of the adventures of Mole and Rat. The singer's powerful bluesy voice has a beautiful counterpoint in the acoustic instrumentation, with the haunting sound of uilleann pipes suggesting the god's presence at the end. His inclusion of these traditional bagpipes is also an act of cultural translation, a distinctly Irish reimagining of Grahame's Edwardian English idyll in a more positive way than in James Stephens's *The Crock of Gold*. 'Pan' by Paul Weller, former lead singer of the Jam and the Style Council, appears on his solo album *As Is Now* (2005). The song begins by praising Pan as god of the dawn, and ends by wondering if he is in fact the Creator. Pan is invoked by the subtle flute music that winds through the song's piano and choral accompaniment. Like Van Morrison's, Weller's Pan is very much the Piper at the Gates of Dawn, and it is perhaps fitting that the singer dubbed 'the Modfather' should be drawn to this quintessentially English vision of the god.

Given his outsider status, Pan has also proven attractive to several alternative bands, as well as to the British electronic music that has come to be known as 'hauntology'. As its name suggests, such music is haunted by the sounds of decades past, suggesting possible futures that never came to be. One artist central to musical hauntology is the Focus Group, a project of the musician and graphic artist Julian House, who runs the label Ghost Box with the producer and composer Jim Jupp. The music of the Focus Group is characterized by sonic arrangements that incorporate looping and sampling of television, film and radio from the 1960s and '70s, including soundtracks to Hammer films and public information programmes.[92] On its website, Ghost Box describes itself as 'a record label for a group of artists exploring the misremembered musical history of a parallel world'.[93] That world is clearly one in which Pan feels at home. The title of the Focus Group's album *We Are All Pan's People* (2007) alludes to the dance troupe Pan's People, a staple on British television in the 1970s. Its cover art centres on a bright blue Pan figure, dancing and holding a musical pipe, surrounded by other dancers; an image suggestive of a horned figure appears in the accompanying booklet, where Pan's name is given in a mysterious context on the final page. The 49-second track 'Pan Calling' features several flute tracks looping eerily against one another; the flute motif continues on the next track, the enigmatically titled 'Through the Green Lens', evoking a natural scene replete with bird songs and splashing – perhaps the sound of a mole and rat paddling down a river. The album's title track repeats an electronic beat-melody over which are heard a variety of hard-to-define sounds (including, possibly, the bleating of a goat), culminating with what sounds like a harpsichord. That 'misremembered musical history' continually opens up vistas on a world presided over by the Great God, evoked through a variety of uncanny soundscapes.

Jupp's own musical project, Belbury Poly, has recorded two Pan-themed tracks infused with a haunting atmosphere. 'Pan's Garden,' from *The Owl's Map* (2006), takes its title from a book of nature stories by Algernon Blackwood. The track overlays clarinet and flute over a jaunty, galloping rhythm, which dissolves into a mysterious collage of electronic and animal sounds. *The Belbury Tales* (2012) features 'Goat Foot', with a pounding bassline and archaic-sounding melody suggesting Pan's followers. In an interview about his most recent album, *The Gone Away* (2020), Jupp describes trying to capture in music the experience of 'A sudden burst of fear. It doesn't build up, it just hits you. I think it's what they used to call "panic terror" in old, weird fiction stories.'[94] Jupp also cites Arthur Machen as an influence, and *The Owl's Map* includes a track called 'The Scarlet Ceremony', an allusion to Machen's story 'The White People'. As we saw in Chapter Four, that story also provided the title for John Ireland's piano piece 'The Scarlet Ceremonies'.

Other twenty-first-century artists drawn to Pan have tended to come from an experimental or explicitly Pagan perspective. Animal Collective, an alternative American band from Maryland, tapped into the visionary tradition with 'I See You Pan', from the album *Hollinndagain* (2002). The first three-and-a-half minutes of this ten-minute track sound like a radio trying to tune in to another world, before the gradual emergence of what sounds like an electronic pan pipe. Against this soundscape, we begin to hear a short lyric cryptically urging Pan to look away. The Wisconsin-based electronic musician Sd Laika (Peter Runge) included a track called 'Great God Pan' on his album *That's Harakiri* in 2014. For much of the track a synthesized panpipe melody hints at the god against a background of digital sounds. The Canadian rock band Blood Ceremony makes what its British label Rise Above Records describes as 'flute-tinged witch rock'.[95] Deeply immersed in occult literature as well as the folk and rock music of the late 1960s and early 1970s, Blood Ceremony has recorded two Pan-themed tracks, 'Hymn to Pan' and 'The Great God Pan'. As these titles suggest, the band is attracted to the darker side of the god explored by Aleister Crowley and Arthur Machen. In 'Hymn to Pan', the final track on the band's self-titled debut from 2009, pounding electric guitar and flute combine with Alia O'Brien's vocals to question the disappearance of the gods and to summon Pan in all his hard-rocking glory. 'The Great God Pan' (from *Living with the Ancients*, 2011) describes a ritual evocation of the god in a heavy-metal-inflected performance that culminates in a haunting organ melody accompanied by bass and drums. If the Focus Group and Belbury Poly tune in to sounds from a parallel world, Blood Ceremony broadcasts directly from a dimension created by *The Wicker Man*, Black Sabbath, Arthur Machen, M. R. James and Sylvia Townsend Warner, whose *Lolly Willowes* inspired their 2019 single of that name.

COMICS AND CHILDREN'S FICTION

Pan has made occasional appearances in American comic books, and in a few stories he is a major presence. The Marvel Comics series *Tales to Astonish* (1959–68) featured bizarre tales of alien and supernatural encounters, emerging from the same cultural milieu as *The Twilight Zone*. Issue no. 6 (1959) featured a classic Pan story written by Stan Lee and illustrated by Steve Ditko, 'I Laughed at the Great God Pan'. The narrator is a rather sleazy figure named Norman who pretends to be an art critic in order to impress young women. He takes his date, a woman named Diane, to the museum, where he claims people value paintings because they are too ignorant to see that most art is ugly or ridiculous. When he singles out a portrait of Pan for especial ridicule, Diane protests that she actually likes it.[96] (It's worth noting that Diane's name suggests the moon goddess, who as Selene was more literally seduced by Pan.) A security guard interrupts, chastising the man for his criticism of the painting. The guard recounts Pan's exploits helping the other gods to defeat the Titans by instilling panic in them, as well as his assistance at the Battle of Marathon.[97] In Lee's retelling, Pan turns the Persian weapons into harmless things such as flowers and bananas.[98] As a result of their victory, the Athenians worship Pan in a cave on the Acropolis. Norman is distinctly unimpressed, but when he meets Diane a few weeks later, he has lost his moustache and much of his hair. Now he knows that he should never have mocked the painting of Pan, and recalls turning to look back at the guard as they left the gallery. In place of boots, Norman saw an anatomical detail (surely familiar by now) that revealed the guard's true identity.[99] As with many Pan stories from the early twentieth century, a failure to understand and honour the god has unwanted consequences for the offender, although in this case the effect is comical rather than harmful.

In 1987–8, DC Comics' *Wonder Woman* featured a story arc called 'Challenge of the Gods', written and illustrated by George Pérez, that offers an original take on the theme of Pan's death. Pan had first appeared in the story immediately before, 'Rebirth', in which the Olympians are celebrating Wonder Woman's restoration of their world after defeating Ares, but at a terrible cost to herself.[100] Hermes suggests sending her to the Paradise Island of Themyscira to be healed, and Pan's salacious interest is awoken by the thought of an island of women.[101] This Pan is the pastoral god in his most debased, goat-like aspect. Pérez draws Pan in his traditional form, but with a hairy back and a receding hairline suggestive of middle-aged lechery. After being healed in the ocean, Wonder Woman is sent back to Themyscira, where she is the

Princess Diana (bearing the name of a moon goddess), daughter of Queen Hippolyte.[102] Part iii of 'Challenge of the Gods', 'Paradise Lost', opens with Pan playing joyfully on his pipes. Dionysus suggests to Eos that Pan hopes to advise Zeus regarding the Amazons, in whom he has taken a prurient interest.[103] Pan succeeds in persuading Zeus to direct his amorous attention towards the Amazons, and the goddesses Artemis and Hestia plan to stop him with the help of Hera and Athena.[104] When Zeus attempts to seduce Diana she refuses, and the divine wrath is directed first against her and then at her mother Hippolyte, who has come to rescue her. Only the divine intervention of Hera spares the two Amazons.[105] Diana is summoned to Mount Olympus, where Zeus decrees her punishment: she is to fight the demons that live below Paradise Island, a punishment Pan claims is a waste of her beauty.[106] In the opening scene of Part iv, 'Fire Torment', Pan counsels Zeus that the defeat of Diana will make the remaining Amazons less likely to resist his advances.[107] Meanwhile, Diana lies exhausted from fighting a seven-headed Hydra, and is kept in a healing sleep by the god Morpheus.[108] Hippolyte, interpreting the arrival of a vulture as an omen, departs to help her daughter – a move that is viewed with suspicion by Pan, who fears having his real motives exposed to the other gods.[109]

In Part v, 'Echoes of the Past', Pan has descended to the Cavern of Doom, where he plays on his pipes to animate a skeleton army to fight Hippolyte as she follows the vulture deep underground.[110] She succeeds in fighting them off, and proceeds deeper into the cavern to face new challenges. Diana soon encounters Pan herself, not realizing his evil intentions, and he sends her to the Green Lantern's citadel for her next adventure, warning her to beware of the Manhunters. In the next issue, 'Demonplague', Heracles discovers a horned skull deep in the Cavern of Doom. When he returns to Olympus, Zeus and the other gods are shocked – the skull is that of Hermes' son, the god Pan himself![111] Hermes journeys to the citadel of the Green Lantern, where he reveals to Wonder Woman that she has been tricked by an imposter.[112] Back on Olympus, Zeus and the other gods lament being deceived by this Pan-pretender, who turns out to be a kind of 'Anti-Pan', to use Roc's phrase.[113] Diana returns to the cavern, where she rescues her mother from a Cyclops, slays a half-woman, half-serpent demon called Echidna, and is saved from the Minotaur when said Cyclops eats it.[114] The vulture that led Hippolyte turns out to be the goddess Harmonia, who tells the two Amazons that Zeus had long been aware of Pan's cave of demons, but in his madness did nothing.[115] She gives Diana an amulet containing the demonic powers released by Pandora, which she in turn surrenders to Ares.[116] At the end of the issue, Hermes appears to Diana, asking her to avenge the slaying of Pan by a Manhunter.[117]

The false Pan of Pérez's story definitely belongs to Patricia Merivale's 'sinister Pan' tradition, a lecherous and malevolent deceiver – but of course, he's not really Pan at all. The fate of the real Pan is narrated by Hermes in a story called 'Tribute', which appeared in the *Wonder Woman Annual* for 1989.[118] In it, we learn that Pan was attacked by a Manhunter who suddenly appeared on Olympus.[119] Although he fought bravely, Pan was killed and his body cast down into the caves below Themyscira, where it was devoured by the blind cyclops Polyphemus.[120] The shape-shifting Manhunter assumes the form of Pan and the remaining Olympians are none the wiser.[121] The imposter Pan is finally slain by Wonder Woman in the *Millennium* crossover series (no. 7), when she slices the disguised android Manhunter in half with her magic lasso.[122]

An authentic but fading Pan appears in the popular series of children's books *Percy Jackson and the Olympians* (2005–9) by the American author Rick Riordan. Pan has gone missing, and the satyrs are trying to locate him. Percy's best friend, the satyr Grover Underwood, receives a 'searcher's license' in the first book in the series, *Percy Jackson and the Lightning Thief* (2005), entitling him to join the hunt for the goat-foot god.[123] Pan actively intervenes – although he does not appear – in the third book of the series, *Percy Jackson and the Titan's Curse* (2007). After slaying the Nemean lion, Percy and his companions flee to Cloudcroft, New Mexico, where Grover senses that it is Pan who has sent the Erymanthian boar that enables them to flee the pursuing 'spartoi', fearsome skeleton warriors.[124] The experience of Pan causes Grover to pass out. In the fourth book in the series, *Percy Jackson and the Battle of the Labyrinth* (2008), Grover and Tyson, Percy's cyclops half-brother, team up to go in search of Pan. After a harrowing encounter with Kronos in the fortress of the Titans, Percy and his companions flee into the Labyrinth of Daedalus, where they find Grover lying unconscious with Tyson watching over him; he has had a powerful sense that Pan is nearby.[125] They cross an underground river and enter a cavern encrusted with crystals and filled with exotic flora and extinct animals.[126]

At its centre is a bed, upon which reclines the Great God Pan, with piercing blue eyes: 'His curly hair was white and so was his pointed beard. Even the goat fur on his legs was frosted with grey.'[127] This is an elderly Pan, with a shimmering form. He has large horns and his pipes lie beside him. When Grover apologizes to Pan for taking so long to find him, the god's laughter inspires joy and hope. Pan tells his visitors that he has slept for ages and had sinister dreams, but now his time is nearly finished.[128] Grover protests, but

Pan tells him that he had previously sent another satyr, two millennia ago, to make that announcement, and Percy's friend Annabeth (who is Athena's daughter) briefly retells the story of Pan's death recorded in Plutarch.[129] Riordan is original in making the source of this story Pan himself, announcing his death to the world through a satyr proxy. It turns out to be the refusal of the satyrs to accept his death that is keeping Pan in this state of half-life. He explains that as a god, his death is more of a fading away.[130] He has vanished from the world because the wilderness has all but disappeared, and tells them it is now up to others to restore the wild to the world: 'The spirit of the wild must pass to you now. You must tell each one you meet: if you would find Pan, take up Pan's spirit. Remake the wild, a little at a time, each in your own corner of the world. You cannot wait for anyone else, even a god, to do that for you.'[131] Riordan's Pan leaves us with a strong ecological message, urging us each to make our own contribution to rebuilding the wilderness. As his form finally disperses, the plants and animals that had surrounded Pan's bed turn to dust, but not before the spirit of Pan has entered Percy and his friends – although Percy thinks Grover may have received a little more than the others. The satyr will go on to use his Pan energy to sow confusion among their enemies.

FILM AND TELEVISION

Pan has had a rather spotty career in film and television, usually appearing in his darker aspects and often in ways that blur his real identity. *The Magician*, directed by Rex Ingram, features a hallucinatory vision of Pan, played by the American dancer Hubert Julian Stowitts. The film is based on a novel from 1908 by W. Somerset Maugham, in which a young woman named Margaret Dauncey is seduced by the magician of the title, a sinister occultist named Oliver Haddo. The character of Haddo is a satirical portrait of none other than Aleister Crowley, who was not amused – he wrote a scathing review of the novel for *Vanity Fair* (under the pseudonym 'Oliver Haddo'!) that accused Maugham of plagiarism.[132] The scene in the film vividly dramatizes a bacchanal set in a hellish landscape, in which Margaret sees an uncanny-looking tree torn by wind and storms:

> in a moment she grew sick with fear, for a change came into the tree, and the tremulousness of life was in it; the rough bark was changed into brutish flesh and the twisted branches into human arms. It became a monstrous, goat-legged thing, more vast than the creatures of nightmare. She saw the horns and the long beard, the great hairy legs with their hoofs, and the man's rapacious hands. The face was horrible with lust and cruelty, and yet it was divine. It was Pan, playing on his pipes, and the lecherous eyes caressed her with hideous tenderness.[133]

As played by Stowitts, Pan is human-sized, and the tree has become a bizarre, expressionist-looking backdrop for the god's prancing. He initially appears playing his pipes atop a twisted scene of human suffering. When we next see him, his shaggy legs and hooves have become human legs, and he is carrying the body of a woman in his arms. As soon as he sees Margaret (played by Alice Terry), he drops the body and rushes towards her with leering eyes, grabbing at her until she suddenly wakes to find herself back in Haddo's presence.[134] Although Maugham's novel and the film itself clearly identify this figure as Pan, he is Pan in his most devilish guise.

Hubert 'Jay' Stowitts (1892–1953) as a diabolical Pan
in *The Magician* (1926), directed by Rex Ingram.

In film, just as in fiction, Pan can play his part in comedy as easily as in horror. In the musical comedy *Merry Andrew* (1958), directed by Michael Kidd, Danny Kaye plays a school-master and would-be archaeologist named Andrew Larabee, who hopes to find a statue of Pan that he believes was buried by the Romans in Sussex. Larabee believes that if he can locate the statue he can become a professional archaeologist and afford to marry his fiancée, Letitia (played by Patricia Cutts). The film includes one lively song about the goat-foot god, 'The Pipes of Pan', which Larabee sings with his pupils to teach them about the god. As the convoluted plot unfolds, Larabee finds himself engaged to the daughter of a circus ringmaster. Her name, tellingly, is Selena (she is played by Pier Angeli), the name of the moon goddess seduced by Pan. The statue of Pan is eventually found by a chimpanzee, and subsequently recovered by Larabee's brothers, who are able to track him down to the circus. There, he must choose between respectability and marriage to Letitia, or following his heart and a life in the circus with Selena.

Pan is one of several forms taken by the enigmatic Dr Lao in the comic fantasy 7 Faces of Dr Lao, directed by George Pal and based on a novel by Charles G. Finney, The Circus of Dr Lao (1935). Played by a heavily made-up Tony Randall, Dr Lao arrives in Abalone, a town in the Old West, to advertise his circus in the local paper run by Ed Cunningham (played by John Ericson). Cunningham is challenging the business-man Clint Stark (played by Arthur O'Connell), who wishes to buy the whole town, and unsuccessfully woos the town schoolteacher and librarian, Angela Benedict (played by Barbara Eden). Lao's circus holds up a mirror to the towns-people, and each encounter with one of Lao's '7 faces' reveals the truth about the visitor. When Angela enters Pan's tent, he begins playing on his pipes and dancing with wild aban-don, until his form changes to resemble Ed Cunningham – still Pan, but with Ed's face. Angela becomes increasingly hot and bothered, unbuttoning her blouse as the transformed Pan dances around her. He eventually places a grape in her mouth, but just as they are about to kiss, a group of visitors enters the tent and Pan's form reverts to Tony Randall. Angela flees, and when the guide introduces Pan to the new group, he lets out a comical bleat. The novel had a satyr rather than Pan, but Pal's alteration works well in the film and offers a rare comic portrayal of the god. His lascivious behaviour with Angela serves a deeper purpose, making her realize her feelings and desire for Ed. Later in the film, Angela is tor-mented by the sound of Pan's music, which she cannot get out of her head as she tosses and turns in bed. When we last see Pan, he is riding a donkey and playing his pipes in Lao's grand finale. Pan's face does, however, make an appearance alongside the other six faces of Lao on the Loch Ness monster as it chases two of Stark's henchmen out of town. We also hear the music of Pan's pipes as Ed and Angela are united in the film's final scene. The film's use of racist stereotypes in portraying Dr Lao (as well as in having a Chinese character played by a white actor) is both offensive and dated, but *7 Faces* is original in playing up the comedic potential inherent in Pan's pastoral character.

Two British horror films take inspiration from the modern cult of Pan, even if he is not represented directly. The cultural historian David Huckvale, in his book *A Green and Pagan Land* (2018), suggests that the figure of Pan lurks behind 'the Goat of Mendes' who appears in the Hammer film *The Devil Rides Out* (1968).[135] Although glimpsed only briefly, the shaggy

Tony Randall as Pan in *The 7 Faces of Dr Lao* (1964). Pan was one of Dr Lao's seven 'faces'. He helps a repressed school teacher named Angela Benedict realize the strength of her feelings for newspaperman Edward Cunningham.

goat looms over a Satanic ritual conducted by the evil Mocata (Charles Gray). Tigon British Film Productions' *The Blood on Satan's Claw* (1971; released as *Satan's Skin* in America) tells the story of a village that gradually comes to serve a demon who has been awakened from his sleep beneath an English field. Huckvale notes several plot parallels between the film and the novel *The Blessing of Pan* by Lord Dunsany.[136] Just as Tommy's piping first lures the young people of the village to worship Pan in Dunsany's novel, Angel Blake (Linda Hayden) initially brings her young neighbours into her Satanic cult. Both novel and film culminate in a sacrifice, although in *The Blessing of Pan* it is a bull rather than a young woman who is offered up.[137] The demon himself is barely seen in the film, though his hair-covered face and large claws suggest a very different creature from Pan.

The concluding story of the eighth season of *Doctor Who* (1971), 'The Daemons', written by Guy Leopold, features a goat-legged, horned alien named Azal who is being reawakened by the Master (disguised as the new vicar) in a village ominously named Devil's End.[138] Leopold's story adapts Margaret Murray's theory of the Horned God for science fiction. In episode 3, the Doctor (played by Jon Pertwee) presents a slide show to explain to the UNIT officers and local witch Miss Hawthorne (played by Damaris Hayman) that the horned gods of world mythology are in fact memories of the Daemons. His slides include the Egyptian god Khnum, a Hindu demon, Palaeolithic cave art and Goya's painting *Witches' Sabbath*. The Doctor explains that such creatures have been seen throughout history and that 'man has turned them into gods or devils, but they're neither. They are in fact creatures from another world.'[139] Although he is not named, one of these gods is clearly Pan, a possibility supported by the Daemons' activity while on Earth. The Daemons, from the planet Daemos, initially arrived on Earth to help *Homo sapiens* displace Neanderthals, then intervened in Greek civilization, the Renaissance and the Industrial Revolution. The reference to their intervention in ancient Greece suggests Pan's appearance to Philippides and his assistance against the Persians. Although we can imagine Pan encouraging the rebirth of Greek culture, as the god of nature he would certainly not inspire the Industrial Revolution, an intervention that shows the Daemons are to some extent distinct from him. Despite leaving a giant hoofprint in a farmer's field, Azal himself does not have any special connection to pastoral life, and his summons by the Master and his coven closely resembles a demonic invocation. 'The Daemons' belongs to the same British cultural moment as *The Wicker Man* or *The Blood on Satan's Claw*, complete with witchcraft and Morris dancers. Although he resembles Pan physically, Azal is a genuinely

Pan's People was a popular British dance troupe that performed on *Top of the Pops* in the 1960s and '70s. Pictured here (from left to right) are Barbara 'Babs' Lord, Sue Menhenick, Dee Dee Wilde, Cherry Gilllespie and Ruth Pearson.

sinister figure who plans to destroy humanity as a failed
experiment.

Viewers of *Top of the Pops* from the late 1960s to the mid-
1970s enjoyed the groovy dance moves of Pan's People, a
troupe whose core members included Babs Lord, Dee Dee
Wilde, Ruth Pearson, Louise Clarke and Cherry Gillespie.[140]
Emerging out of a dance group simply called the Beat Girls,
they adopted the name at the end of 1966 after rejecting
'Dionysus's Darlings'.[141] The dancers performed to pop music,
particularly songs by artists who were unavailable to perform
on the show. Although tame by today's standards, in their
time the troupe's dance moves and sexy costumes were considered risqué. (Several of their performances can be viewed
on YouTube, uploaded by admiring fans.) They captured the
glamour and sexual freedom associated with early 1970s rock
and disco. Just as Pan's troupe of nymphs entranced the male
viewer with their dancing, Pan's People cast an alluring spell
over many in the *Top of the Pops* family audience – teenagers
and fathers alike.

In twenty-first-century film, the dark fantasy released in
English as *Pan's Labyrinth* (2006), directed by Guillermo del
Toro, is further on the outskirts of the Pan tradition. Its original Spanish-language title is *El laberinto del fauno*, literally
'The Labyrinth of the Faun', and del Toro himself has said
that the film has nothing to do with Pan.[142] The change in title
probably has to do with the fact that in English 'faun' is a
homonym for 'fawn', inappropriately conjuring up images
of Bambi for anglophone audiences. In the film, the strange
and sinister-looking faun sets three tasks for a young girl
named Ofelia (played by Ivana Baquero) to complete in order
to regain her immortality and be restored to her original
kingdom, where she was once Princess Moanna. The faun
proves to be a helper and a guide, rather than an antagonist,

but the film as a whole plays with Patricia Merivale's 'sinister Pan' tradition, provoking fear and more than a few moments of panic on Ofelia's behalf. Del Toro later wrote the foreword to a selection of tales by Arthur Machen published in 2011, revealing his own deep immersion in the work of a major precursor in tales of supernatural terror.[143]

A lecherous and leering Pan (also known as 'Satyre') appears in *Sa majesté minor* (His Majesty Minor; 2007), directed by Jean-Jacques Annaud. Pan/Satyre is played with grotesquely comic relish by Vincent Cassel. Set on an Aegean island before the dawn of Greek civilization, the film is a celebration of hedonism and unrestrained sexuality. Its protagonist is the hapless Minor (played by José Garcia), a rustic innocent raised by pigs, who falls in love with the beautiful Clytia (Mélanie Bernier). Clytia is already engaged to Karkos (Sergio Peris-Mencheta), and Minor finds himself driven out of the village along with his swine. He meets Satyre/Pan, who takes a sexual interest in him (along with any other humans he encounters). When Minor returns to his village, he has learned the power of eloquent speech, attracting the attention of Clytia and the wrath of Karkos. The film was a critical and commercial failure, in spite of Annaud's bold attempt to adapt the pagan sensuality of Pan's world for the cinema.

DEPTH PSYCHOLOGY

With its interest in mythology as a repository of archetypal images and patterns, it is no surprise that the depth psychology pioneered by Carl Jung (1875–1961) has turned to Pan to gain insight into the human psyche. In the *Vision Seminar*, 1930–31, Jung offered some reflections on Pan in light of the god's appearance in the visions of a puritanical young woman, who saw herself 'worshipping a sort of Pan, a huge satyr, a god of nature'.[144] These visions compensated for her conscious attitude, which took a negative view of her instinctive life. For Jung, 'the god Pan is obviously a nature spirit, a sort of philosophical nature god.'[145] He not only identifies Pan with the phallic god Priapus, but compares him to the Roman god Saturnus, who like Pan rose from humble origins to become a more cosmic god, in Saturnus' case one identified with Chronos.[146] Jung's attitude to Pan is positive, and he refers to him as 'the life-giver, the great god Pan'.[147] Nonetheless, Pan also embodied the primal experience of sudden fear as it was first known in pastoral Arcadia, which Jung surprisingly identifies with Pan's music: 'Pan's flute created the panic fear of the shepherds. The word panic comes from Pan. He went about whistling or playing his pipe and frightening the shepherds. The shepherd's fear is like the stampede of the herds.'[148] Just as a herd of animals can suddenly be overwhelmed by fear, so 'one is suddenly seized with terror without knowing why. Sometimes it is a particularly lonely and uncanny spot, but at other times one cannot say what it is, a kind of animal fear seizes one. It is the great god Pan that causes the panic terror.'[149] Pan gives life, but life can at times be a source of terror, particularly if approached with an attitude of mistrust or hostility. Jung's notion that Pan used his music to frighten shepherds is not borne out by classical sources, but the connection he draws between Pan and 'a kind of animal fear' like that which causes a herd to stampede is consistent with what we know the ancients attributed to the god. As we have seen, E. M. Forster also plays with this connection in the stampede of tourists that takes place in 'The Story of a Panic' (see Chapter Four).

James Hillman (1926–2011) developed his own 'Archetypal Psychology' out of Jung's ideas, emphasizing the role of myth in revealing the many fantasies that form our psyches, and the role of the psyche in shaping those fantasies. He is a controversial figure among Jungians for rejecting Jung's developmental framework and treating the psyche as a shifting network of fantasies.[150] Jungians are particularly critical of Hillman's claim to offer the archetypal perspective of the *puer eternus*, the 'eternal youth' who never grows up or develops, the archetype behind such figures as Peter Pan. Given Hillman's commitment to this point of view, it is no surprise that he was particularly drawn to the god Pan himself. In *Pan and the Nightmare* (1972; revised 2007), Hillman explores the way Pan manifests in the individual modern psyche. He begins by arguing that the polytheism of Greece offers the possibility of reintegrating 'unconscious imagination' into psyches unbalanced by Western emphasis on the unified conscious ego, itself a product of centuries of monotheistic culture.[151] Hillman looks back to the pioneering work of Wilhelm Heinrich Roscher, whose *Ephialtes* he includes in translation as the second part of his book. For Hillman, Roscher's key psychological insight is his recognition that the Pan archetype embodies 'panic and nightmare'.[152] Considering Pan as a god of nature, Hillman argues that he is the embodiment of 'behaviour at its most nature bound'.[153] Such behaviour is 'wholly impersonal, objective, ruthless', and as such belongs to the non-human worlds of the animal and the divine.[154]

To make sense of the irrationality of dreams and myth, Hillman insists that we must acknowledge the non-verbal imagery that arises in the unconscious and produces such strange figures as Pan. Our rejection of nature and the imaginal world of the unconscious is symbolized in Plutarch's account of the death of Pan. For Hillman, this tale signals a major break in the human psyche: 'nature had become deprived of its creative voice. It was no longer an independent force of generativity. What had had Soul, lost it; or lost was the psychic connection with nature.'[155] As the god of nature, Pan is also the god of nature within us, which manifests as instinct. The feeling of panic that he induces 'will also be seen to be the right response to the numinous', experienced most vividly in nightmares when the dreamer is paralysed amid seemingly autonomous dream presences.[156] Hillman devotes a chapter to masturbation, a habit that Pan allegedly taught to solitary shepherds. He notes that while it is a practice shared by humans and animals, for humans it is associated with both fantasy and guilt – inspired by Pan but threatened with punishment by the Judaeo-Christian God, who in the Bible famously struck down Onan for spilling his seed.[157] Hillman's discussion of rape is the most disturbing part of his analysis. He confronts us with the mythical reality of Pan's attempted rapes, noting that these included the shepherd Daphnis as well as nymphs.[158] Considering Pan's attempted rapes of several nymphs, Hillman writes that 'Pan brings body, goat-body. He forces the sexual reality of physical generation upon a structure of consciousness that has no personal physical life, whose life is all "out there" in physical nature.'[159] Although Hillman is careful to identify the nymphs with preconscious nature, the gender dynamics his interpretation implies here are problematic, to say the least, as is his insistence that, for the psychologist, rape can only ever be a 'metaphor' for the inner world of fantasy.

Hillman does offer a more nuanced account of the nymphs in his chapter devoted to them, noting that 'Syrinx, Echo, and Pitys – who sighs . . . or moans when the wind blows through the pine trees – are the sounds of nature. The nymphs reflect nature to the ear. They teach listening, and listening stops compulsion.'[160] That compulsion is, of course, embodied by Pan, who also spends much of his time listening and watching, so the different instincts embodied by Pan and the nymphs are inextricably linked. Within our psyche Pan and the nymphs provoke reflection, which transforms raw stimulus into meaningful experience and is therefore crucial to the development of culture.[161] Hillman argues that the mythical contest between Pan and Eros symbolizes the contest between impersonal instinct and love itself, but that the reflection provoked by Pan is also a central impetus to consciousness and civilization. Hillman claims that we reject Pan whenever we choose civilized values over brutal experience: 'The struggle between Eros and Pan, and Eros' victory, continues to put Pan down each time we say a nightmare is a bad dream, rape violates relatedness, masturbation is inferior to intercourse, love better than fear, the goat uglier than the hare.'[162] As twenty-first-century readers, we may well resist some of these claims (when *doesn't* rape violate relatedness?). For Hillman, however, these Pan experiences precede ethical reflection, which is precisely why they are usually judged as threatening civilized values. The psychologist, he says, must deal with them on their own terms. Hillman points to Pan's connection to our growing ecological awareness, noting that some American officials (in the 1970s, when he was first writing about Pan) were threatened by the environmental movement in part because they saw it as fundamentally pagan in character. The panic and instinctual responses inspired by Pan reveal his close connection to the experience of spontaneity, a source of joy in life and a necessary adaptive response. In his final chapter, Hillman suggests that coming to terms with the power of nature both inside and outside ourselves will help to heal the gap between them – as Socrates prayed.

In her study *The Archetypal Pan in America: Hypermasculinity and Terror* (2018), the psychotherapist Sukey Fontelieu turns to the myths of Pan to help us understand America in the twenty-first century. She observes that contemporary American culture oscillates wildly between 'panic and apathy', responses that correspond to the terror induced by Pan as well as the god's self-absorption in his own desires. As an example, she points to the American response to the terrorist attacks on 9/11 – attacks by the military on Afghanistan (and Iraq) and an immersion in consumerism by the civilian population.[163] For Fontelieu, the pattern of panicked and apathetic responses to public crises such as mass shootings and rape in the military point to a cultural complex animated by the Pan archetype. After an overview of Plutarch's story of Pan's death, noting that the scholars of Tiberius concluded that the Pan who died must be a *daemon* distinct from the god, she observes that Eusebius took the process even further, making this *daemon* a 'demon' or evil spirit: 'The voices of the earlier polytheistic religions advocating for the plurality of the psyche, were overpowered by the Christian myth of one god and one devil, especially in the New Testament.'[164]

Fontelieu's interpretations of the myths of Pan are rooted in an attentive reading of the surviving texts, allowing for a corrective to some of Hillman's generalizations. Although Hillman and other Jungians have frequently identified Pan as a rapist, Fontelieu notes that Pan's attempts always fail.[165] She connects Pan's affinity for the wilderness with his isolation, while observing that his association with caves connects him to the chthonic powers within the earth.[166] Fontelieu points out that collectively the nymphs are able to soothe Pan's aggressions through music and dance, but that as individuals they become his sexual prey. Despite this, 'Pan's conquests were only successful when the desire was mutual.'[167] She also cites less common versions of the myths, such as Nonnos' story that Syrinx escaped being a reed forever and joined the retinue of Dionysus, regaining her freedom.[168] Reflecting on the militarism of American culture, Fontelieu turns to the stories of Pan's own military interventions, where he instilled panic in armies of invading Persians and Gauls, much as the United States attempted to create panic in its aptly named 'Shock and Awe' invasion of Iraq in 2002.[169] Pan's influence is felt domestically as well, with large increases in the number of Americans diagnosed with anxiety disorders over the last two decades.[170] Although the myths of Pan often focus on his violence and self-absorption, Fontelieu emphasizes that he can also be an inspiring dancer and musician when in balance with the nymphs. The ancient Arcadian ritual of beating an image of Pan with squills when hunting was unsuccessful suggests the practice of scapegoating, but at the same time highlights Pan's archetypal connection to fertility and strength.

Pan's presence in our contemporary era embodies many contradictions, as he has from his earliest emergence into history. As we come closer to the present day, some of the ways he has been imagined have become less tenable; Frank O'Hara, for example, was the last major poet to treat him as a symbol of sexual liberation. His mythological role as a would-be ravisher of nymphs makes him a figure whom contemporary feminist writers reject, focusing instead on the experience of those nymphs he pursues. For the tradition of depth psychology, Pan's problematic sexuality and its connection to fear and violence make it urgently necessary to explore the implications his archetype has for ourselves and for society. These darker aspects of the Pan tradition inform some of his appearances in popular culture, while others focus on the god's role as guardian of the wild. Pan's traditional role of protector of the flocks was extended by Kenneth Grahame to include all animals; for many New Age practitioners, Pan's guardianship now extends to the world of plants and flowers. He continues to challenge us to consider the boundaries between the wilderness and civilization, between non-human nature and the spaces we have carved out for ourselves.

Where can Pan be found? You have been searching for him for a long time, have felt his presence deep in the darkness of the forest, and once thought you heard his pipes down by the river. Yet the god himself remains elusive, retreating along with the wild places that were once just a short walk from town. These days, you feel closest to Pan when working in the garden, with the palpable surge of life that emerges with the flowers each spring, and you have even let a corner of the garden run wild in his honour. You can feel Pan's frenzied and ecstatic side in some of the rock music you still enjoy, while the eerier aspects of the god come through in the haunting electronic music you've recently started listening to. The psychologists you've read suggest that Pan resides deep in our unconscious mind, but you wonder if he might also be present in the outer world of nature – a bridge between our psyche and the wilderness.

You decide to return to the wild, walking through the old forest that recedes further from town with every passing year, making your way down to the river. If nothing else, there you can enjoy the sound of the water as it eddies around the rocks, and listen to the wind rustling the reeds. As you walk, you recall the myths of Pan and his unsuccessful pursuit of the nymphs. How to reconcile that would-be ravisher with the cosmic god of all? Perhaps there is no way; the contradictions of Pan's traditional appearance, part goat and part man, suggest that his divine nature combines extremes that for us can never be reconciled. And yet, before you begin your journey home, you pause and wonder about those nymphs. What would they say about Pan? What would those myths look like from their point of view? You turn back to the reeds, thinking of Syrinx and her sad fate. You would like to hear her story.

CONCLUSION

As I write this in the autumn of 2020, the world is still in the grip of the global coronavirus pandemic. That word, with its familiar prefix *pan-*, meaning all, implies a disease that has spread everywhere, reflecting the worldwide reach of the virus. The pandemic teaches us that in the twenty-first century we are all interconnected, and no amount of exclusion or scapegoating will alter that fundamental condition of contemporary life. And the scapegoating is real: in America, as President Trump and members of his administration describe SARS-COV-2 as the 'Chinese' or 'Wuhan' virus and COVID-19 as 'Kung flu', threats and actual violence against Asian Americans have increased dramatically. At the same time, Black Lives Matter protestors are being demonized as 'anarchists' and targeted with overwhelming force by federal agents, while immigrant children are isolated from their parents to languish in steel pens at the southern border. In the ancient world, scapegoats were banished to the wilderness, Pan's habitation, whether actual goats – as in Israel – or individuals identified as different or undesirable, as in Greece. They bore the guilt and bad luck of the whole community, although for the Greeks the *pharmakon* could also be a cure. The plight of those scapegoated, symbolically exiled to Pan's wilderness, invites our empathy, but also provides us with the opportunity to reconsider our relationship to 'all' – to choose to co-operate and work towards the greater good rather than to blame and exclude.

That sense of 'all' must extend to Pan's domain, the natural world and its inhabitants. While it is not clear exactly how the coronavirus first spread to humans in the Chinese province of Wuhan, the presence of similar viruses in local bat populations has led some epidemiologists to suggest contact through human encroachment into bat territory, or through intermediary species sold in the illegal wildlife trade. Both possibilities point to an exploitative relationship with other species, mirrored in Western countries where meat-packing plants have been sites of major COVID-19 outbreaks. Those same plants are often staffed by workers belonging to scapegoated populations, such as undocumented immigrants; social and environmental justice are inextricably linked. Kenneth Grahame described 'The Piper at the Gates of Dawn' as 'Friend and Helper', a protector of the wild who can none-theless be a source of fear as well as awe. As global temperatures increase dramatically, with wildfires and rising ocean levels, that fear can easily give way to growing panic. It is up to us whether we allow that panic to overwhelm us, or accept it as a gift from Pan and respond by taking responsibility for the well-being of our planet.

REFERENCES

1 MYTHIC PAN

1 'To Pan', in Homer and Hesiod, *Hesiod. The Homeric Hymns, and Homerica*, trans. Hugh G. Evelyn-White (Loeb Classical Library) (Cambridge, MA, 1914), Hymn XIX, pp. 443–7.
2 Philippe Borgeaud, *The Cult of Pan in Ancient Greece*, trans. Kathleen Atlass and James Redfield (Chicago, IL, 1988), pp. 42–3.
3 Ibid., p. 42.
4 Robert Graves, *The Greek Myths* (Harmondsworth, Middlesex, 1960), vol. I, p. 101.
5 Borgeaud, *Cult of Pan*, pp. 8–9, 19–22.
6 Pausanias, *Description of Greece*, trans. W.H.S. Jones (Loeb Classical Library) (Cambridge, MA, 1918), 8.36.8, p. 83.
7 Ulrich Hübinger, 'On Pan's Iconography and the Cult in the Sanctuary of Pan on the Slopes of Mount Lykaion', in *The Iconography of Greek Cult in the Archaic and Classical Periods: Proceedings of the First International Seminar on Ancient Greek Cult, Organised by the Swedish Institute at Athens and the European Cultural Centre of Delphi (Delphi, 16–18 Novembre 1990)*, ed. Robin Hägg (Liège, 1992), pp. 189–207, https://books.openedition.org.
8 John Boardman, *The Great God Pan: The Survival of an Image* (London, 1997), pp. 29–30.
9 Borgeaud, *Cult of Pan*, pp. 185–7.
10 Edwin L. Brown, 'The Divine Name "Pan"', *Transactions of the American Philological Association*, 107 (1977), pp. 57–61.
11 Willy Alfred Borgeaud, 'Appendix', in P. Borgeaud, *Cult of Pan*, pp. 185–7.

12 Borgeaud, *Cult of Pan*, p. 182.
13 Wendy Doniger, trans., *The Rig Veda* (London, 1981), pp. 194–5.
14 Aaron J. Atsma, 'Pan Cult', www.theoi.com, accessed 6 August 2020.
15 Borgeaud, *Cult of Pan*, p. 65.
16 Atsma, 'Pan Cult'.
17 Peter McDonald, *The Homeric Hymns* (Manchester, 2016), p. 314.
18 'To Pan'.
19 McDonald, *Homeric Hymns*, p. 118.
20 'To Pan'.
21 Borgeaud, *Cult of Pan*, pp. 70–71.
22 'To Pan'.
23 Pindar, *Olympian Odes, Pythian Odes*, trans. William H. Race (Loeb Classical Library) (Cambridge, MA, 1997), Pythian Ode III, p. 253.
24 Herodotus, *The Persian Wars*, trans. A. D. Godley (Cambridge, MA, 1920), VI.105.1, www.perseus.tufts.edu.
25 Plato, *Phaedrus*, trans. Christopher Rowe (London, 2005), p. 68.
26 Boardman, *Great God Pan*, p. 27.
27 Ibid., p. 29.
28 Pausanias, *Description of Greece*, 10.23.7, p. 503.
29 Boardman, *Great God Pan*, p. 29.
30 Ibid., p. 32.
31 Ibid., pp. 33, 36.
32 Ibid., p. 36.
33 Ibid., pp. 36–7.
34 Ibid., p. 34.
35 Robin Lane Fox, *Pagans and Christians* (Harmondsworth, Middlesex, 1998), p. 130.
36 'Pan and Goat', www.theoi.com, accessed 8 August 2020.
37 Mary Beard, 'Pan and the Goat', *Times Literary Supplement*, 2019, www.the-tls.co.uk.
38 Boardman, *Great God Pan*, p. 40.
39 Andrea M. Berlin, 'The Archaeology of Ritual: The Sanctuary of Pan at Banias/Caesarea Philippi', *Bulletin of the American Schools of Oriental Research*, 315 (1999), pp. 27–45.
40 Israel Ministry of Foreign Affairs, 'Bronze Mask of Pan

Uncovered at Hippos-Sussita', www.mfa.gov.il, 19 March
2015.
41 Quoted in Borgeaud, *Cult of Pan*, pp. 23–5.
42 Ibid., p. 26.
43 Ibid., p. 28.
44 Ibid., pp. 29–31.
45 Ibid., p. 42.
46 Ovid, *Metamorphoses*, trans. Mary M. Innes
(Harmondsworth, Middlesex, 1955), pp. 47–8.
47 Ibid., pp. 250–51.
48 Borgeaud, *Cult of Pan*, p. 85.
49 Longus, *Daphnis and Chloe*, trans. The Athenian Society
(1896), https://en.wikisource.org.
50 Nonnos, *Dionysiaca*, trans. W.H.D. Rouse (Loeb Classical
Library) (Cambridge, MA, 1940), 48. 670–88, p. 473.
51 Borgeaud, *Cult of Pan*, pp. 78–9.
52 Ibid., p. 78.
53 Virgil, *Eclogue, Georgics, Aeneid I–VI*, trans. H. Rushton
Fairclough (Loeb Classical Library) (Cambridge, MA, 1916),
Georgics, 3. 390–93, p. 205.
54 Borgeaud, *Cult of Pan*, pp. 57–8.
55 Ibid., p. 100.
56 Nonnos, *Dionysiaca*, I. 368–530, pp. 29–41; 'Aigipan',
www.theoi.com, accessed 8 August 2020.
57 'Panes', www.theoi.com, accessed 8 August 2020.
58 Philostratus, *Apollonius of Tyana*, trans. F. C. Conybeare
(Loeb Classical Library) (Cambridge, MA, 2005), III. 13,
p. 253.
59 'Panes'.
60 Quoted in Patricia Merivale, *Pan the Goat-God: His Myth
in Modern Times* (Cambridge, MA, 1969), p. 2.
61 Theocritus, 'Idyll I, "Thyrsis"', trans. J. M. Edmonds,
www.theoi.com, accessed 8 August 2020.
62 Ibid.
63 Ibid.
64 Theocritus, 'Idyll VII, "Harvest Home"', trans.
J. M. Edmonds, www.theoi.com, accessed
8 August 2020.
65 Virgil, *Eclogue II*, trans. H. R. Fairclough, 'Virgil, Eclogues',
www.theoi.com, accessed 8 August 2020.
66 Ibid.

67 Virgil, *Eclogue x*, trans. H. R. Fairclough, 'Virgil, Eclogues', www.theoi.com, accessed 8 August 2020.

68 Virgil, *Georgics*, 3, 390–93, p. 205.

69 Borgeaud, *Cult of Pan*, pp. 164–8.

70 Menander, *Dyskolos*, trans. Carroll Moulton (New York, 1977), p. 15.

71 Ibid., p. 17.

72 Ibid., p. 21.

73 Ibid., p. 28.

74 Ibid., p. 31.

75 Ibid., pp. 43–51.

76 Ibid., pp. 42–65.

77 Lucius Apuleius, 'The Most Pleasant and Delectable Tale of the Marriage of Cupid and Psyche', in *The Golden Ass*, trans. William Adlington (1566), Books iv–vi, http://sites.fas.harvard.edu/~chaucer.

78 *Daphnis et Chloé*, www.wikipedia.org; *Daphnis and Chloe*, Obelisk, www.arthistoryproject.com, accessed 23 December 2020.

79 Longus, *Daphnis and Chloe*.

80 George Hart, 'Min', in *The Routledge Dictionary of Egyptian Gods and Goddesses* (London, 2005), p. 94.

81 George Hart, 'Benebdjetet', ibid., pp. 44–5.

82 Herodotus, *Persian Wars*, ii.46, p. 2.

83 Ibid.

84 Livy, *History of Rome*, trans. Benjamin Oliver Foster (Loeb Classical Library) (Cambridge, MA, 1919), i.v, p. 21.

85 Harry Thurston Peck, 'Faunalia', in *Harper's Dictionary of Classical Antiquities* (1898), www.perseus.tufts.edu.

86 Apostolos N. Athanassakis and Benjamin M. Wolkow, 'Introduction', in *The Orphic Hymns* (Baltimore, MD, 2013), p. xiv.

87 Robert Graves, *The Greek Myths* (Harmondsworth, Middlesex, 1960), vol. i, pp. 111–15.

88 Athanassakis and Wolkow, 'Introduction', p. xvi.

89 Ibid., p. x.

90 Merivale, *Pan the Goat-God*, p. 29.

91 Athanassakis and Wolkow, 'Introduction', p. xvii.

92 Thomas Taylor, 'The Orphic Hymn to Pan', in Merivale, *Pan the Goat-God*, p. 233.

93 Ibid., pp. 233–4.
94 Ibid., p. 234.
95 Quoted ibid., p. 10.
96 Ibid.
97 Virgil, *Eclogue x*.
98 Plutarch, *De defectu oraculorum*, trans. Frank Cole Babbitt, in *Moralia*, vol. v (Loeb Classical Library) (Cambridge, MA, 1936), 17, pp. 401–3.
99 Graves, *Greek Myths*, vol. i, p. 103.
100 Stephanie Dalley, *Myths from Mesopotamia: Creation, the Flood, Gilgamesh, and Others* (Oxford, 2009), p. 320.
101 Merivale, *Pan the Goat-God*, p. 13.
102 Quoted ibid., p. 13.
103 Ibid.
104 Quoted in Eusebius of Caesarea, *Praeparatio Evangelica*, Book v, trans. E. H. Gifford (1903), www.tertullian.org.

2 Medieval and Early Modern Pan

1   John Boardman, *The Great God Pan: The Survival of an Image* (London, 1997), p. 8.
2   Edgar Wind, *Pagan Mysteries in the Renaissance* (New York, 1968), p. 191.
3   Ibid., chapters 7 and 8.
4   Quoted in Boardman, *Great God Pan*, p. 9.
5   Quoted in Patricia Merivale, *Pan the Goat-God: His Myth in Modern Times* (Cambridge, MA, 1969), p. 13.
6   François Rabelais, *Gargantua and Pantagruel, Complete* (1532–64), trans. Sir Thomas Urquhart of Cromarty and Peter Antony Motteux, www.gutenberg.org.
7   Sir Philip Sidney, *The Countess of Pembroke's Arcadia* (1590), Book i, www.luminarium.org.
8   John Lyly, *Midas* (1592), www.elizabethandrama.org.
9   Merivale, *Pan the Goat-God*, p. 20.
10 Edmund Spenser, *Shepheardes Calender vii: Julye* [1592], in *Spenser and the Tradition: English Poetry, 1579–1830*, comp. David Hill Radcliffe, http://spenserians.cath.vt.edu.
11 Matthew 25:32, King James Version.
12 Andrea Alciato, 'Emblem 98 Nature', in *Book of Emblems* (1621), trans. William Barker, Mark Feltham and Jean Guthrie, www.mun.ca/alciato.

13 Francis Beaumont and John Fletcher, *The Faithful Shepherdess* (c. 1608), www.gutenberg.org.
14 Ben Jonson, *Pan's Anniversary; or, The Shepherd's Holiday*, in *English Masques*, ed. Herbert Arthur Evans (London, 1897), p. 161.
15 Ibid., p. 166.
16 Ibid., pp. 166–7.
17 Ibid., p. 167.
18 Ibid., p. 169.
19 Francis Bacon, *The Wisdom of the Ancients*, https://en.wikisource.org.
20 Boardman, *Great God Pan*, pp. 13–14.
21 Ibid., p. 14.
22 See www.peterpaulrubens.net.
23 Poussin, *The Triumph of Pan*, London, National Gallery, www.nationalgallery.org.uk; Picasso, *La Bacchanal* (1944), Canberra, National Gallery of Australia, https://cs.nga.gov.au.
24 Boardman, *Great God Pan*, p. 15.
25 John Milton, *Comus* (1634), www.dartmouth.edu/~milton.
26 John Milton, *Paradise Lost* (1674), www.dartmouth.edu/~milton.
27 John Milton, 'On the Morning of Christ's Nativity' (1629), www.dartmouth.edu/~milton.
28 Ibid.
29 Andrew Marvell, 'Clorinda and Damon' (1650–52), www.luminarium.org.
30 Andrew Marvell, 'The Garden' (1682), www.luminarium.org.
31 Ibid.
32 Andrew Marvell, 'The First Anniversary of the Government under O.C.' (1655), www.luminarium.org.
33 John Dryden, 'The Lady's Song' [1704], in *The Poems of John Dryden* (1913), ed. John Sargeaunt, www.bartleby.com.
34 Alexander Robertson of Struan, 'The Consolation: An Eclogue', in *Poems, on Various Subjects and Occasions* (Edinburgh, 1751), p. 89.
35 Ibid., p. 91.
36 John Gay, *Fables* (London, 1761), p. 146.
37 Ibid., p. 147.
38 Ibid., p. 148.

3 PAN'S ROMANTIC REBIRTH

1 Quoted in Philip J. Cardinale and Joseph R. Cardinale,
'A Newly Discovered Blake Book: William Blake's Copy
of Thomas Taylor's *The Mystical Initiations; or, Hymns of
Orpheus*' [1787], *Blake: An Illustrated Quarterly*, XLIV/3 (2011),
www.blakearchive.org.

2 William Blake, 'An Imitation of Spenser' [1793], in
Poetical Sketches (1868), ed. Richard Herne Shepherd,
https://en.wikisource.org.

3 William Blake, 'Fable XII, Pan and Fortune' (1793),
www.britishmuseum.org.

4 William Blake, *The Marriage of Heaven and Hell* (*c*. 1790),
https://en.wikisource.org.

5 William Wordsworth, *The Prelude, or Growth of a Poet's
Mind; An Autobiographical Poem* (1850), Book VIII,
https://en.wikisource.org.

6 William Wordsworth, *The Excursion* (1814), Book IV,
https://en.wikisource.org.

7 Blake, *Marriage of Heaven and Hell*.

8 Wordsworth, *The Excursion*, Book VII.

9 Samuel Taylor Coleridge, *The Notebooks of Samuel Taylor
Coleridge*, vol. II, ed. Kathleen Coburn (London, 1962),
p. 2661, https://books.google.com.

10 Samuel Taylor Coleridge, *Biographia Literaria* (1817),
chapter XXI, www.gutenberg.org.

11 John Keats, *Endymion* (1818), https://en.wikisource.org.

12 Mary Shelley, *Proserpine and Midas* [1820], ed. A. Koszul
(1922), www.gutenberg.org.

13 Percy Bysshe Shelley, 'Hymn of Pan' [1820], in *The Complete
Poetical Works of Percy Bysshe Shelley*, ed. Thomas
Hutchinson, vol. II (1914), www.gutenberg.org.

14 Percy Bysshe Shelley, 'Ode to the West Wind' [1820],
in *Complete Poetical Works*, ed. Thomas Hutchinson, vol. I
(1914), www.gutenberg.org.

15 Mary Shelley, *Proserpine and Midas*.

16 Percy Bysshe Shelley, 'The Witch of Atlas' (1820),
www.gutenberg.org.

17 Percy Bysshe Shelley, 'Pan, Echo, and the Satyr' [1824],
in *Complete Poetical Works*, ed. Thomas Hutchinson, vol. III
(1914), www.gutenberg.org.

18 George Gordon, Lord Byron, 'Aristomenes' [1823], in
   The Works of Lord Byron, ed. Ernest Hartley, vol. IV (1905),
   https://en.wikisource.org.
19 Wordsworth, *Prelude*, Book VIII.
20 Quoted in Patricia Merivale, *Pan the Goat-God: His Myth in
   Modern Times* (Cambridge, MA, 1969), p. 63.
21 Leigh Hunt, 'The Universal Pan' [1825], in *The Poetical
   Works of Leigh Hunt*, ed. H. S. Milford (Oxford, 1923),
   p. 746, https://books.google.com.
22 Ibid., pp. 746, 747.
23 Ibid., p. 747.
24 Thomas Love Peacock, *Calidore: A Fragment of a Romance*
   [1816], ed. Richard Garnett (1891), https://d.lib.rochester.
   edu.
25 Merivale, *Pan the Goat-God*, p. 67.
26 Thomas Love Peacock, *Melincourt; or, Sir Oran Haut-Ton*
   [1817] (London, 1896), pp. 50–51, https://books.google.com.
27 Ibid., p. 51.
28 Ibid., p. 52.
29 Thomas Love Peacock, *Rhododaphne, or, The Thessalian Spell*
   [1818], in *The Works of Thomas Love Peacock*, vol. III,
   ed. Henry Cole (Oxford, 1875), p. 172, https://books.google.
   com.
30 Ibid., p. 173.
31 Thomas Love Peacock, note to 'Pan in Town' [1825],
   in *The Works*, vol. III, p. 222.
32 Peacock, 'Pan in Town', p. 222.
33 Peacock, note to 'Pan in Town', p. 222.
34 Felicia Hemans, 'Modern Greece: A Poem' [1817], in
   Spenser and the Tradition: English Poetry 1579–1830, comp.
   David Hill Radcliffe, https://spenserians.cath.vt.edu.
35 William Hazlitt, *Hazlitt on English Literature*, ed. Jacob
   Zeitlin (1913), www.gutenberg.org.
36 Elizabeth Barrett Browning, 'The Dead Pan' (1843),
   www.ebbarchive.org.
37 Elizabeth Barrett Browning, 'A Musical Instrument' (1860),
   https://en.wikisource.org.
38 Robert Browning, 'Pan and Luna' (1880), https://en.wiki-
   source.org.
39 Virgil, *Eclogue X*, trans. H. R. Fairclough, 'Virgil, Eclogues',
   www.theoi.com, accessed 8 August 2020.

40 Robert Browning, 'Pan and Luna'.
41 Amby Burfoot, 'Oct. 26: The Truth about Pheidippides and the Early Years of Marathon History', www.runnersworld. com, 26 October 2010.
42 Robert Browning, 'Pheidippides' (1879), https://en.wiki-source.org.
43 Burfoot, 'Oct. 26'.
44 Walter Savage Landor, 'Pan and Pitys', in *The Hellenics of Walter Savage Landor* (Edinburgh, 1859), p. 80, https://books. google.com.
45 Ibid., p. 81.
46 Ibid., p. 82.
47 Ibid., pp. 82–3.
48 Ibid., p. 83.
49 Ibid., p. 84.
50 Walter Savage Landor, 'Pan', in *The Works and Life of Walter Savage Landor*, vol. VIII (London, 1876), p. 306.
51 Walter Savage Landor, 'Cupid and Pan', in *Hellenics*, p. 85.
52 Ibid., p. 86.
53 Ibid., p. 89.
54 Ralph Waldo Emerson, *Nature* (1849), www.gutenberg.org.
55 Ralph Waldo Emerson, 'Woodnotes II' [1841], in *Poems by Ralph Waldo Emerson* (1904), www.gutenberg.org.
56 Merivale, *Pan the Goat-God*, pp. 91–2.
57 Ralph Waldo Emerson, ['The Patient Pan'], in *Poems*.
58 Ralph Waldo Emerson, 'Natural History of Intellect', in *The Natural History of the Intellect and Other Papers* (Boston, MA, 1904), p. 36.
59 Ibid., p. 35.
60 Ibid., p. 36.
61 Nathaniel Hawthorne, *The Marble Faun* (1860), www.gutenberg.org.
62 Ibid.
63 Robert Louis Stevenson, 'Pan's Pipes', in *Virginibus Puerisque and Other Papers* (1881), https://en.wikisource.org.
64 Oscar Wilde, 'The Decay of Lying', in *Intentions* (1913), www.gutenberg.org.
65 Oscar Wilde, 'Pan' [1881], in *Poems* (1913), www.gutenberg.org.
66 Ronald Hutton, *The Triumph of the Moon: A History of Modern Pagan Witchcraft*, new edn (Oxford, 2019), p. 168.

67 Merivale, *Pan the Goat-God*, p. 96.
68 Charles Algernon Swinburne, 'Pan and Thalassius,' in *Poems and Ballads*, Third Series (1917), www.gutenberg.org.
69 Philippe Borgeaud, *The Cult of Pan in Ancient Greece*, trans. Kathleen Atlass and James Redfield (Chicago, IL, 1988), pp. 104–7.
70 Charles Algernon Swinburne, 'A Nympholept', in *Astrophel and Other Works* (1917), www.gutenberg.org.
71 Charles Algernon Swinburne, 'The Palace of Pan,' in *Astrophel and Other Works*.
72 Knut Hamsun, *Pan*, trans. Sverre Lyngstad (London, 1998), p. 4.
73 Ibid., p. 12.
74 Ibid., p. 20.
75 John Boardman, *The Great God Pan: The Survival of an Image* (London, 1997), pp. 16–18.
76 See https://artsandculture.google.com.
77 See https://commons.wikimedia.org.
78 Ibid.
79 Ibid.
80 See www.wikiart.org.
81 Ibid.
82 See www.mutualart.com.
83 See https://commons.wikimedia.org.
84 Aubrey Beardsley, 'A Footnote', *The Savoy*, I/2 (1896), p. 185, www.archive.org.
85 Aubrey Beardsley, ['Pan Reading to a Woman'], *Studio Magazine*, XIII/62 (1898), p. 259, https://babel.hathitrust.org.
86 Aubrey Beardsley, *The Story of Venus and Tannhäuser* (1907), www.gutenberg.org.
87 See www.artgallery.nsw.gov.au.
88 See www.deutscherandhackett.com.
89 See www.artgallery.nsw.gov.au.
90 Kurt Gänzl, 'The "Voix de Flûte": Offenbach's Star Comedian Léonce (1820–1900)', www.operetta-research-center.org, 1 January 2001.
91 Jens Malte Fischer, *Mahler* (New Haven, CT, 2011), p. 275.
92 Bruno Walter, *Gustav Mahler*, trans. James Galston [1941] (Mineola, NY, 2013), p. 28.
93 Henry-Louis de la Grange, *Gustav Mahler*, vol. II: *Vienna: The Years of Challenge, 1897–1904* (Oxford, 1995), p. 712.

94 Wilhelm Heinrich Roscher, *Ephialtes*, trans. A. B. O'Brien, in *Pan and the Nightmare*, ed. James Hillman, revd edn (Putnam, CT, 2007), p. 98.
95 Ibid., p. 107.
96 Quoted ibid., pp. 128–9.
97 Ibid., p. 130.
98 Ibid., p. 142.

4 PAN IN THE TWENTIETH CENTURY

1 R.D.S. Jack, 'Barrie, Sir James Matthew, baronet', in *Oxford Dictionary of National Biography*, www.oxfordndb.com, accessed 11 August 2020.
2 James Barrie, *Peter Pan in Kensington Gardens* (1906), www.gutenberg.org.
3 James Barrie, *Peter Pan* [*Peter and Wendy*] (1911/1991), www.gutenberg.org.
4 Kenneth Grahame, 'The Rural Pan', in *The Pagan Papers* (1894), https://en.wikisource.org.
5 Kenneth Grahame, *The Wind in the Willows* (1908), www.gutenberg.org.
6 Kenneth Grahame, *The Wind in the Willows* (London, 1908).
7 Kenneth Grahame, *The Wind in the Willows* (New York, 1913).
8 E. H. Shepard, 'The Piper at the Gates of Dawn', in Kenneth Grahame, *The Wind in the Willows* (London, 1931).
9 Arthur Rackham, 'The Piper at the Gates of Dawn', in Kenneth Grahame, *The Wind in the Willows* (London, 1940).
10 Charles van Sandwyk, 'The Piper at the Gates of Dawn', in Kenneth Grahame, *The Wind in the Willows* (London, 2008).
11 Eden Phillpotts, *Pan and the Twins* [1922], ebook (New York, 2012).
12 William Hazlitt, *Hazlitt on English Literature*, ed. Jacob Zeitlin (1913), www.gutenberg.org.
13 W. Somerset Maugham, *Cakes and Ale* (1930), www.gutenberg.ca.
14 Helen H. Law, *A Bibliography of Greek Myth in English Poetry* (New York, 1932).
15 Walter de la Mare, 'They Told Me', in *Collected Poems, 1901–1918* (1920), https://en.wikisource.org.
16 Walter de la Mare, 'Sorcery', in *Collected Poems*.

17 Bliss Carman, 'The Pipes of Pan' [1902], in *The Pipes of Pan* (Boston, MA, 1906), p. 4; italics in original.

18 Ibid., p. 7.

19 Ibid., p. 8.

20 Ibid., p. 23.

21 D.M.R. Bentley, 'Carman, William Bliss', in *Dictionary of Canadian Biography*, vol. xv, www.biographi.ca.

22 Bliss Carman, 'A Young Pan's Prayer' (1902), in *The Pipes of Pan*, p. 100.

23 Michael Matthew Kaylor, 'Introduction', in *The Garden God: A Tale of Two Boys* (Richmond, VA, 2007), p. xli.

24 Forrest Reid, *The Garden God* (1906), www.gutenberg.org.

25 E. F. Benson, 'The Man Who Went Too Far' [1912], in *Collected Stories* (2006), gutenberg.net.au

26 'Saki' [H. H. Munro], 'The Music on the Hill', in *The Chronicles of Clovis* (1911), www.gutenberg.org.

27 Quoted in Nicola Beauman, 'Forster, Edward Morgan', in *Oxford Dictionary of National Biography*, www.oxforddnb.com.

28 E. M. Forster, 'The Story of a Panic', in *The Celestial Omnibus and Other Stories* (1912), www.gutenberg.org.

29 E. M. Forster, *The Longest Journey* (1907), www.gutenberg.org.

30 E. M. Forster, *A Room with a View* (1908), www.gutenberg.org.

31 Peter Hunt, *The Making of The Wind in the Willows* (Oxford, 2018).

32 James Stephens, *The Crock of Gold* (1921), www.gutenberg.org.

33 Mark Williams, *The Irish Immortals* (Princeton, NJ, 2016), p. 453.

34 D. H. Lawrence, 'Pan in America', in *The Bad Side of Books: Selected Essays*, ed. Geoff Dyer (New York, 2019), p. 194.

35 Ibid., p. 195.

36 Ibid., p. 196.

37 William Wordsworth, 'Lucy Gray' [1799], in *Wordsworth's Poetical Works*, ed. William Knight (1896), www.gutenberg.org.

38 Lawrence, 'Pan in America', p. 196.

39 Ibid., p. 197.

40 Ibid., p. 198.

41 Ibid., p. 199.
42 Ibid., p. 200.
43 Ibid., p. 201.
44 Ibid., p. 203.
45 Ibid., p. 204.
46 Ibid., p. 206.
47 D. H. Lawrence, *St Mawr*, in *The Woman Who Rode Away/
St Mawr/The Princess*, ed. Brian Finney, Christa Jansohn
and Dieter Mehl (London, 2006), p. 84.
48 Ibid., p. 85.
49 Ibid., p. 86.
50 Ibid., p. 87.
51 Ibid., p. 93.
52 Lawrence, 'Pan in America', p. 206.
53 Lawrence, *St Mawr*, p. 127.
54 Ibid., p. 134.
55 Mark Kinkead-Weekes, 'Re-Dating "The Overtone"',
D. H. Lawrence Review, xxv/1–2 (1995), pp. 75–80.
56 D. H. Lawrence, 'The Overtone', in *The Complete Short
Stories*, vol. iii (Harmondsworth, Middlesex, 1977), p. 755.
57 Ibid., p. 756.
58 Ibid., p. 757.
59 Ibid., p. 758.
60 Ibid., p. 759.
61 D. H. Lawrence, 'The Last Laugh', in *Complete Short Stories*,
vol. iii, p. 631.
62 Ibid., pp. 639–40.
63 D. H. Lawrence, *Lady Chatterley's Lover* (New York, 2005),
p. 324.
64 Aldous Huxley, 'Cynthia', in *Limbo* (1920), www.guten-
berg.org.
65 Stephen McKenna, *The Oldest God* (Boston, ma, 1926), p. 72.
66 Ibid., p. 347; italics in original.
67 Ibid., p. 348; italics in original.
68 Lord Dunsany, 'The Death of Pan', in *Fifty-one Tales* (1915),
https://en.wikisource.org.
69 Lord Dunsany, 'The Prayer of the Flowers', in *Fifty-one
Tales*.
70 Lord Dunsany, 'The Tomb of Pan', in *Fifty-one Tales*.
71 Lord Dunsany, *The Blessing of Pan* (New York, 1926), p. 7.
72 Ibid., p. 10.

73 Ibid., p. 69.
74 Ibid., p. 156.
75 Ibid., p. 172.
76 Ibid., p. 210.
77 Sylvia Townsend Warner, *The True Heart* [1929] (London, 1978), p. 125.
78 Ibid., p. 130.
79 Ibid., p. 131.
80 Ibid., unpaginated Preface.
81 William Faulkner, 'Black Music', in *The Collected Stories of William Faulkner* (New York, 1995), p. 805.
82 Ibid., p. 811.
83 Ezra Pound, 'Pan Is Dead', in *Canzoni and Ripostes* (London, 1913), www.gutenberg.org.
84 Robert Frost, 'Pan with Us', in *A Boy's Will* (London, 1913), https://en.wikisource.org.
85 Patricia Merivale, *Pan the Goat-God: His Myth in Modern Times* (Cambridge, MA, 1969), p. 220.
86 E. E. Cummings, '[in Just-]', www.poetryfoundation.org.
87 W. B. Yeats, 'News for the Delphic Oracle', in *The Collected Poems of W. B. Yeats*, ed. Richard Finneran (New York, 2008), pp. 363–4.
88 'La Flûte de Pan', www.windrep.org, accessed 16 August 2020.
89 Andrew Barnett, *Jean Sibelius* (New Haven, CT, 2007), p. 175.
90 Julie McQuinn, 'Exploring the Erotic in Debussy's Music', in *The Cambridge Companion to Debussy*, ed. Simon Tresize (Cambridge, 2003), p. 126.
91 *Joueurs de flûte*, www.wikipedia.org, accessed 16 August 2020.
92 Quoted in Timothy Judd, '"Daphnis and Chloe": Ravel's Shimmering "Symphonie Chorégraphique"', 5 June 2019, https://thelistenersclub.com.
93 'Myths Op. 30 – Karol Szymanowski', www.culture.pl.
94 Ibid.
95 Jerrold Northrop Moore, *Edward Elgar: A Creative Life* (Oxford, 1984), pp. 270–71.
96 Edmund Gosse, 'To a Traveller', in *The Collected Poems of Edmund Gosse* (London, 1911), p. 277.
97 Matthew Riley, 'Rustling Reeds and Lofty Pines: Elgar and

the Music of Nature', *Nineteenth-century Music*, xxvi/2
(2002), p. 162.

98 Ibid., p. 163.

99 Quoted ibid., pp. 157–8.

100 Eric Saylor, *English Pastoral Music, 1900–1955*, ebook
(Urbana, IL, 2017).

101 Michael Kennedy, *The Works of Ralph Vaughan Williams*
(Oxford, 1992), p. 64.

102 *The Arcadians* (1907), www.wikipedia.org, accessed
16 August 2020.

103 Graham Parlett, 'The Pagan World of Arnold Bax' (1999),
www.arnoldbax.com.

104 Fiona Richards, 'The Goat-god in England: A Musical
Context for Lawrence's Fascination with Pan', *D. H.
Lawrence Review*, XL/1 (2015), p. 96.

105 Quoted in Colin Scott-Sutherland, *Arnold Bax* (London,
1973), p. 41.

106 Richards, 'The Goat-god', pp. 96–7.

107 Ibid., p. 91.

108 *Six Metamorphoses after Ovid* [1951], www.wikipedia.org,
accessed 16 August 2020.

109 Fiona Richards, *The Music of John Ireland* (Abingdon,
Oxfordshire, 2000), p. 66.

110 Ibid., pp. 66, 68.

111 Ibid., p. 66.

112 Ibid., p. 69.

113 Ibid., p. 63.

114 Quoted ibid., p. 76

115 Quoted ibid., p. 72.

116 Ibid., p. 73.

117 Quoted ibid., p. 67.

118 H. Orsmond Anderton, *Granville Bantock*
(London, 1915).

119 Saylor, *English Pastoral Music*.

120 Ibid., p. 132.

121 Ibid., p. 134.

122 Ibid., p. 135.

123 Ibid., pp. 135–6.

124 Ibid., pp. 136–7.

125 Ibid., p. 137.

126 Ibid., p. 138.

127 Ibid., p. 139.
128 Ibid.

5 PAN AS OCCULT POWER

1 Christian Wildberg, 'Neoplatonism' (2016), *Stanford Encyclopedia of Philosophy*, https://plato.stanford.edu.
2 Ronald Hutton, *The Triumph of the Moon: A History of Modern Pagan Witchcraft*, new edn (Oxford, 2019), pp. 69–70.
3 Edgar Wind, *Pagan Mysteries of the Renaissance*, revd edn (New York, 1968), chapters 7–8.
4 Athanasius Kircher, *Obeliscus Pamphilius* (1650), https://digi.ub.uni-heidelberg.de; for a mildly censored reproduction with English translation, see the version by Manly P. Hall, *The Secret Teaching of All Ages* (1928), https://commons.wikimedia.org.
5 Éliphas Lévi, *Dogme et rituel de la haute magie* (Paris, 1861); Éliphas Lévi, *Transcendental Magic* [1896], trans. A. E. Waite (Boston, MA, 1972) p. xiv.
6 Francisco de Goya, *El Aquelarre (The Witches' Sabbath)* (1798), www.flg.es.
7 Zrinka Stahuljak, *Pornographic Archaeology: Medicine, Medievalism, and the Invention of the French Nation* (Philadelphia, PA, 2013), p. 79.
8 Lévi, *Transcendental Magic*, p. 307.
9 Ibid., pp. xiv–xv.
10 Avi Selk, 'A Satanic Idol Goes to the Arkansas Capitol Building', www.washingtonpost.com, 17 August 2018.
11 Hutton, *Triumph of the Moon*, p. 48.
12 Stanislas de Guaita, *La Clef de la Magie Noire* (Paris, 1897).
13 David Huckvale, *A Green and Pagan Land: Myth, Magic and Landscape in British Film and Television* (Jefferson, NC, 2018), p. 115.
14 Albrecht Dürer, *Witch Riding Backwards on a Goat* (1501–2), www.collections.tepapa.govt.nz.
15 Nevill Drury, *Stealing Fire from Heaven: The Rise of Modern Western Magic* (Oxford, 2011), pp. 43–4.
16 Liz Williams, *Miracles of Our Own Making: A History of Paganism* (London, 2020), p. 204.

17 Quoted in Arthur Machen, *The Great God Pan and Other Horror Stories*, ed. Aaron Worth (Oxford, 2018), p. 379.
18 Ibid.
19 Susan Johnston Graf, *Talking to the Gods: Occultism in the Work of W. B. Yeats, Arthur Machen, Algernon Blackwood, and Dion Fortune* (Albany, NY, 2015), pp. 60–61.
20 Quoted in Machen, *Great God Pan*, pp. 354–5.
21 Ibid., p. xiii.
22 Ibid., p. xv.
23 Arthur Machen, *The Great God Pan* (1895), www.gutenberg.org.
24 Drury, *Stealing Fire*, p. 55.
25 Ibid., p. 86.
26 Ibid., p. 90.
27 Aleister Crowley, 'Hymn to Pan', *The Equinox*, III/1 (1919), p. 5, https://keepsilence.org.
28 Ibid., p. 6.
29 Ibid., p. 7.
30 Paul Newman, *Aleister Crowley and the Cult of Pan* (London, 2004), p. 36.
31 Victor Neuburg, 'The Triumph of Pan', in *The Triumph of Pan* [1910] (Austin, TX, 2009), p. 7.
32 Ibid., p. 8.
33 Ibid., p. 9.
34 Victor Neuburg, 'The Lost Shepherd', in *Triumph of Pan*, p. 49.
35 Hutton, *Triumph of the Moon*, p. 51.
36 Neuburg, 'Triumph of Pan', p. 9.
37 Ibid., p. 10.
38 Aleister Crowley, 'Prologue of the Unborn', *Liber VII (Liberi Vel Lapidis Lazuli) and Liber IX (Liber e Vel Exercitiorum)* [1907] (n.p., 2020), p. 1.
39 Ibid., pp. 2–3.
40 Ibid., p. 3.
41 'Night of Pan', www.thelemapedia.org, accessed 16 August 2020.
42 Ibid.
43 Aleister Crowley, *The Book of Lies* [1913] (York Beach, ME, 1962), p. 12.
44 Ibid., p. 13.
45 Ibid., p. 19.

46 Graf, *Talking to the Gods*, chapter 5.
47 Algernon Blackwood, 'The Touch of Pan', in *Day and Night Stories* (1917), www.gutenberg.org.
48 Graf, *Talking to the Gods*, p. 103.
49 Dion Fortune, *The Winged Bull* (London, 1935), p. 12.
50 Dion Fortune, *The Goat Foot God* [1936] (York Beach, ME, 1980), p. 68.
51 Ibid., p. 69.
52 Ibid., p. 164.
53 Ibid., p. 171.
54 Ibid., p. 184.
55 Ibid., pp. 253–4.
56 Ibid., p. 293.
57 Ibid., p. 294.
58 Ibid.
59 Ibid., p. 303.
60 Ibid., p. 304.
61 Ibid.
62 Ibid., pp. 319–20.
63 Ibid., p. 362.
64 Ibid., p. 381.
65 Dion Fortune, *Dion Fortune's Rites of Isis and of Pan*, ed. Gareth Knight (Cheltenham, Gloucestershire, 2013), p. 8.
66 Ibid., p. 41.
67 Ibid., p. 42.
68 Ibid., p. 43.
69 Ibid., p. 44.
70 Ibid., p. 46.
71 Ibid., p. 52.
72 Ibid.
73 Charles Leland, *Aradia; or, The Gospel of the Witches* [1899] (Newport, RI, 2010).
74 Mélusine Draco, *Pan: Dark Lord of the Forest and Horned God of the Witches* (Alresford, Hampshire, 2016), p. 64.
75 Hutton, *Triumph of the Moon*, pp. 148–54.
76 Ibid., pp. 208–9.
77 Margaret A. Murray, *The Witch Cult in Western Europe* (Oxford, 1921).
78 Hutton, *Triumph of the Moon*, p. 203.
79 Margaret A. Murray, *The God of the Witches* [1921] (Oxford, 1977), p. 23.

80 Ibid., p. 28.
81 Ibid.
82 Ibid.
83 Ibid., p. 113.
84 Williams, *Miracles of Our Own Making*, p. 257.
85 Hutton, *Triumph of the Moon*, p. 328.
86 Ibid., pp. 220–32.
87 Ibid., pp. 215–20.
88 Gerald Gardner, *Witchcraft Today* [1954] (New York, 1970).
89 Gerald Gardner, *The Meaning of Witchcraft* [1959] (York Beach, ME, 2004), p. 13.
90 Ibid., p. 23.
91 Ibid.
92 Ibid., p. 115.
93 Ibid., p. 161.
94 Nevill Drury, *Pan's Daughter: The Magical World of Rosaleen Norton* (Oxford, 2016), pp. 19–20.
95 Ibid., pp. 23–5.
96 Ibid., p. 147.
97 Rosaleen Norton, 'Witches Want No Recruits', *Australasian Post*, 10 January 1957, p. 35; quoted in Drury, *Pan's Daughter*, p. 150. Italics in original.
98 Norton, 'Witches Want No Recruits'.
99 Ibid.
100 Ibid.
101 Ibid.
102 Drury, *Pan's Daughter*, p. 34.
103 Ibid., pp. 38–41.
104 Norton, 'Witches Want No Recruits', quoted in Drury, *Pan's Daughter*, p. 148.
105 Norton, 'Witches Want No Recruits'; italics in original.
106 Drury, *Pan's Daughter*, p. 197.

6 CONTEMPORARY PAN

1 Robert Graves, *The Greek Myths*, vol. I, revd edn (Harmondsworth, Middlesex, 1960), p. 101.
2 Ibid.
3 Ibid., p. 102.
4 Ibid.
5 Ibid.

6 Ibid., p. 103.
7 Ibid.
8 Herbert A. Leibowitz, 'A Pan Piping on the City Streets: *The Collected Poems of Frank O'Hara*', *New York Times Book Review*, 28 November 1971, www.nytimes.com.
9 Frank O'Hara, 'Oranges: 12 Pastorals', in *The Collected Poems of Frank O'Hara* [1971], ed. Donald Allen (Berkeley, CA, 1995), p. 5.
10 Ibid.
11 Ibid.
12 Ibid., p. 7.
13 Frank O'Hara, 'Ode for Saint Cecilia's Day', in *Collected Poems*, p. 27.
14 Ibid., p. 28.
15 Ibid., p. 29.
16 Frank O'Hara, 'The Pipes of Pan', in *Collected Poems*, p. 81.
17 John Ashbery, 'Syringa', www.poetryfoundation.org.
18 Kenneth Koch, 'Io', in *After Ovid* (New York, 1996), p. 62.
19 Ibid., p. 63.
20 James Merrill, '"Syrinx" Text and Notes' (1970), ed. Timothy Materer, http://omeka.wustl.edu.
21 Ibid.
22 Allen Curnow, 'Fantasia and Fugue for Pan-pipe', in *Collected Poems*, ed. Elizabeth Caffin and Terry Sturm (Auckland, 2017), pp. 351–5.
23 Ibid., p. 374.
24 Ibid.
25 Ibid., p. 351.
26 Ibid., p. 352.
27 Ibid., p. 353.
28 Ibid., p. 355.
29 Quoted in Zoë Brigley, 'Dryad', in *Hand & Skull* (Newcastle, 2019), p. 18.
30 Ibid.
31 Zoë Brigley, 'Syringe', in *Hand & Skull*, p. 44.
32 Stephen King, 'The Lawnmower Man', in *Night Shift* (New York, 1978), pp. 309–23.
33 Tom Robbins, *Jitterbug Perfume* (New York, 1985), p. 57.
34 Ibid., p. 307.
35 Ibid., p. 320.
36 Ibid., p. 325.

37 Ibid., p. 326.
38 Nina MacLaughlin, *Wake, Siren: Ovid Resung* (New York, 2019), p. 84.
39 Ibid.
40 Ibid., p. 85.
41 Ibid., p. 86.
42 Ibid., p. 87.
43 Amy Herzog, *The Great God Pan* (New York, 2014), p. 47.
44 Ibid., p. 68.
45 See 'About the Findhorn Foundation', www.findhorn.org, accessed 16 August 2020.
46 Eileen Caddy, *Flight into Freedom and Beyond: The Autobiography of the Co-founder of the Findhorn Community*, revd edn (Forres, Moray, 2007), pp. 109–12.
47 Ibid., p. 131.
48 Mike Scott, 'Prologue', in R. Ogilvie Crombie, *The Gentleman and the Faun: Encounters with Pan and the Elemental Kingdom* (Forres, Moray, 2009), pp. xi–xii.
49 Ibid., pp. xii–xiii.
50 Ibid., pp. xiii–xiv.
51 Crombie, *The Gentleman and the Faun*, pp. 2–3.
52 Ibid., p. 3.
53 Ibid., pp. 7–8.
54 Ibid., pp. 12–13.
55 Ibid., p. 13.
56 Ibid., p. 14.
57 Ibid., p. 22.
58 Ibid., p. 23.
59 Ibid., p. 24.
60 Ibid., p. 104.
61 Gordon Lindsay, *The Occult Diaries of Robert Ogilvie Crombie*, ed. David Spangler (Everett, WA, 2011), pp. 116–17.
62 Crombie, *The Gentleman and the Faun*, p. 99.
63 Ibid., p. 114.
64 Machaelle Wright, MAP: *The Co-creative White Brotherhood Medical Assistance Plan* (Jeffersonton, VA, 2006), p. 11.
65 Machaelle Wright, *The Perelandra Garden Workbook*, 2nd edn (Jeffersonton, VA, 2020), p. 13.
66 Wright, MAP, p. 11.
67 Ibid.

68 Wright, *Perelandra Garden Workbook*, p. 13.
69 Ibid., p. 17.
70 Ibid.
71 Leo Vinci, *Pan: Great God of Nature* (London, 1993).
72 Nicholas Goodrick-Clarke, *The Western Esoteric Traditions: A Historical Introduction* (Oxford, 2008), chapter 2.
73 Ibid., pp. 42–3.
74 Vinci, *Pan*, p. 232.
75 Ibid., p. 233.
76 Ibid., p. 234.
77 Ibid., p. 235.
78 Ibid., p. 237.
79 Ibid., p. 238.
80 Ibid., p. 239.
81 Mélusine Draco, *Pan: Dark Lord of the Forest and Horned God of the Witches* (Alresford, Hampshire, 2016).
82 Ibid., p. 67.
83 Ibid., pp. 42–3.
84 Rob Chapman, *Syd Barrett: A Very Irregular Head* (London, 2011), p. 148.
85 Rob Young, *Electric Eden: Unearthing Britain's Visionary Music* (New York, 2010), pp. 454–5.
86 Ibid., pp. 287, 509.
87 Mike Scott, *Adventures of a Waterboy Remastered* (London, 2017), p. 209.
88 Ibid., p. 115; italics in original.
89 Ibid.; italics in original.
90 Scott, 'Prologue', pp. xi–xvii.
91 Mike Scott, 'My Favourite W. B. Yeats Poem: Mike Scott on "News for the Delphic Oracle"', www.irishtimes.com, 10 June 2015.
92 Young, *Electric Eden*, pp. 585–6.
93 See www.ghostbox.co.uk, accessed 19 August 2020.
94 Bob Fischer, 'Belbury Poly, Jim Jupp and Ghost Box Records', 7 August 2020, www.hauntedgeneration.co.uk.
95 See www.riseaboverecords.com, accessed 19 August 2020.
96 Stan Lee and Steve Ditko, 'I Laughed at the Great God Pan', *Tales to Astonish*, 6 (1959), pp. 1–2.
97 Ibid., p. 2.
98 Ibid., p. 4.
99 Ibid.

100 George Pérez, Len Wein and Bruce D. Patterson, 'Rebirth',
     Wonder Woman, 7 (1987), p. 4.
101 Ibid., p. 5.
102 Ibid., p. 8.
103 George Pérez, Len Wein and Bruce D. Patterson, 'Paradise
     Lost', *Wonder Woman*, 10 (1987), p. 1.
104 Ibid., p. 3.
105 Ibid., pp. 8–10.
106 Ibid., pp. 13–14.
107 George Pérez, Len Wein and Bruce D. Patterson, 'Fire and
     Torment', *Wonder Woman*, 11 (1987), p. 3.
108 Ibid., p. 6.
109 Ibid., pp. 8–9, 16.
110 George Pérez, Len Wein and Bruce D. Patterson, 'Echoes
     of the Past', *Wonder Woman*, 12 (1988), p. 8.
111 George Pérez, Len Wein and Bruce D. Patterson,
     'Demonplague', *Wonder Woman*, 13 (1988), pp. 2–3.
112 Ibid., pp. 4–5.
113 Ibid., p. 5.
114 Ibid., pp. 9–13.
115 Ibid., p. 14.
116 Ibid., p. 21.
117 Ibid., p. 22.
118 George Pérez, Cara Sherman Tereno and Leslie Sternbergh,
     'Tribute', *Wonder Woman Annual*, 1 (1988), pp. 43–52.
119 Ibid., p. 46.
120 Ibid., p. 47.
121 Ibid., p. 48.
122 '*Millennium* vol. 1 7', www.dc.fandom.com, accessed
     19 August 2020.
123 Rick Riordan, *Percy Jackson and the Lightning Thief*
     (London, 2005), p. 357.
124 Rick Riordan, *Percy Jackson and the Titan's Curse*
     (London, 2007), p. 165.
125 Rick Riordan, *Percy Jackson and the Battle of the Labyrinth*
     (London, 2008), pp. 290–91.
126 Ibid., pp. 295–6.
127 Ibid., p. 296.
128 Ibid., p. 297.
129 Ibid., pp. 297–8.
130 Ibid., p. 298.

131 Ibid., p. 300.
132 'Oliver Haddo' [Aleister Crowley], 'How to Write a Novel', *Vanity Fair*, 30 December 1908, www.100thmonkeypress. com.
133 W. Somerset Maugham, *The Magician* (1908), www.gutenberg.org.
134 See www.youtube.com.
135 David Huckvale, *A Green and Pagan Land: Myth, Magic and Landscape in British Film and Television* (Jefferson, NC, 2018), p. 115.
136 Ibid., pp. 120–23.
137 Ibid., pp. 121–3.
138 Guy Leopold, 'The Daemons', dir. Christopher Barry, *Doctor Who* (1971).
139 Ibid., episode 3.
140 'Pan's People', www.wikipedia.org, accessed 16 August 2020.
141 Ibid.
142 Ian Spelling, 'Guillermo del Toro and Ivana Baquero Escape from a Civil War into the Fairytale Land of Pan's Labyrinth', *Science Fiction Weekly*, 25 December 2006, www.webarchive.org.
143 Arthur Machen, *The White People and Other Weird Stories*, ed. S. T. Joshi (London, 2011).
144 Carl Jung, *Visions: Notes of the Seminar Given in 1930–1934*, ed. Claire Douglas (Princeton, NJ, 1997), p. 523.
145 Ibid., p. 580.
146 Ibid.
147 Ibid., p. 178.
148 Ibid., p. 581.
149 Ibid.
150 David Tacey, 'James Hillman: The Unmaking of a Psychologist, Part One: His Legacy', *Journal of Analytical Psychology*, LIX/4 (2014), pp. 503–18.
151 James Hillman, ed., *Pan and the Nightmare*, revd edn (Putnam, CT, 2007), pp. 2–9.
152 Ibid., p. 12.
153 Ibid., p. 16.
154 Ibid., p. 17.
155 Ibid., p. 26.
156 Ibid., p. 34.

157 Ibid., p. 43.
158 Ibid., p. 45.
159 Ibid., p. 51.
160 Ibid., p. 62.
161 Ibid., pp. 66–7.
162 Ibid., p. 69.
163 Sukey Fontelieu, *The Archetypal Pan in America: Hypermasculinity and Terror* (Abingdon, Oxfordshire, 2018), p. 21.
164 Ibid., p. 57.
165 Ibid., p. 79.
166 Ibid., pp. 65–71.
167 Ibid., p. 73.
168 Ibid., p. 76.
169 Ibid., p. 82.
170 Ibid., pp. 85–6.

SELECT BIBLIOGRAPHY

Boardman, John, *The Great God Pan: The Survival of an Image* (London, 1997)

Borgeaud, Philippe, *The Cult of Pan in Ancient Greece*, trans. Kathleen Atlass and James Redfield (Chicago, IL, 1988)

Hillman, James, ed., *Pan and the Nightmare*, revd edn (Putnam, CT, 2007)

Huckvale, David, *A Green and Pagan Land: Myth, Magic and Landscape in British Film and Television* (Jefferson, NC, 2018)

Hutton, Ronald, *The Triumph of the Moon: A History of Modern Pagan Witchcraft*, new edn (Oxford, 2019)

Merivale, Patricia, *Pan the Goat-God: His Myth in Modern Times* (Cambridge, MA, 1969)

Williams, Liz, *Miracles of Our Own Making: A History of Paganism* (Reaktion, 2020)

Young, Rob, *Electric Eden: Unearthing Britain's Visionary Music* (New York, 2010)

ACKNOWLEDGEMENTS

Thanks, first and foremost, to my wife, Natalie, for her love and support while I worked on this project. I could not have written this book without her encouragement. Thanks as well to my stepson Nathan for his patience and for keeping an eye out for Pan.

Thanks to Charles Sandwyk and the Folio Society for permission to reproduce his illustration of 'The Piper at the Gates of Dawn'. Thanks to Jim Jupp of Ghost Box Music for permission to reproduce Julian House's cover art for *We Are All Pan's People* by the Focus Group.

Thanks to my editor, David Watkins, for encouraging me to imagine a more inclusive book than I had originally envisioned. Thanks to the anonymous reader of my proposal for suggesting some additional texts to consider. Thanks to Chris Miller for drawing my attention to the work of Allen Curnow.

PHOTO ACKNOWLEDGEMENTS

The author and publishers wish to express their thanks to the below sources of illustrative material and/or permission to reproduce it. Every effort has been made to contact copyright holders; should there be any we have been unable to reach or to whom inaccurate acknowledgements have been made, please contact the publishers, and full adjustments will be made to subsequent printings.

Alamy: p. 295; British Library, London: p. 62; Cornell University Library: p. 208; Harvard Art Museums/Fogg Museum, Bequest of Grenville L. Winthrop: p. 163; Houghton Library, Harvard University: pp. 164 (top), 165 (top); Julian House © GhostBox 2007: p. 168 (bottom); illustration from the Folio Society edition of *Wind in the Willows* © Charles van Sandwyk 2005, www.foliosociety. com: p. 148; Library of Congress, Gift of Alice and Leslie Schreyer, 1982: p. 132; Metropolitan Museum of Art, New York, Harris Brisbane Dick Fund: p. 64; Metropolitan Museum of Art, New York, Rogers Fund, 1943: p. 15; Museo Lázaro Galdiano, Madrid: p. 166; Museum of Fine Arts, Boston: p. 161 (top); Naples National Archaeological Museum: p. 161 (bottom); National Archaeological Museum, Athens: pp. 22, 33.

INDEX